BEYOND THE

New Directions in Development Theory

Beyond the Impasse

NEW DIRECTIONS IN
DEVELOPMENT THEORY

Edited by

FRANS J SCHUURMAN

ZED BOOKS
London & New Jersey

Beyond the Impasse was first published by
Zed Books Ltd, 7 Cynthia Street, London N1 9JF, UK
and 165 First Avenue, Atlantic Highlands, New Jersey
07716, USA, in 1993.

Second impression, 1996.

Cover designed by Andrew Corbett.
Laserset by Keith Addison.
Printed and bound in the United Kingdom
by Biddles Ltd, Guildford and King's Lynn.

A catalogue record for this book is
available from the British Library.

US CIP data is available from
the Library of Congress.

ISBN 1 85649 209 5 Hb
ISBN 1 85649 210 9 Pb

Contents

Preface

Back in the 1960s and 1970s, lecturing on development theories was a rather well-defined domain of knowledge transfer. Authors on the subject used to be divided into 'the good' (neo-Marxists), 'the bad' (modernisation theorists) and 'the ugly' (the computerised doomsday specialists). Students were tuned in to the often-ritualized discussions and voluntarily read the classical Marxist or neo-Marxist texts which were popular at the time. Non-abiding teachers or fellow-students were called to order with quotes varying from Marx's 'The 18th Brumaire of Louis Bonaparte' to the then increasingly popular work of Samir Amin. Student activism not only involved new democratic university structures but also led to the creation of departments specifically engaging in research on the problem of development and underdevelopment in the Third World.

Now, well into the 1990s, things have changed. The good feel bad, the bad feel good, and the ugly underwent plastic surgery. In the 1980s the subject of development theories moved into what became known as an 'impasse'. Teaching development theories was no longer a relatively clearcut case, for reasons which will be outlined in this book.

In 1991 the Nijmegen Institute of Comparative Development Studies (NICCOS) of the University of Nijmegen, the Netherlands, organised a workshop with the intent to take stock of the fragmented field of development theories. The present volume contains the contributions to that conference supplemented with an introductory chapter. Its aim is to provide university teachers and students alike with an accessible overview of the reasons for the currently fragmented field of development theories, the new approaches and the future challenges. In addition, the bibliographies included constitute valuable reading lists for further reference and study.

According to post-modernism the time for definite answers packed in metanarratives is over. Maybe so. Many questions raised in this book will not receive any definite answers, but they convey the message that it is worthwhile to ask the right questions and not to stop looking for the answers.

I am grateful to Robert Molteno of Zed Books for his general encouragement and his critical editorial support.

– Frans J. Schuurman

1

Introduction: Development Theory in the 1990s

by Frans J. Schuurman

Many developing countries will remember the 1980s as the lost decade. The same assessment could perhaps be applied to the field of development theory. Especially from the mid-1980s onwards, an increasing number of publications outlined the contours of what became known as 'the impasse in development theory'. Major factors contributing to this impasse were post-modern criticism of theory formation in the social sciences, the growing awareness that the emphasis on economic growth – awarded a central role in development theory – resulted in an insupportable burden on the natural environment, and loss of the socialist paradigm as the link between theory and development praxis.

For reasons elaborated later, the development theory impasse especially concerned Marxist and neo-Marxist thinking. Consequently, adherence to the neo-liberal paradigm – the 'counter-revolution' in John Toye's terms (1987) – seems to have reached major proportions. The euphoria on the right concerning Fukuyama's view of 'the end of history' (1989) seems premature at least: many Third World countries continue to have major economic problems, although, in political terms, the ongoing democratisation process would seem to allow for better conditions for the development process.

In spite of the development theory impasse, empirical studies of development themes continued in the Third World. However, they lacked the paradigmatic umbrella of, for example, dependency theory or the modes of production theorem. Given the criticism levelled against these analytical frameworks, it was logical that Third World studies in the 1980s should emphasise empirical research, linked only occasionally to metatheory.

In the meantime, however, attempts were increasingly being made to go beyond the development theory impasse. The contributions in this volume offer an overview of these endeavours, without, however, coming up with a fully-fledged new theory of development. The aim of the anthology is to examine the scientific tools which could be used to construct a post-impasse development theory, and to identify constraints on their application.

This introductory chapter provides the reader with some necessary background to the discussions. It begins with a short overview of the major Marxist and neo-Marxist development theories which were criticised so severely in the 1980s. Next, several contributions to the impasse debate which subsequently arose are dealt with, using David Booth's article on the subject as a central point of reference (1985). In the following section, several attempts to reconstruct development theory will be introduced – e.g., the regulation school and post-imperialism. Attention then shifts to the question of whether the post-modern discourse has anything positive to offer post-impasse development studies, other then a general criticism of theory formation.

Many of the themes discussed will be elaborated in the other contributions to this volume.

An Overview of Neo-Marxist Development Theories

Relevant to any discussion of Marxist and neo-Marxist development theories are their points of similarity and difference. Both Marxism and neo-Marxism regard social and political relations as determined by the primacy of production relations. However, as far as development theory is concerned, the differences between the two schools of thought are considerable. The major points of difference are the following:

1. Marxism is Eurocentric in its approach. It examines imperialism from the perspective of the central capitalist countries (the core), looks for reasons for imperialism's existence (the search for markets, cheap raw materials and labour so as to maintain profits at the core) and, consequently, for imperialism's function in the economic development of the core countries.

Neo-Marxism, on the other hand, looks at imperialism from the perspective of the peripheral countries, studying the consequences on the periphery of imperialist penetration. The best-known neo-Marxist development theories are the dependency theories, the modes of production theories and the world systems theories, which will be dealt with later.

2. Marxism emphasises the historically progressive role of capitalism. Marx and the 'early' Lenin describe the role of the spread of capitalism in Eastern despotic societies as historically progressive. Economic development was stimulated as major feudal landholders transformed themselves into capitalist entrepreneurs. Simultaneously the feudal yoke was lifted from the shoulders of the peasants, who would in due course form a working class (impossible under a feudal system), which could then be recruited for a socialist revolution.

In his later publications, Lenin (1917) pointed out the dangers of exorbitant profits being transferred from the periphery to the core countries, retarding capitalistic development potential. Further, he pointed to the relationships between the local bourgeoisie in the periphery and the bourgeoisie in the core, preventing the genesis of a progressive bourgeoisie (as in Western Europe during the Industrial Revolution).

The unilinearity of orthodox Marxism is obvious: societies evolve from feudalism to capitalism and finally to socialism. This unilinear thinking will be criticised below.

Neo-Marxists disagree with this historically progressive role of imperialism and capitalism, arguing that they are more likely to lead to underdevelopment in the periphery than development. Second, they see other potentially revolutionary actors apart from workers, namely peasants. In the 1980s this vision had to make room for the attention focused on yet other actors, the 'new social movements'. (I will return to this point).

3. Marxists still adhere to a 19th-century development optimism. For example, they view the concept of scarcity as an invention of the bourgeoisie to legitimise economic inequality.

Increasingly, neo-Marxists integrate an ecological consciousness in their vision, although this approach is very recent and rather problematic (Benton 1989).

4. In discussing the appropriation of economic surplus, neo-Marxists look not only at class relations (where one class exploits the labour of another), but also at relations in a spatial sense where appropriation of surplus can play a role, namely between countries. This follows the 'later' Lenin, who signalled the possibility of excessive profiteering in this way.

Dependency Theory

One of the best-known neo-Marxist development theories is the dependency theory. As with most social science theories, this theory was a child of its time (the end of the 1960s), the major characteristics of which were:

1. *The failure of the import substitution strategy.* After World War 2 a number of Latin American countries (Brazil, Chile, Mexico, Argentina) adopted an industrialisation programme emphasising the so-called 'infant industry' argument, that goes back to the 19th-century German economist Friedrich List. Analyses by the Economic Commission for Latin America (ECLA), under the direction of Raul Prebisch, confirmed a deterioration in the terms of trade for traditional Latin American primary product exports compared to imported industrial goods. A number of countries consequently decided to produce industrial goods themselves, both to

limit their dependence on imported goods and to set an autonomous development process in place.

Towards the end of the 1960s it was becoming increasingly clear that this import substitution policy was not decreasing dependency on foreign countries. Foreign companies went behind tariff walls, national industry remained dependent on the import of machinery, and the internal market was too limited (through unequal income distribution) to generate sufficient demand. The dependent countries showed a pattern of increasing influence of foreign capital and increasing dependency. According to the dependency theorists (*dependentistas*), this process led to a growing social, political and economic marginalisation of many Latin Americans. This large-scale marginalisation could not be adequately explained by the then-current modernisation theory, which blamed the traditional (meaning non-functional or even dysfunctional) values of the marginalised population for preventing their integration into the economic dynamic.

A number of political events were also of significance in the birth of dependency theory.

2. The Cuban revolution. In 1959 this event presented Latin America with the possibility of socialist revolution. This created the demand for theoretical support which was not provided by orthodox Marxist writings on revolution.

3. The military coup in Brazil. This coup d'état in 1964 led to a policy that opened the floodgates for foreign capital, resulting in increasing marginalisation of the working population. Many critical academics, among them the future *dependentistas*, were exiled abroad, where they began to examine, and to criticise, the economic model of the Brazilian government.

4. The US invasion of the Dominican Republic. In 1965 this invasion quashed a popular uprising (supported by some enlightened army officers), emphasising that imperialism was prepared to defend its interests in Latin America. Anti-imperialist feelings in Latin America stirred up by this intervention played a distinct role in the development of dependency theory.

Dependency theory drew on a diverse range of earlier theoretic schools.[1] Hence, it is hardly surprising that there has been a diversity of elaborations of the dependency idea.[2] Nonetheless, the common spirit of the time allowed the following consensus to be reached with respect to the dependency concept:

- Underdevelopment is a historical process. It is not a condition necessarily intrinsic to the Third World.
- The dominant and dependent countries together form a capitalist system (a standpoint which would later be developed by world systems theoreticians).
- Underdevelopment is an inherent consequence of the functioning of the world system. The periphery is plundered of its surplus: this leads to development of the core and underdevelopment of the periphery.

There was also a reasonable level of agreement about the role of multinational corporations:

- Multinationals impose a universal consumption pattern, without taking local needs into account.
- They use capital-intensive techniques in areas with large labour resources.
- They out-compete national capital, or undertake joint ventures with local capital.
- They use a variety of methods to transfer capital (e.g., fictitious price systems).
- They involve themselves in national political and economic affairs, via (among others) their relationships with the local bourgeoisie.

In short, the contention was that both a penetration of bank and industrial capital, and a consumption ideology that alienated the periphery from itself and made it dependent on the core, led to large-scale marginalisation and the non-realisation of development potential.

In the beginning there was little criticism from the modernisation school; increasingly, however, orthodox Marxists took the neo-Marxist renegades to task. In the early 1970s the critique concentrated on André Gunder Frank (1967, 1969), not necessarily because he was the most typical of the dependency school, but for a number of other reasons. First, Frank wrote in English – the Spanish of the other *dependentistas* seems to have been too inaccessible to the critics. Second, Frank was both polemical and outspoken in his arguments. He was also sometimes placed with the world systems theorists because he not only wrote about Latin America but also about the historical development of the capitalist world system, and the 'true' world system writers based themselves on his work.

It is beyond the scope of this introduction fully to elaborate Frank's ideas and the criticisms thereof. I will, however, look at one element of this criticism, as it led to the formation of the modes of production theories and emphasised the contrast between Marxists and neo-Marxists.

Frank asserted that Latin America could be characterised as capitalist practically from the start of the colonial period. There was no question of the dual society proposed by modernisation theorists. There was something approximating production for the world market and there was a system for appropriation of the economic surplus. The way in which the surplus was appropriated varied over time (from plunder to unequal trade), but the surplus was always usurped in one way or another.

Frank's assertion that Latin America was capitalist from the beginning of the colonial period brought him under heavy fire, particularly from the Argentinian economist Ernesto Laclau (1971). Laclau argued that Frank had used a mistaken definition of capitalism, that capitalism was a mode of production, rather than a mode of exchange. He concentrated on the sort of labour relations which created a product in the first place, rather than on what happened to the surplus. If, rather than the manner of production, matters such as production for a market and appropriation of the surplus were of prime importance in defining capitalism, reasoned Laclau, then capitalism should be defined as having existed since the Ancient Greeks.[3] According to Laclau, such a definition turns capitalism into a meaningless concept.

In the meantime, the modernisation theorists had recovered from their shock, and began to direct their criticism at the inadequate empirical evidence supporting the dependency thesis that differences in degree of dependency were causally related to differences in economic development (Ray 1973, von Albertini 1980, Bairoch 1980). In general this criticism followed the tactic of erecting a straw man (of dependency theories) which was then knocked down. Soon, however, modernisation theorists became more interested in computerised global growth models (Kahn and Wiener 1967, Rostow 1978, Kahn *et al.* 1979).

Modes of Production Theory

Laclau went further in his criticism of Frank, attempting to develop an idea where the emphasis lay not on the circulation sphere (trade, appropriation of surplus) but on the production sphere. The question of how products were produced (the production relationships) was further examined. In France, especially, the modes of production concept was given a clearer theoretical form, particularly by anthropologists Pierre Philippe Rey (1971, 1973) and Claude Meillassoux (1971, 1972, 1981). The anthropologists found an opportunity to address what they saw as a 'need' in the dependency theories, namely, lack of attention to the local level.

The basic idea of the modes of production theory is that a number of modes of production coexist in a society, and that they have a relationship to each other (regarding exchange of labour, goods, capital, etc.): they articulate with each other. Further, it was thought that a relationship between capitalist and non-capitalist modes of production was favourable for the capitalist mode of production. Apartheid was used as a classic example of an articulation between capitalist and non-capitalist modes of production. The workers lived in their traditional homelands, where they had land that didn't produce enough to live on, and so had to offer their labour to South African industry. Salaries, however, could remain low, because workers had some income from their land.

This example shows that a capitalist mode of production not only relates to existing non-capitalist modes of production, but it can also create new ones. The conclusion was that in many developing countries capitalism articulated with non-capitalist modes of production and so retarded the development of these countries.

From the time this concept became known in international literature there was a boom in the number of modes of production identified by anthropologists. In addition to Rey's colonial (see also Banaji 1972), lineage and transitional modes of production, other modes of production were 'discovered', such as the peasant mode of production (Bartra 1975, Harrison 1977), the African mode of production (Coquery-Vidrovitch 1969) and the petty-commodity mode of production (Poulantzas 1975, Amin 1974, 1976). Eventually it appeared as if every village could be identified as having its own unique mode of production, and the concept threatened to become meaningless (Foster-Carter 1978).

The Marxists argued that this neo-Marxist interpretation of modes of production was incorrect. Marx's standpoint was that 'mode of production' was a concept that had to be used at a national level, and that at any one point in time, there was only one mode of production.

Opinions on the articulation of production modes also diverged among supporters of the theory. Some felt that non-capitalist modes of production had resisted capitalist penetration, others argued that the non-capitalist production modes were kept alive by capitalism, if not even created by capitalism.[4]

The modes of production concept maintained itself successfully for a reasonably long time; however, interest in it began to wane in the 1980s. Nonetheless, the development of this concept offered many fruitful studies during the 1970s, above all because these discussions offered insight into why development projects can be problematic.[5]

World Systems Theory

Just as the dependency school was a child of its time, so were the world systems theories. This approach was developed in the mid-1970s, when East Asian countries were experiencing swift growth that could no longer be described as dependent development, particularly as they had begun to challenge the economic superiority of the USA in a number of areas.

Another factor conducive to the rise of world systems theories was the oncoming crisis in socialist countries. The failure of the Cultural

Revolution in China and economic stagnation in the Eastern Bloc led to an opening in the direction of international capital. Previously unthinkable alliances were formed: for example between Washington and Peking. These were developments to which revolutionary Marxism could contribute nothing. It could be said that developments were happening on a world scale that were not covered by existing development theories.

Wallerstein was the most outspoken figure in this new terrain. His work from the mid-1970s onwards was strongly based on the ideas of André Gunder Frank and other *dependentistas*. Unequal trade, the exploitation of the periphery by the core, and the existence of a world market were concepts taken from dependency school thinking.

Like Frank, Wallerstein argued that a capitalist world economy had existed since the 16th century, that is, since the beginning of the colonial era. He saw non-capitalist modes of production as a part of capitalism, the definition of which (based on 19th-century England) he saw as too narrow. Increasingly, countries which were previously isolated and self-supporting became involved in the world economy. The final result is the creation of a core and a periphery, with a number of semi-periphery countries in between.

The core consists of the industrialised countries, the periphery of the agricultural export countries. The semi-peripheral countries (like Brazil), which act as a buffer between the core and the periphery, are differentiated from the periphery by their more significant industrial production. The semi-periphery functions as a go-between: it imports hi-tech from the core, and in return exports semi-manufactured goods to the core. It imports raw materials from the periphery and exports to it industrial end-products.

Wallerstein saw the Newly Industrialised Countries (NICs) as examples of the semi-periphery. A peripheral country can achieve the status of semi-periphery and in this way can be brought into the core. The spread of as large a market as possible is essential to his reasoning. These were areas where Wallerstein clearly diverged from dependency school thinking, if only in that *dependentistas* did not reason in terms of a semi-periphery.

The world systems concept was seen, in this period, as a handy solution to a problem that *dependentistas* were increasingly confronted with: how to differentiate between internal and external factors as explanations for underdevelopment. The world systems theory offered a simple solution: in moving to a more abstract level (with countries as global analysis units) there are no more external factors. There are also no longer different sorts of capitalism, such as core capitalism and peripheral capitalism; instead there is one capitalist world system. The origin of development and underdevelopment is then found in the incorporation of countries within the world system. Underdevelopment occurs because countries are subject to a trade regime and produce for a world market that is characterised by unequal trade.[6] Wallerstein was criticised by followers of the modes of production theory, who argued that there were a number of production modes, each articulating in its own way with the dominant capitalist mode.[7]

Another world systems author is Samir Amin, who began publishing on this topic in 1976. In contrast to Wallerstein, Amin did not agree with the presence of a capitalist mode of production in Latin America from the 16th century. He did agree with the existence of a non-capitalist mode of production which saw its surplus appropriated through unequal trade. This unequal trade led to a stagnation in the expansion of the national market and thus to a disarticulated economic system.[8] Like Wallerstein, Amin argued for the existence of the go-betweens, the semi-peripheral countries.

In general, the criticism of the world systems approach is the same as that of the dependency theories: the neglect of class analysis, the neglect of the diversity of the Third World, and the assumption of non-workable political options such as self-reliance and a socialist world government. In taking a global view, the findings are difficult to translate to the concrete realities of Third World countries.

As with previous approaches, the world systems theory was also pushed to the background in the 1980s.

Some Causes of the Impasse in Development Theories
The criticism of Marxist and neo-Marxist development theories as well as of modernisation theories led to a theoretical vacuum in the 1980s, which for many Third World countries was a decade of economic crisis.

In the past 30 years (the period of the existence of development theories) developing countries have realised an improvement in life expectancy, child mortality and literacy rates. However, these are averages only and are less valid for lower socio-economic groups. In the 1980s there was actually a reversal in these indicators (the outbreak of cholera epidemics in Latin America and Africa point to this). With the current per capita growth of 1.3–1.6 per cent it will take another 150 years for Third World countries to achieve half the per capita income of Western countries, and that is without taking into consideration the sometimes negative growth figures of the 1980s. Instead of a self-sustained growth (to use Rostow's terms), many developing countries are up to their ears in debt. Problems such as unemployment, housing, human rights, poverty and landlessness are increasing at alarming rates. UNICEF estimated a fall of 10–15 per cent in the income of the poor in the Third World between 1983 and 1987. In 1978 the Third World received 5.6 per cent of the world's income; in 1984 that had fallen to 4.5 per cent. The 'trickle-down' process had failed absolutely. Two hundred years ago the income ratio between the world's rich and poor countries was 1.5:1, in 1960 it was 20:1, in 1980 it went up to 46:1 and in 1989 the ratio was 60:1 (Trainer 1989, World Bank 1991).

From the mid-1980s the vacuum in development theories was raised in an increasing number of publications in terms of a crisis, an impasse, for the following reasons:[9]

1. The realisation that the gap between poor and rich countries continued to widen and that the developing countries were unlikely to be able to bridge that gap whatever strategy they would follow.

2. The realisation that developing countries, in the 1980s, were preoccupied with short-term policies aimed at keeping their heads above water in terms of debt. Policies did not take intermediate or long-term goals into consideration, nor did it seem likely that they would be able to do so in the future.

3. The growing awareness that economic growth has had, and is having, a catastrophic effect on the environment. It was calculated that if developed countries maintained their current level of growth, by 2050 they would need an output eight times higher than the current level. That this would cause an ecological disaster is obvious. Advocates of sustainable development argued that growth = development is not only invalid for the Third World, but also for the wealthy industrialised countries – and why wait for a major ecological catastrophe before we realise this? The 'zero growth' option increasingly came into the picture, but found no foundation in any of the already discredited development theories.

4. The delegitimisation of socialism as a viable political means of solving the problem of underdevelopment. Although Marxist and neo-Marxist development theories were never particularly strong in presenting realisable policy alternatives, socialist-inspired development trajectories were now totally removed from the policy agenda.

5. The conviction that the world market is an over-arching whole which cannot be approached using development policies oriented at the national level. Individual nation-states are assigned an increasingly smaller function. Development theories, however, still used the nation-state as a meaningful context for political praxis.

6. The growing recognition of differentiation within the Third World that could no longer be handled by global theories assuming a homogenous First and Third World. The 1980s saw an avalanche of books on the subject of whether or not 'the' Third World exists as an entity.

7. The advancement of post-modernism within the social sciences, where there has been a tendency to undermine 'the great narratives' (capitalism, socialism, communism, etc.) by arguing that there is no common reality outside the individual. Political alternatives, which always exist by the grace of a minimum of common perception, are in this way manoeuvred out of sight. Development theories based on metadiscourses have no right to exist, according to post-modernists.

At the end of the 1980s, the only group not touched by the crisis (and who reacted with a sometimes irritating and unfounded triumphalism) were the neo-liberal adherents of the open market ideology. This post-Keynesian vision (also known as Reaganomics) has, since the middle of the 1970s, turned the crisis to its advantage.

Neo-Liberalism

From the mid-1970s this development ideology enjoyed increasing popularity. The oil crisis at the beginning of that decade and the subsequent restructuring of international capitalism led to a redefinition of the role of the state. This meant the end of Keynesianism and the idea of the welfare state. Publications by Bauer (1981, 1984), Little (1974, 1982), Lal (1983) and Balassa (1982) gave substance to what John Toye (1987) labelled the counter-revolution in development thinking. What started in the 1970s as a neo-monetarist vision on the problem of hyperinflation in many Third World countries, grew into a new development ideology.

State interference with the market mechanism was considered ineffective, counterproductive and basically inconsistent. According to David Lehmann (1990), Chile under Pinochet exhibited one of the clearest examples of neo-liberal policy. The state should primarily endeavour to lower the fiscal deficit through devaluation, deregulation of prices and decreasing state subsidies. The circumstances in Chile at the time – a military dictatorship – were highly suitable for the introduction of this neo-liberal and neo-monetarist economic policy. The rounds of applause which Chile earned in international financial circles encouraged many currently democratising governments in developing countries to follow Chile's example. Limiting the role of the state, a liberal economy and a strict monetary policy according to the guidelines of the International Monetary Fund (IMF) and the World Bank, are the major policy options in many Third World countries.

However, as Chossudovsky (1991) rightly observes, the structural adjustment package of the IMF can increasingly be considered as the cause rather then the solution to the economic problems experienced in the Third World. The withdrawal of the state led to the increasing impoverishment of low-income groups. Liberalisation of the economy and the growing emphasis on export-led industrialisation resulted in a dual economy, with one sector producing for the international market and another sector producing for a shrinking national market. Euphoric interpretations of Mexico's and Argentina's recent economic upsurge seem rather premature because the state deficit has been cut back primarily by large-scale privatisations which cannot go on indefinitely.

As a development ideology, neo-liberalism most resembles the well known modernisation paradigm, but in fact it has less to offer because the role of the state has been minimalised.

After so many years of oligarchic, restricted democratic or military regimes which neglected the basic needs of their people, many Third World countries in Latin America, Africa and Asia alike have currently entered a process of transition to democracy which could create the conditions for states finally to start caring for the poor and the excluded. However, the neo-liberal trajectory denies the Third World states the policy tools to intercede actively in favour of those without jobs, houses, health care, schooling and food. Instead, national assets are sold out on a large scale to (inter)national private capital, leading to a recolonisation of the Third World. The current status of the concept of modernisation – and modernisation theory for that matter – seems increasingly to refer only to political aspects of the transition to democracy in the Third World (Apter 1987).

Substantiating the Impasse

Although in the preceding section some criticism of neo-Marxist development theory has already been dealt with, it must be pointed out that much of this criticism has been generated within the (neo)Marxist camp itself. In 1985, David Booth published an article in which he approached the problem somewhat more thoroughly, raising questions over both the neo-Marxist and Marxist development theories as such. This article has since functioned as an important reference for the theoretical substantiation of the impasse in the sociology of development.

Stuart Corbridge (1989) identifies three dimensions in Booth's critique of (neo)Marxist development studies: 'essentialism', 'economism' and 'epistemology'. Regarding the first dimension, Booth argues that (neo)Marxists, from the perspective of their metatheory, attempt to prove the necessity of economic development *casu quo* underdevelopment as such, instead of attempting to explain the underlying dynamics. In this respect, Booth criticises both the circulationists and productionists in the Marxist camp.[10] According to Booth, the similarity between these two schools of thought is that capitalism is defined in terms of laws that produce inescapable and fixed outcomes (for example, a socialist revolution). Theories with this characteristic have been named teleological. The publications of Bill Warren (1980), which have a structural Marxist character wherein Warren positions himself against the *dependencia* theories, are also placed by Booth under the 'teleological' banner. The dependency school was further criticised on the basis of the tautological relationship between underdevelopment and dependency.[11] It is worth mentioning here that modernisation theory also exhibited a teleological trait: the example of the United States was held up to developing countries as an end goal that was reachable by following the rules laid down by the modernisation theory.

The second dimension in Booth's critique refers to the economism in Marxist development studies. With this he means that the complex of political, social and cultural factors in developing countries is seen as a consequence of the national and international economic structure. According to Booth, this interpretation interferes with the study of these factors as independent dimensions. To interpret culture patterns in developing countries exclusively in terms of the functional needs of the metropolitan capital is meaningless in Booth's eyes.

The third dimension, that of epistemology, concerns Booth's comment that Marxists have closed their eyes to relevant issues in what he calls 'mainstream' literature. They have ignored, for example, literature about industrialisation processes in the Third World, where the state fulfils a pioneering role. Booth claims that Marxists were placed in an epistemological confrontation with 'mainstream' literature that led to concepts (such as unequal trade and exploitation) which were rarely based on empirical data, were almost never calculable and, on top of that, were wrapped in pseudo-scientific jargon.[12]

Although Booth's article attracted much attention, the basis of his critique was not in itself new. In 1979 Henry Bernstein was already moving away from the *dependentistas* and the modes of production school. Bernstein reproached the then-radical development theorists for wanting to have their cake and eat it too. The fundamental difference between the developed core in the industrialised world and the underdeveloped periphery was, according to Bernstein, cast in terms (respectively) of autonomous and dependent development processes. On the other hand, there is talk of exploitation of the periphery by the core to oppose the fall in the rate of profit. According to Bernstein this logic is not consistent: one cannot describe the development process of the core as independent if that process depends on exploitative relations with the periphery in order to keep the dynamics of its own development going.

Further, Bernstein scorns the modes of production school for the 'shopping list' of production modes which turns it into an empty concept. His conclusion – that underdevelopment is not a uniform process with uniform causes and consequences – led to Bernstein's conviction that a theory of underdevelopment was not possible. He sees attempts to construct such a theory as ideologically coloured. With this critique, Bernstein in fact pre-empted both Booth and post-modernist thought. However, neither Bernstein in 1979 nor Booth in 1985 (contrary to his chapter in this volume) offered a concrete way out of the impasse in radical development theories.

Continuation of the Impasse Debate

In an article published in 1988, Leslie Sklair added weight to Booth's argument for a temporary shift of attention within development studies from the level of theory to the level of *meta*theory.

Sklair sees the only way out of the impasse described by Booth as the combination of metatheory, theory and empirical research in one project.[13] According to Sklair, the impasse arose from the confusion of metatheory and theory, where attempts were made to test a metatheory which was, by definition, untestable. On top of that is the problem that diverse, and sometimes divergent, theories can be derived from one metatheory. These can be internally consistent, but are not necessarily consistent with each other.

As an example Sklair cites the historic-materialist metatheory from which were derived theories of 'dependent underdevelopment' (Frank 1976, 1969), 'dependent development' (Cardoso and Faletto 1970) and 'dependency reversal' (Warren 1980). Sklair follows the same reasoning for gender theories such as liberal feminism, socialist feminism and radical feminism, which he sees as deriving from the same historic-materialist metatheory, and which take as their central substantive element the conflict between 'patriarchy and the liberation of women under capitalism'. Sklair argues for a cross-fertilisation between theories that are derived from the same metatheory, for example, between 'dependent development' and particular gender theories that can then be empirically tested by a study of the role of women in the internationalisation of production.

Sklair's differentiation between theory and metatheory is not in itself new; however, it is worth bringing it to the fore again in the light of the development theory impasse. The suggestion of cross-fertilisation can also be useful. However, two problems are still with us. First is the post-modernist criticism of metatheoretical assumptions, such as those inherited from the Enlightenment. (I shall return to this point later in this chapter.) Second, I get a hint in Sklair's article of a not-unknown manoeuvre, namely, that if a theory is untestable, or falsified through testing, then it can be promoted to the rank of metatheory. That looks to me like merely shifting the problem, rather than solving it. I say a 'not-unknown manoeuvre' as it puts me in mind of the way world systems theorists 'solved' the problem confronting the *dependentistas*: the difficult empirical difference between internal and external factors that play a role in (under)development. This problem was solved by world systems theorists by shifting their analysis to a higher level. On a world level we are no longer confronted with the problematic differentiation between internal and external factors.

Vandergeest and Buttel (1988) have also picked up the thread of Booth's critique of the underlying metatheoretical assumptions of Marxism. Furthermore, they have established that neo-Marxism sets itself against an orthodox Parsonian version of Max Weber (Parsons 1937) that was subsequently annexed by the modernisation theory. They feel that this version does not do justice to Weber's thinking, and point to a recent school of neo-Weberians to which Claus Offe (1985), Charles Tilly (1984), Pierre Bourdieu (1977) and Anthony Giddens (1981, 1984), among others, belong.

According to Vandergeest and Buttel, Weber accused Marxists of failing to see their model as an ideal type and attempting to identify reality with the model. At the same time Weber held the opinion that socio-political analyses should put more emphasis on the 'historic-interpretative specificity'. This approach stands firmly against the way Parsons and the modernisation theory have reified Weber's concept of ideal type.[14] Neo-Weberians handle the concept of ideal type as neither outcome deterministic (teleological) nor as explanatory of reality. The identification of obstacles to development (as happens in Marxism and the modernisation theory) is irrelevant, according to neo-Weberians, because this assumes a particular, identifiable route to a defined end-situation that is called 'development'. Thus, in the modernisation theory, culture is seen as something static and, in the Third World, a possible obstacle to development. In Marxist analysis, on the other hand, culture is seen as being determined by the economy. The neo-Weberian approach, however, sees culture as a creative process that must be studied in locally oriented research.

Vandergeest and Buttel also label analysis of the state, where political power is placed in a cultural context, as belonging to the neo-Weberian approach. As a possible disadvantage they cite Weber's lack of attention to practical political intervention. Concerning what must be done with a quantity of locally oriented research, Vandergeest and Buttel point to the possibility, in fact the necessity, of looking within the heterogeneity of developing countries for common denominators.

It is a pity that these authors have not developed this line of thought further. The necessity of historical comparative research is, for me, precisely the point here, and something Vandergeest and Buttel correctly refer to in their introduction.

Mouzelis (1988) takes up the baton handed on by Vandergeest and Buttel. So as not to become bogged down in generalities such as 'the reality in the Third World is so complex and diverse', Mouzelis proposes ' ... to go beyond the case study, without sacrificing context in terms of time and space'. He proposes an attempt to analyse specific development trajectories and use that analysis as a basis for typologies, as Barrington Moore (1966) has done for industrialised countries. Mouzelis assumes that if development trajectories plotted for Argentina, Chile and Brazil (for example) are compared to those of the Asian NICs (Newly Industrialised Countries), we would then be presented with essential factors that influence the development process, such as the amount and form of state dirigism, the influence of agrarian reform, relations between agriculture and industry, and the development of the internal market.

Mouzelis's approach emphasises that it is not necessary to limit comparisons to regional studies; for example, it is valid to place Greece in the same catagory as the countries of the Latin American southern cone. He argues here for a more autonomous position for the political dimension in the analysis.[15] Thus he sees military regimes in Latin America more as independent actors than as promoters of ruling class interests. According to Mouzelis, development trajectories in the Third World are more often characterised by competition for the means of domination and coercion than competition for means of production. He refers explicitly to concepts developed by the French regulation school, namely regime of accumulation and mode of regulation, which is discussed in the following section.

Initiating Post-Impasse Development Theory

The continuation and development of the debate begun by Booth (detailed above) over the impasse in (neo)Marxist development theories has shed light on a number of attempts to give substance to post-impasse development theories. It is remarkable that a number of these attempts are not particularly recent and even predate the generally felt impasse.

In this section I will discuss the French regulation school, the actor-oriented approach, post-imperialism, gender studies, and finally the research agenda on sustainable development, which is in fact more concerned with defining development strategies than with theoretical explorations.

The Regulation School

The French regulation school, led by Lipietz and Aglietta, formulated its thinking in the early 1980s. The essence of the regulation school was clearly presented in a succinct article by Lipietz in 1984. Like Mouzelis, Lipietz is of the opinion that regularities in development trajectories are observable through historical comparative research. He explicitly warns against the deduction of a concrete reality from supposed regularities that are themselves deduced from a universal concept such as imperialism or dependency.

According to Lipietz, regularities (that is, a sequence of contradictions, crises and transformation) in development trajectories can be abstracted in two concepts: 'regime of accumulation' and 'mode of regulation'. A regime of accumulation describes the way in which the economic product is allocated between consumption and accumulation. In Marxist terminology this leads to a particular stabilised reproduction scheme.[16] This is coupled with a particular mode of regulation: regulating norms, values and laws – in short, a set of internalised rules and procedures that integrate social elements in individual behaviour.[17]

Lipietz cites Fordism as an example of a regime of accumulation and a mode of regulation.[18] He warns against the approach that a predictable dynamic in capitalism produces a particular consecutive combination of his dyadic concepts. He opts for *a posteriori* functionalism, where the furthest one can go is to assert that a particular combination of regime of accumulation and mode of regulation can reproduce itself for a period without crisis. The stability and consistency of an economic world system is therefore not the consequence of the working of the 'invisible hand' of capitalism: rather it is the result of the interaction between relatively autonomous national regimes of accumulation. Thus the functioning of multinational corporations leads to an international division of labour; however, there is still the prerequisite of the cooperation of the individual countries, which can be further complicated by involvement in a completely different project.[19]

Lipietz's approach can offer a way of giving a more precise form to the historical comparative research supported by a number of authors previously discussed. In any case, it prevents Argentina falling into the same category as the 'banana republics' because of the export of primary products. Nevertheless, Lipietz finds it difficult to heed his own warning that the theory of international relations is extremely sensitive to functionalism and holism. He suggests that so-called peripheral Fordism, just as Fordism is a particular combination of a regime of accumulation and a mode of regulation.[20] At the same time he argues, justifiably, that there are vast differences in the mode of regulation between, for example, South Korea and Mexico (in terms of land reform, for instance).

Lipietz's observation that development strategies cannot be seen out of the context of the position the countries ('social formations' in Lipietz's terms) take in the international circuit, leads us to two other attempts to go beyond the development theory impasse.

The Actor-Oriented Approach

In contrast to the work of Lipietz and Aglietta, which concentrates on the level of nation-state and internationalisation, sociologist Norman Long (1990) is more interested in the relationships between the meso level (the 'habitus': the wider context wherein access to power and resources plays a role) and the micro level. In his 'actor-oriented approach' Long asserts that the actors' behaviour is not derived from their structural position – a similar standpoint to Lipietz, but on a lower analytical level. Long argues that both the modernisation theory and the neo-Marxist approach are too deterministic, that their vision of development trajectories is too linear, and that they see social change as emanating from external impulses (such as state policy or a dynamic in the market system). For Long, human (re)action and consciousness play a central role.

Long indicated his actor-oriented approach as early as the 1970s, in his work with Brian Roberts in Long and Roberts, 1978. On the basis of his research in Peru and Mexico, Long came to the conclusion that even where structural conditions and types of external impulses are relatively constant, behaviour of actors can take a diverse range of forms. He expressly did not reduce behaviour of individual actors to individual motives and interests. This would lead to an empty voluntarism. Instead, Long is interested in the interface between the meso level and the individual actor. He suggests that the latter has a wider range of actions available than is usually presumed. Furthermore, these actions can have an effect on a meso level, contrary to the widely-held view that it is primarily meso-level impulses that determine the behaviour of individual actors.

Referring to Hindess (1986), Long asserts that actors have access to a variety of discourses upon which to base their actions. Long labels not only individuals as actors (or 'agents') but also corporations, the church and the state bureaucracy. On the other hand, he does not see gender or class as actors or agents. He denies having reverted to the trap of ethnographic particularism, because he specifically concentrates on the relation between the meso and micro levels.

Reacting to Long's actor-oriented approach, David Slater (1990) asserts that Long correctly refutes the Marxist 'econocentric' vision of class as actor. Class is an abstract concept and is therefore not capable of social action. However, he finds Long's rendering of the neo-Marxist dependency idea somewhat one-sided, in his neglect of Cardoso's concept of dependent development, for example. Moreover, Slater – *à la* Leslie Sklair – would like to see more attention paid to the integration of metatheory, theory and empirical research, and to social movements and resistance on a regional/local level.

Post-Imperialism

The third proposal for a renewal in development theories, which I would like to cover briefly, is that of post-imperialism, which has its most important exponents in David Becker and Richard Sklar (1987). The latter began to develop his ideas in 1976.

Post-imperialism is not actually a development theory, but rather a set of ideas about the political and social organisation of international capitalism. Becker and Sklar begin with a critique of the standard neo-imperialist theories. In the first neo-imperialist variant that they identify, capitalism is seen to be the root of all evil (surplus extraction, inappropriate technology, anti-democratic bourgeoisie in alliance with international capital, etc.). The second neo-imperialist theory they argue against is Cardoso's 'dependent development', the viewpoint of which was that the Third World was industrialising (also Warren's position) but that it remained structurally incomplete. Developing countries then must bring themselves into line with a world economy dominated by transnational corporations, which could supply the missing inputs, and as such would also be in a position to exercise decision-making power. The authors reproach Cardoso for underestimating the NICs' capacities for technical innovation, and for presenting an unrealistic alternative in the form of total autonomy and a state that would have to represent the will of the people.

Becker and Sklar contend that neo-imperialism in general is based on the false assumption that international capitalist expansion is of necessity imperialistic in its nature. In their vision the transnational corporations (TNCs) offer Third World countries access to capital, markets and technology. There is a harmony of interests between politically autonomous countries, in spite of differences in phases of economic development. There is then no question of a growing international domination. Everywhere in the Third World the elite will form stable relationships with the TNCs, according to Becker and Sklar. Thus there is a 'managerial' bourgeoisie consisting of a 'corporate wing' and a 'local wing', which in general have common interests. The only danger for this coalition occurs when the 'local wing' expresses overly nationalistic rhetoric. The TNCs tend to behave as 'good corporate citizens'. Becker and Sklar call this adaptation to the local political climate the 'doctrine of domicile'.[21]

Furthermore, Becker and Sklar contend that the members of the international bourgeoisie are also influenced by development values in the host country, and that communication is not simply one-way traffic between international and national bourgeoisie.[22] By assertively and prágmatically interacting with foreign investment and the corporate managerial elite, a new local bourgeoisie has, in many Third World countries, managed to usurp political power from the old oligarchical elite. The new local bourgeoisie no longer needs an authoritative administration to be able to exercise their class domination. Becker and Sklar feel that their post-imperialist interpretation corresponds with the beginning of a post-nationalist period.

In a certain sense, post-imperialism seems to show some similarity to Long's actor-oriented approach, in that the spotlight is on the actors in the development process, and not so specifically on mechanistic processes. Still, Becker and Sklar employ a much more structuralist approach. Their class analysis is characterised by awarding important weight to the political context in comparison to the economic over-determinism in the orthodox Marxist class analysis.[23]

In a critical comment, Frieden (1987) praises the post-imperialists for drawing attention to the assertive pragmatism with which Third World countries can respond to foreign capital investments. Frieden (justifiably) comments that these ideas have not yet reached the level of development theory, and that much analysis still has to be done. Class formation and the dialectics of class struggle are central in the analysis of post-imperialism, but Frieden warns not only against political determinism, but also against underestimating the economic levers available to international capital to gain entrance to certain countries. In addition, he establishes that the case studies used (Zambia and Peru) concentrate on TNCs in the mining sector (copper). In comparison to other economic activities this is a very specific sector and not particularly representative of the behaviour of foreign capital in the Third World.[24]

Frieden's criticism is justified. Post-imperialism is not a development theory; at most it is a theory regarding a recently arisen international oligarchy. This 'managerial' bourgeoisie is a new class which defends its interests against the proletariat and the old oligarchic classes. In the Third World this results in a great diversity in relations between the state and (international) capital. Although attention to the behaviour of the corporate and 'local' part of the managerial bourgeoisie is a useful element within post-imperialism, it places too much emphasis on the political element in the analysis, and not enough on the economic element.[25] Despite criticism by Becker and Sklar of the historical *dependencia* school of Cardoso *et al.*, the strength here was the connection, on a national level, of an economic analysis to an analysis of the variety in class alliances and class oppositions.

The post-impasse development studies dealt with up to now vary in regard to the formal object (the explanatory framework) and the material object (what needs to be explained). Despite their differences, the development theories discussed have at least one common feature, namely positivism. The world is regarded as it is and not as it should be. There are also, however, post-impasse approaches of a more normative nature, the most important of which concern gender studies and sustainable development.

Gender Studies

Gender studies show a dialectical relation to development theories. On the one hand, gender studies contributed to the impasse in development theories by consistently criticising the 'invisibility of women' in these theories. However, gender studies, on the other hand, used metatheories which they shared with the heavily criticised development theories. In other words, gender studies chose a material object (e.g., the position of women, gender relations), using as a formal object the same inspirational source (Marxist metatheory) as many development theories. Gender studies were thus confronted with a similar impasse, which took some time to materialise because of the epistemological confrontation which gender studies saw itself engaged in. Thus, according to Komter (1991), feminist theory in the past had constantly looked for a structuralist approach, and moved into a crisis when the material object opened more space for the study of pluralism and diversity among women. The subsequent liaisons with Marxism, psychoanalysis and post-modernism only led gender studies to growing theoretical fragmentation.

Komter limits herself to commenting upon gender studies in Western industrialised countries, but Marnia Lazreg (1988) goes beyond that. She accuses Western feminism of a Eurocentric view of the position of women in the Third World in general, and women in Islamic countries in particular. According to Lazreg, women in the Third World are considered the helpless victims of systems reigned by tradition, patriarchy and religion. Post-modern Western studies, based on the theories of Foucault and Derrida, tend to ignore totally the daily reality of women in the Third World.

Considering the analogy of the impasse in development theories and that in gender studies, the shift to post-modernism in gender studies does not come as a surprise (Delsing 1991, Risseeuw 1991). Given Lazreg's criticism, the recent attention feminist analyses have paid to Giddens's structuration theory seems most promising (Davis 1991, Wolffensperger 1991).

The theoretical field of gender studies is moving beyond the impasse but a clear post-impasse approach has yet to emerge.

Sustainable Development

Sustainable development is most often defined as a strategy to satisfy the needs of the present generation without interfering with the needs of future generations. The definition itself and the way it is used in practice offer a rather heterogeneous picture. The term sustainable development encompasses development strategies which range from light-green to dark-green, from romantic and nostalgic conservatism to utopian socialism, from absolute-zero growth in the economy to maintaining the present world economic growth rate. As a result, the 'green' notion of sustainable development could be incorporated without effort into both the 'blue' development model (neo-liberal) and the 'red' development model (socialist, and these days social democratic). In a number of cases one can therefore hardly speak of an *alternative* development model.

Employing the common terms mentioned above increasingly leads to interconnections between the discourse of sustainable development and that of women's emancipation. Exploitative behaviour towards nature, it is argued, is a typical patriarchal attitude, in which both women and nature are given a subordinate role (Mies 1986, Shiva 1988). Women's emancipation would, therefore, also lead to less exploitative relations with nature. In addition, attention to ethnic minorities in the Third World – who generally are considered to treat nature in a less damaging manner – can give further shape to sustainable development.

The different ways industrialised countries on the one hand and developing countries on the other hand regard the substantiation of sustainable development strategies point to the danger of ethnocentric handling of this concept.[26]

Bill Adams (in this volume) finds sustainable development to be a flag for many ships, and because of this the concept does not enjoy an accepted theoretical foundation. Yet, the power of the concept lies in the insights derived from micro-level praxis. Thus, Adams favours a theory formation of sustainable development which includes the macro as well as the micro: the transnational corporation and the peasant, the biosphere and the field. The fragmented praxis of ecological research, planning and policy, in developed as well as in underdeveloped countries, indicate the necessity of theory formation for sustainable development.

In his criticism of neo-Marxist development theories, Booth concluded that the problems and the solutions lay particularly at a metaphysical level. However, since the mid-1980s, criticism from post-modernism of the social sciences in general has taken a position against metatheories in any shape or form. In the present case, the impasse in development theories is increasingly attributed to a modernity discourse with untenable metaphysical starting points. The question which arises next is the extent to which post-modernism can contribute to the further shaping of post-impasse development studies. Or is post-modernism simply a fashionable ethnocentric phenomenon which manoeuvres development studies into a cul-de-sac?

Before answering this question, the next section will first briefly outline the contours of post-modernism.

Post-Modernism

Within the framework of this introduction there is no room for an extensive discourse on post-modernism.[27] I will limit myself to those elements which in the ensuing sections are directly or indirectly relevant to post-impasse development theories.

Post-modernism is a reaction to the Enlightenment narrative of the development of scientific knowledge, along lines laid out by Galileo and Newton, which should lead to a rational control by man (sic) over his natural and social surroundings. The notion of a transcendental God allowed the view that society was 'makeable'. The Enlightenment narrative is given shape in the assumed emancipation of humankind: liberation from poverty, slavery and ignorance. Since the French Revolution, liberty, equality and fraternity have been held high as a banner of modernity.

Post-modernists react against this modernity discourse. Thus Lyotard (1984, 1985) believes that Auschwitz and Stalin heralded the ultimate fiasco of the modernity project. Science is not employed to emancipate humanity, but enlisted by capital and subjugated to efficiency rather than truth. There is no one single truth, as depicted by modernity philosophy; rather there is a plurality of perspectives, each with its own language, its own rules and myths. French post-structuralists such as Derrida (1973, 1976), Deleuze and Guattari (1983, 1987) developed the thesis that language consists of a set of 'signifiers' which do not give access to reality, and where the existence of one reality is moreover doubted.[28] Symbols become more important than the message they must convey. There is no longer a distinction between truth and lie, between reason and rhetoric, between essence and semblance, between science and ideology. An apparent reality is created by mass media through an endless circulation of symbols. Production no longer sets the tone in society, consumption of symbols replaces it. Universal values do not exist and metatheories (both Marxism and modernisation theories) which take universal values as given and see society as 'makeable' are suspect and merely contribute to an apparent reality. The Enlightenment ideal of the emancipation of humanity has not been achieved nor can it be achieved.

There are three currents which fall under the term post-modernism, originating respectively from art, from literature and language philosophy (the post-structuralists), and from social sciences (the post-industrialists). The oldest claims to the title post-modernism lie with the arts, which, in the 1950s, reacted against the abstract in paintings and the International Style in architecture.

Of particular importance here is the philosophy of post-industrialism. The basic idea is that Western countries entered a post-industrial phase whereby the concentration on production of goods was replaced by production of technical knowledge (Bell 1973, Touraine 1974). Post-industrial society is a 'knowledge' society, in which a growing part of the labour force is used for the production of technical know-how. Basically, the argument goes as follows. Fordism reached a crisis in the 1970s, heralding a late-Fordist phase for capitalism, which exhibited the following features:

- increasing internationalisation of capital, especially through the spread of assembly activities;
- a decrease in importance of the nation-state, and an absolute and relative decrease of the traditional core of the working class;
- a marked increase in the service class through the increased role of management, research and financial transactions;
- increasing unemployment and a growing distinction between skilled and unskilled labourers;
- an increasing difference in consumer patterns;
- a larger role of mass media in the process of socialisation.

According to the post-industrialists, late Fordism displayed such distinct contours during the 1980s that it is legitimate to talk of a post-Fordist period. Here, the development of micro-electronics provides the industrial sector with an even more flexible organisation, with a hard core of well-paid labourers in the areas of research and development and in management. The role of the state is reduced to keeping the whole internationally competitive.[29] The individualisation of society increases (e.g., the increase in single-person or childless households). Consumption is characterised by stressing constant renewal of the products on offer. This consumer hedonism leads to 'disposable life-styles' (Berman 1982). The functionalistic aesthetic of Fordist use values, which were related to the norms of rigid Taylorist mass production, belongs permanently to the past.

I have discussed post-industrialism in some detail here because it provides a good background to understanding post-modernist schools of thought.[30] Thus Callinicos (1989, 1990) argues that it is not coincidental that post-modernism is particularly fed by French philosophers and social scientists. In these circles a number of events in Europe at the end of the 1960s and start of the 1970s were greeted as accelerations of class struggle. Euphoria over the revolts of 1968 in France and 1969 in Italy, the Portuguese revolution of 1974–75 and the end of the Franco regime in Spain in 1975-76 turned into bitter disappointments at the end of the

1970s. According to Callinicos, the tightly-laced corset of Althusserian Marxism did not offer space for any reaction other than an exodus in the direction of post-modernism.

The manner in which post-modernism subsequently took shape is much more heterogenic than I have suggested so far. The notion about the end of the Enlightenment narrative of growth and emancipation is substantiated in three post-modern sub-directions:

1. A neo-conservative communitarianism. Social anomie must be opposed by a return to tradition and history, a type of neo-romantic nature philosophy.

2. A progressive communitarianism. The Marxist adage of the socialist revolution must be forgotten. This would only lead to a new kind of Stalinism. Instead one must search for other types of local sources of resistance against the governing power and knowledge system. One must hereby think of new social movements. Michel Foucault also wants to involve hospital patients, prisoners and gypsies – in short, groups familiar with the effect of hegemonic power.

3. Nihilism. Truth and reason have been lost sight of and simulation is the 'name of the game'. Jean Baudrillard (1975) is the most outspoken exponent of this philosophy. The only hope cherished by this sceptic is that the masses will become so numbed by media bombardment that they can no longer be indoctrinated because of their 'unresisting imbecility'.[31]

In the following section post-modernism (and post-Marxism for that matter) will be critically examined, delimiting its possible relevance for post-impasse development theory.

Post-Modernism and Post-Marxism: A Critique

If we consider labour as the principle of modernity and communication as the principle of post-modernity, then the post-modern is the name of the transition from Labour to Communication as the fundamental power of structuration and social formation. Marx is dead, the workers are not a class destined to emancipate itself and thereby everyone else. In short: the dialectic of the Enlightenment has been defeated, the grand narratives are over. I suspect that this enthusiasm is premature, or rather, that those who want to shout with joy should hurry up and do it now, before the minor narratives they are so jubilant about begin to grow again.

(Flogstad, in Albertsen 1988: 339)

Post-modernism has shifted from awkward neologism to derelict cliche without ever attaining to the dignity of concept.

(Hassan, in Boyne and Rattansi 1990: 9)

My position in this section will be that, however relevant it may be to characterise the industrial North as post-modern or post-industrial, the developing countries in the South cannot be characterised as such. On the contrary, what typifies those countries is an aborted modernity project, whereby the Ideals of Enlightenment such as Freedom, Equality and Fraternity are further out of reach than they ever were in the North. The equating of the failure of the modernity project in the South to a post-modern situation exhibits a far-reaching naivety and leads to a political demobilisation and conservatism.[32] Nevertheless, the post-modern debate has resulted in an understanding which can benefit development studies, without it being necessary to adopt the entire baggage of post-modern ideas.

One of the most central notions in the post-modernism debate is *deconstruction*. I interpret this notion in three related ways:

1. It points to the delegitimisation of Enlightenment discourses (liberalism and socialism) which had not resulted in general emancipation of humankind.

2. Deconstruction entails the dismantling of structures to find the actors within these structures. Structures are considered to be reified notions (e.g. the world system) which have merely an apparent value. Deconstruction in this sense eventually leads to the individual actor as the only valid unit of analysis.

3. Deconstruction is the quest for the hidden metaphors in some central concepts within the Enlightenment discourse. An example is given by Derrida with his notion of logocentrism, mentioned above.

Another example offering even more insight can be found in Lummis (1991), who deconstructs the notion of 'development' which stands so central in Enlightenment discourse. According to Lummis the term 'development' contains a number of metaphors which lead to evolutionary, universal and reductionist interpretations. The first metaphor he observes is development in the sense of making something visible which is latently present, as if a positive print is made of a negative. The positive, then, already exists in the shape economic development has adopted in the industrialised societies. In the structure of developing countries this image is latently present (as a negative), and can only be made visible through a number of actions (development policy).

Another semantic metaphor Lummis observes in 'development' is the interpretation of a literal process: something develops in the sense of unfurling, becoming visible piece by piece. That which slowly becomes visible is, however, already embedded in the structure (the 'genes'). The result of the 'development process' is thus fixed – it is merely a matter of speed. Here, as well, policy can help out, in the case of developing countries. This policy is then formulated by those who pretend to know the building blocks ('genes') of the structure, as well as the final outcome. This interpretation also leads to an evolutionary and reductionist view of the developing process in Third World countries, one devoid of reality.[33]

The current attraction of Lummis's article is that he deconstructs the notion of development in a post-modern manner, without becoming trapped in political nihilism. On the contrary, he ventures a political alternative (albeit a utopian one).

Although my first interpretation of deconstruction given above seems to imply political nihilism, the second and third interpretations are of importance to a more detailed shaping of post-impasse development theory. An attempt to deconstruct structures into actors has already been indicated in the preceding section, in the shape of the actor-oriented approach of Norman Long. An attempt at objectifying notions relevant to development (without ethnocentric connotations) can be found in Rawls (1972).

Direct application of post-modern views with respect to research themes within the Third World have, up to now, been limited to the new social movements as expressions of resistance against modernity.[34] In a contribution on social movements in this volume I have argued that this is an unrealistic interpretation of social movements in the Third World. In order not to repeat all the arguments here I will only reproduce my principle objection, as it further clarifies the position in the beginning of this section, namely that the Third World does not consist of post-modern societies.

Social movements (new and old) in the Third World are not expressions of resistance against modernity; rather, they are demands for access to it. There are enough reasons to characterise many Third World countries as aborted modernity projects, if only because of the exclusion of large parts of the population. When those excluded unite in groups and forge ties of solidarity, this must not be seen as an embryonic form of a new society, but rather as a survival strategy. Citizenship and Participation (Enlightenment ideals!) are (directly or indirectly) highly regarded by these social movements; participants want access to welfare and well-being. They are no longer prepared to be shifted to the sidelines. Romantic post-modern interpretations, where it is stressed that autonomy must be maintained, do not do justice to the essence of these movements. In addition, they disregard the historical origin of many of these movements.[35]

Similar criticisms can be levelled at post-modern treatises of emancipation movements in industrial societies. Thus Sabina Lovibond in her article about feminism and post-modernism stated: 'How can anyone ask me to say goodbye to "emancipatory metanarratives" when my own emancipation is still such a patchy hit and miss affair?' (Lovibond in Boyne and Rattansi 1990).

This brief exposé of social movements leads us to a less direct link between post-modernism and development theory, via post-Marxism. Anthony Giddens (1976) with his structuration theory, and Ernesto Laclau and Chantal Mouffe (1985) with their notion of radical democracy, are known exponents of post-Marxism.[36] As is the case with post-modernism, post-Marxist studies are rather heterogeneous. Nevertheless there are certain points of departure in common, and as far as these are relevant here, I will briefly mention them.

To a large extent, post-Marxists go along with post-modern character-isations of contemporary Western societies, but they do not conclude from this an intrinsic post-modern condition. According to Giddens, the central process is the radicalisation of modernisation 'as it is uni-versalised by the global spread of its distinctive institutions'. These 'institutions' are capitalism, industrialism, and administrative and military powers. The hegemony of each of these institutions is disputed by several forms of social movements. Giddens rejects the analytical centrality of class and the capitalist mode of production.

Laclau and Mouffe also question the structural centrality of the class notion. They no longer accept that consciousness, culture and politics can be derived from structural positions within society. The search for a metadiscourse leads to theoretical confusion and political dogmatism. In their discourse theory Laclau and Mouffe stress the autonomy of the existing discourses and argue this as follows:
- Societies are characterised by a variety of social conflicts, of which one is not by definition more important than another.
- The groups involved (social movements) do not necessarily have a unified/single goal and not necessarily the same opponent.
- The outcome of the conflicts is not pre-determined by structural factors but by the interaction between the internal dynamics of social movements on the one hand and the reaction of external actors on the other.

An important conclusion here is that Giddens and Laclau/Mouffe doubt the possibility of a coherent socialist policy based on class or on (new) social movements. At this point Laclau and Mouffe replace the notion of socialism with the more vague term of radical democracy, which departs from a marked reduction of the hegemony of the insti-tutionalised discourses. Given their vague elaboration of the concept of radical democracy and their emphasis on the autonomy of discourses,

Laclau and Mouffe are perilously close to approaching the political nihilism of post-modernism – which leads Scott (1990) to disqualify Laclau and Mouffe's discourse theory as an 'anti-theory' theory.

Laclau and Mouffe are correct in arguing for the heterogeneity of discourses within social movements, but this does not exclude that (i) certain emancipatory goals, such as Citizenship and Participation, are found in all social movements, and as such (ii) there is a feasible basis for meaningful relations between social movements, which (iii) can further substantiate the concept of radical democracy.

Although, as mentioned above, Laclau and Mouffe are known as post-Marxists, it is not clear to me from the above which elements of the Marxist frame of reference they try to save through the introduction of their central concept of radical democracy. Giddens, with his four 'institutional axes of modernity', is much more clearly a post-Marxist in this respect than Laclau and Mouffe (see also Bromley 1991).

Diversity and Inequality, Universalism and Specificity, Determinism and Voluntarism:
The Narrow Path of Post-Impasse Development Theory
How does the preceding affect post-impasse development studies? In answering this question I return to the differentiation between formal and material object mentioned in an earlier section *(see Post-Imperialism, page 19)*.

According to Buttel and McMichael (1991), it is necessary to change the *explanandum* (that which needs to be explained) in order to substantiate post-impasse development theory.[37] They argue that in the diagnosis of the impasse in development theory unilateral attention was paid to the *explanans* (the explaining framework). The stated problems with the *explanans* in development studies (functionalistic, teleological, reductionist, etc.) originate from the *explanandum*, where the understanding of an assumed homogeneity within the Third World is important. The solution Buttel and McMichael offer is then relatively obvious: alter the *explanandum*! In other words: not the homogeneity but the *diversity* within the Third World should become the new research theme.

The authors offer as *explanans* a certain type of historical-comparative framework ('incorporated comparison') leading to a typology of development trajectories. This argument seems so amazingly simple that one wonders why no one had came up with it before. If the *explanans* is criticised, then you must not in the first instance alter the *explanans*, but rather the *explanandum* – and in such a way that the ensuing *explanans* can no longer be accused of misplaced teleology, evolutionism and reductionism. Instead of homogeneity within the Third World we now concentrate on explaining the diversity, the result of which is that we are less likely to develop a universal metatheory. Post-modern and post-Marxist notions such as deconstruction, autonomous discourses and pluralism can subsequently be incorporated without much effort into the Buttel and McMichael approach (although they do not regard themselves as post-modernists). In addition, their proposal is reminiscent of certain post-impasse approaches previously mentioned (Mouzelis, the regulation school).

Nevertheless, Buttel and McMichael all too easily disregard two important points, and some aspects of their proposal must be questioned. In the first place, their *explanandum* (diversity within the Third World) suggests a contradiction in terms. If one maintains the term 'Third World' as part of the *explanandum*, this means that the Third World countries have certain features in common, which allow them to be characterised as such. It appears illogical to me then to turn immediately to studying diversity, without first finding a more detailed definition and explanation of these common features. Second (and I have previously tried to make this clear), I object to this rather voluntary use of the term diversity. In my opinion, development theory must not only be concerned with studying diversity, but also with *inequality* – this in spite of the fact that usage of this term is overlaid with negative post-modern connotations. Studying diversity solves a lot of the problems in post-impasse development theory that post-modernism and criticism à la Booth have pointed to. In my opinion, too great an emphasis on diversity and specificity leads to a voluntarist, pluralist approach to the development problem, allowing no space for a universalistic emancipation discourse. Buttel and McMichael find a rather easy solution because they argue a separation between development theory and development praxis. They feel the latter is a millstone around the neck of development theory.[38]

I feel that a new *explanandum* for development studies should not be restricted to 'diversity' but be explicitly concerned with 'inequality': inequality of access to power, to resources, to a humane existence – in short, inequality in emancipation. If we were to let go of this, there would be no justification for the existence of development theory. We must not be afraid to work normatively on a theoretical level as is argued in several contributions to the present volume. However, we have not yet answered the question of which theoretical framework belongs to such an *explanandum*. In this respect, the proposed approaches to post-impasse development theory dealt with so far should pay more attention to the *explanandum*, as this is often a problematic area. Only Norman Long's actor-oriented approach conveys the impression that not just diversity but also inequality is manifest. In addition, the theoretical framework (the *explanans*) of Long's approach takes into account the criticisms of

Booth and of post-modernism. Nevertheless, Long's approach also has drawbacks when we discuss inequality.

Whichever theoretical corner we may choose to sit in, it cannot be denied that development on a global scale is of importance to the inequalities within the Third World, and between the First and Third Worlds. The debt burden of the Third World and the influence of international financial organisations on policies in these countries are known examples. Lesser known, though not less important, is the increasing triadisation of the world economy, whereby Europe, the U.S. and Japan 'play ball' with each other and increasingly large parts of the Third World stand on the sidelines, while summoned at the same time to throw themselves at the mercy of the world market. Inequality is thus a relevant concept, not only on a micro-level (the household) or meso-level (social categories), but also on a supranational level.

Thus the central question for post-impasse development theory is to design a theoretical framework that links these analytical levels. One of the problems to be faced is that, while the micro- and the meso-levels are primarily defined using socio-cultural variables, and the spatial dimension is present only implicitly, analyses of diversity and inequality on a national or supranational level have an explicit spatial dimension which, in turn, does not tell us very much about the actors involved. A meaningful connection between all the analytical levels can only be made if the relevant actors are displayed. For example, national and supranational structures are not organic entities, but consist of interrelated actors such as the state bureaucracy, the national and international bourgeoisie, political parties, international financial institutions, etc. In other words, the analytical framework of post-impasse development theory would have to involve the relationship between power, actors and structure, which subsequently would have to be substantiated at the various analytical levels using historical comparative research. Diversity and inequality would then form the *explanandum*.

More narrowly defined, development theories address situations where large parts of the human population suffer from substantial inequalities in emancipation. I interpret emancipation not in a teleological sense as a narrowly defined concept using certain (Western) standards as absolute criteria in terms of development of the production forces, standards of living, etc. In my opinion, emancipation should be defined dynamically in terms of a process whereby social actors try to liberate themselves from structurally defined hierarchical relations which are discriminatory and as such give unequal access to material (e.g., land, housing, services) and immaterial resources (e.g., ideology, political power). In a structure characterised by hierarchical relations, some actors extract more value from a set of relations than others.

Value must be interpreted here in a rather wide sense: economic, financial, social, psychological, political, etc. The reason some actors extract more value from the interaction is that they have more power – power which is as multi-faceted as the value being extracted. Multi-levelled structures characterised by a generalised low degree of emancipation do have things in common, but, as has been emphasised in this section, inequality (and the struggle against inequality for that matter) takes very diverse forms.

So power, actors, multi-levelled structure, inequality and diversity are the key concepts in the construction of post-impasse development theories. Many of these concepts can be detected, implicitly or explicity, in the new approaches to post-impasse development theories treated in this introduction. What is lacking, however, is an attempt to cross-fertilise these approaches, which differ at the spatial level of analysis. Mouzelis's concept of 'mode of domination', the dyadic concepts 'regime of accumulation' and 'mode of regulation' of the regulation school, and the 'actor-oriented approach' of Norman Long remain unrelated. In addition, only Long's analysis attempts to reformulate development policies on the local/regional level.

The point is not to strive for one grand and glorious development metatheory *per se* but rather to stress that a lot of new ground has already been covered, but that the plots still remain rather isolated. In addition, the argument here is not solely concerned with the attempt to provide post-impasse development theory with a new *explanans* (e.g., historical comparative research) and *explanandum* (e.g., inequalities in emancipation, or differences in development trajectories). This must be accompanied by an attempt to develop a meaningful development policy (a political praxis) which avoids being dogmatic, which in the past was a consequence of unilinear and universalistic views of development issues.

The construction of a post-impasse development theory on a non-reductionist and non-teleological basis is the challenge of the 1990s. Much of the groundwork has been done in the last decade, but this must not remain as isolated empirical research, nor as the construction of concepts which on a higher level of abstraction do not result in relevant development praxis.

The Contributions
In the first few chapters in this volume the conditions necessary to move beyond the impasse in development theory are further specified. In his contribution **David Booth** suggests that the heavy atmosphere of intellectual stagnation and self-imposed insulation from practical issues that was so prevalent in development research in the early 1980s seems to have cleared. Fresh and exciting work is being carried out at a variety

of levels and on a host of different topics. However, identifying what effectively distinguishes the new research agenda is no easy matter, given the variety of substantive concerns and cross-cutting intellectual influences that have played a role in its emergence. One thing is obvious: whereas formerly influential theories more or less deliberately ignored the complex diversity of the real world of development, the style of research that has come into prominence since the early 1980s takes as its central task the explanation of significant variations in patterns of development in different local, regional and national settings. As such, social study of development is brought back into touch with the alternatives facing real actors – governments, business enterprises, mass organisations, local communities, etc.

At the same time, Booth notes that the revival of interest in the diversity of development is related to a rather heterogeneous set of related intellectual developments, with different perspectives and priorities. The chapter gives a systematic consideration of these perspectives along lines of:

– theory and method;
– agency, structure and explanation;
– deconstruction and concept formation;
– relevance.

Michael Edwards, representing the voice of development praxis, takes as his point of departure the need for development studies to contribute in a practical way to the resolution of the problems and issues facing poor and powerless people around the world. Conventional development studies have largely failed to do this, and the chapter analyses the factors underlying this situation.

New directions in development studies, such as participatory research and growing links between NGOs and academics, are explored to see what hope they offer for the future. The chapter updates the author's earlier article, *The Irrelevance of Development Studies* (Edwards 1989), and attempts to answer some of the criticisms levelled at it.

David Slater specifies some themes connected to the political dimension of the research agenda for the 1990s. One of the current trends in the discussion of Third World development is characterised by a return to the social dimension. It is no longer sufficient to talk of economic growth, privatisation, rolling back the state and freeing the market; equity has also to be firmly placed on the agenda, just as, previously, structural adjustment had to be given a 'human face'.

Slater argues, first, that neo-liberal discourse, including monetarist imperatives, has a deep political meaning that is rooted in possessive individualism, and, second, that, in stark contrast, mainstream Marxism has prioritised class struggle and state control over the individual citizen. In an era of shifting meanings, the re-contextualisation of critical development theory needs to include a re-thinking of the political imagery.

The chapter illustrates this position in relation to four themes:
- the periphery as subordinated other;
- state power and democracy;
- civil society and movements of resistance;
- the eclipse of revolutionary rupture.

Ronaldo Munck also discusses the political agenda for post-impasse development theory, though specifically for Latin America. The chapter focuses on the question: since Leninism operated as developmentalist ideology in many Third World countries, why not social democracy? During the re-democratisation of Latin America in the 1980s, social democracy began to act as a point of reference for virtually all progressive forces. Whereas in the 1970s dependency theory pointed towards socialism as the way to development, now social democracy is stressed.

The question is, though, whether the methods of social democracy will be able to achieve its traditional objectives. Structural heterogeneity and unstable political cycles still characterise Latin America. An alternative of radical democracy or revolutionary reforms has been proposed as a more viable alternative to the present impasse. Modernisation theory is now resurgent in the new world order. Dependency theory is no longer seen as a viable radical alternative. Although Munck offers some suggestions on how social democracy may provide a way out of the impasse, he warns against magic answers or bold new 'ways forward'.

Stuart Corbridge considers how attention to development ethics might inform our accounts of the developing countries' debt crisis *and* how our accounts of development ethics might be informed by our knowledge of the developing countries' debt crisis.

He begins his contribution with some remarks on development ethics and its possible relation to a continuing, and much-remarked, crisis in development studies and policy. He next outlines a standard narrative account of the debt crisis. The third and fourth parts of the contribution re-examine the debt crisis from the viewpoint of some propositions derived from development ethics. No simple conclusions are drawn, nor solutions put forward; rather, the chapter concludes by reflecting on the difficulties of attending to the dilemmas of development without lapsing into either an unhelpful pessimism or an unwarranted certainty about 'what should be done'.

Norman Long and **Magdalena Villarreal** examine existing attempts to theorise and investigate the nature of knowledge processes inherent in development intervention. Their chapter opens with a discussion of current struggles to integrate theoretical understanding and practical concerns, leading to a critical view of systems models, particularly as applied in extension science.

The need for a more sophisticated analysis of how knowledge and power are socially constructed is identified through the presentation of three cases, exploring organisational and strategic elements involved in development interfaces. This points to the centrality of power differentials and struggles over social meaning for an understanding of knowledge processes, which are interwoven with actors' accumulated social experiences, commitments and culturally-acquired dispositions.

Long and Villarreal argue that an actor-and-interface perspective, which challenges interventionist thinking, can revitalise the sociology of development, thus building a better bridge between theory and practice and at the same time bringing the study of development into more direct contact with mainstream sociological and anthropological theory and debate.

The last three chapters shed some light on more specific themes in post-impasse development research: gender, social movements and the environment.

The chapter by **Janet Townsend** draws on Caroline Moser's analysis of research on women in development (World Development, 1989) and the author's own research experience in land settlements in Latin America.

Townsend examines the following topics: empowerment as a leading development strategy; the difficulties of cross-cultural comparison; the silencing of the poor; the silencing of women; the role of the researcher; alternatives to academic centralism and control of knowledge; and the uses of extensive and intensive research.

Her contribution adopts significant parts of post-modern critique, but accepts the validity of development studies and gender studies, which is denied by certain forms of post-modern thought.

In his chapter on social movements research, **Frans Schuurman** also takes post-modern-inspired interpretations to task. Disillusionment with respect to the progressive role of the labour proletariat and the virtual disappearance of socialism as a political project led to a scramble of radical social scientists for either a post-Marxist or a post-modern position. Attention increasingly fell upon the so-called new social movements in the North as well as in the South as collective attempts within civil society to create new identities and to thwart attempts of the mainstream ideology to hegemonise the inner life-spaces.

After rescuing some valuable notions of post-Marxism (the concept of discourse) and post-modernism (the concept of deconstruction), Schuurman takes issue with the interpretation of these new currents concerning new social movements in the South. It is argued that, contrary to being post-modern, these movements are engaged in a new modernity project where Citizenship and Participation are central values. The arguments put forward are illustrated by the case of Chile.

Bill Adams discusses the problems connected with the 'greening' of post-impasse development theory. The rhetoric of sustainable development is widely used by very different actors in the development process. Some use it to promote a radical restructuring of priorities with regard to environmental development and economic growth. Others simply intend a change in attitudes, emphasis and, in some cases, project appraisal methods. Such approaches are sometimes labelled 'dark green' and 'light green' respectively.

The chapter argues that the diversity of sustainable development ideologies reflects reformist/radical divisions within post-1970s environmentalism. The influences of technocentrist and ecocentrist/biocentrist thinking in environmentalism can be distinguished, and related to the reformism/radicalism continuum in sustainable development.

Divergent radical environmental ideologies, particularly Deep Ecology and Social Ecology, compete for claims to define a coherent 'green' development ideology. The confusion inherent in sustainable development thinking creates serious problems for practical application on the ground in the Third World, and the implications of this for the longevity of the rhetoric and ideologies behind it are considered.

Notes

1. Of influence were: i) publications by Marx and Lenin on class analysis, and the relation between imperialism and capitalism; ii) Rosa Luxemburg on the penetration of the capitalist mode of production in non-capitalist societies, and its consequences on the dismantling of the 'natural economy'; iii) Raul Prebisch and Gunnar Myrdal with their analyses in terms of core and periphery; iv) the French structural Marxists who in the 1970s strongly advocated the modes of production concept; v) Paul Baran, who as early as the 1950s wrote about the negative consequences of monopoly capitalism for the periphery. He stressed the transfer of economic surplus, which checked the development of the periphery. Baran is also known as the first neo-Marxist.
2. The differences between the *dependencia* authors can be found, among

others, in Hunt (1989), Larrain (1989) and Hettne (1990). For a critique of the various ways of categorising the *dependentistas*, see Frank (1991).

3. This opposition between those who emphasise the 'mode of production' and those who emphasise the 'mode of exchange' is also sometimes referred to as the argument between the 'productionists' and the 'circulationists' respectively. The basic idea of the circulationists is that underdevelopment is caused by and maintained by surplus transfer (for instance by the mechanism of unequal exchange) from the periphery to the centre. Productionists on the other hand argue that the question which must be addressed is the way surplus is produced in the periphery and the class formation that results. For further discussion of these 'schools' and criticisms see Hoogvelt (1982).

4. For a useful discussion see Peet (1980) and Brewer (1980).

5. Many rural development projects in the 1960s and 1970s were begun on the basis of the idea that the peasants involved would produce in a capitalist manner. Using the concept of peasant mode of production it was shown that peasants had their own form of logic to connect the production factors of land, labour and capital.

6. The term unequal exchange was especially elaborated upon in that period by Arghiri Emmanuel in his book *Unequal Exchange: A Study of the Imperialism of Trade*, London, 1972.

7. See Brenner (1977) and Larrain (1989).

8. A disarticulated economic system is described by Amin using a refinement (as far as I know derived from the Polish economist Kalecki) of the distinction that Marx made between Departments I and II of the economy: Ia – capital goods, Ib – raw materials, IIa – mass consumer goods, IIb – luxury consumer goods.

   In the core, economic development is the result of the relation between Departments Ia and IIa. The periphery, on the other hand, is characterised by the occurrence of Departments Ib (export of raw materials) and IIb, which cannot result in independent economic development. Amin argues that this disarticulation of the economy is maintained by the changing coalitions within elite circles.

9. In contrast to the 1970s (Hettne 1990), when Southern scholars published their share on development theories, it seems that from the 1980s onwards publications on the crisis and new directions of development theories have been almost hegemonically controlled by Northern scholars (the present volume hardly excepted).

   This is not to say that these publications, by definition, represent a Eurocentric view on the current status of development theory. Eurocentrism, in this case, is a state of mind, a political-philosophical view on the problem of development and underdevelopment; in other words it is not *per se* an attitude determined by geographic location.

   Still, it is worthwhile to elaborate briefly on the 'silence from the South' on the impasse in development theory. With some exceptions (e.g., Soja 1989, Raji Kothari publishing in the Indian journal *Alternatives*), the attention of

Southern scholars in the 1980s shifted from an abstract approach to the problem of underdevelopment to more pragmatic issues. The worsening economic crisis (heightened by the debt burden) on the one hand, and political changes (i.e., transition to democracy) on the other, induced Southern scholars to concentrate their research on issues such as the role of social movements (especially women's organisations) and of NGOs in the democratisation process, the acceleration in environmental degradation, the economic consequences of structural adjustment policies, etc.

Many of these publications have been of great importance to those who are currently trying to manoeuver development theories on a more abstract level out of their impasse.

10. Regarding the distinction between circulationists and productionists, see note 3 above.

11. Booth accuses the *dependentistas* of a tautological argument because underdevelopment was defined in terms of the degree of dependence, while at the same time dependency was cited as the cause of underdevelopment. Corbridge also criticises the tendency (particularly of advocates of the modes of production concept) to present auto-referential evidence, such as: if a pre-capitalist mode of production survives contact with the dominating capitalist mode of production, then this was obviously so because it was functional for capitalism. If the pre-capitalist mode of production disappears, it was obviously not functional.

12. Although Booth does not mention the 'bluff concepts' in the modernisation theory, it is worth mentioning at least one: the 'trickle-down' mechanism. To activate economic growth, one must concentrate capital spatially and economically, which at first results in increasing geographical and social inequality. This polarisation, however, is reversed in the last instance by a 'trickle-down' mechanism from the most dynamic sectors and regions to the periphery. In many developing countries this critical turning-point is far from being reached. Rather there is increasing regional and social polarisation.

13. Sklair provides the following definitions of metatheory, theory and empirical research. Metatheory is 'a set of assumptions about the constituent parts of the world and about the possibility of knowledge about them'. A metatheory can therefore not be tested empirically, but can give rise to the development of testable theories. A theory, then, is 'a set of propositions derived directly or indirectly from a metatheory not logically incompatible with it'. Successful testing of a theory gives the related metatheory greater plausibility. Empirical research, finally, is the 'practice of manufacturing explanations and predictions about real objects ... guided by the abstractions of the theory and its hypotheses ...'

14. The concept of reification refers to the tendency to interpret abstract notions (e.g., ideal types) as existing in real life. See Taylor (1979) for a thorough criticism of the way Parsons considered his ideal typical approach, based on

Tönnies and Weber, as universally applicable in analysing social and political transformation processes.

15. Mouzelis (1988: 39) argues that '… neglect of the political – as a major, if not the major, base for explaining the varied capitalist trajectories in the Third World – constitutes the Achilles heel of all development theory'.

16. Marx distinguished two economic sectors, called Department I and II, producing respectively capital goods and consumer goods. Both types of goods are sold in both Departments, giving rise to a set of particular economic relations within and between the two basic economic sectors. This set of relations, when expressed in economic symbols, is called a reproduction scheme which determines the dynamic in the reproduction of the capitalist system.

17. Lipietz hereby refers to Bourdieu's notion of 'habitus'. It seems to me, however, that Lipietz in his description of mode of regulation also adopted elements which in Bourdieu fall under the concept of 'doxa' (the un-mentioned).

18. Fordism is characterised by mass production, consumption of standardised goods, a significant growth of labour productivity because of a Taylorist division between managers and labourers, and finally, an important role of the Keynesian welfare-state.

19. National states can, for instance, build tariff walls to stimulate the process of national industrialisation. Multinationals can circumvent tariff walls by producing in the country itself, resulting in a new international division of labour. The national state and the MNOs differ in this in the nature of their project. For criticism of Lipietz's emphasis on the autonomy of the state see McMichael and Myhre (1991).

20. With peripheral Fordism, Lipietz refers to the Newly Industrialised Countries such as South Korea, Mexico and Brazil.

21. The 'doctrine of domicile' has three aspects. First, it refers to the nature of the ideology of the modern bourgeoisie, which tends to shape its interest in terms of moral values which have a wide societal base. The second aspect refers to the operation of the transcorporative oligopoly. This entails making mutual price agreements, market regulation, etc. Here, as well, there is an ideological component, because the TNCs are of the opinion that their operations are in the general interest. The last aspect concerns the internal organisation of a TNC, whereby the authors stress not so much the economic element, as the ideological motivation of the staff of the TNC in the developing country. In particular, they point to the legitimising of relations between the company and society. For further elaboration of these aspects see Stander and Becker (1990).

22. Becker and Sklar go one step further when they raise the question of whether it shows misplaced optimism to expect that this form of communication could contribute to world peace, because it transcends national and ideological antagonisms. In short, the transnational corporation as channel for international brotherhood!

23. The post-imperialist emphasis on national and international bourgeoisie reminds one of the concept of 'Strategische Gruppen' (strategic groups) developed by the German authors Evers and Schiel (1988).

24. Foreign investments in the mining sector are much more dependent on the national political and economic climate than investments in other sectors. The transnational mining corporation, for instance, is tied to specific locations and is thus rather dependent on the state for providing and maintaining the necessary infrastructure. In other words, if the profits of these TNCs come under threat, they will first try within the national political arena to avert this threat. Withdrawal of investments is, after all, accompanied by large-scale capital loss.

25. This criticism is illustrated by the type of theoretical sources which inspired Becker and Sklar: political theories of modern enterprises, and class analyses of political power in Third World countries.

26. Thus the zero-growth option has more supporters in the polluted, Western consumer societies than in the developing countries. Although many developing countries also have serious environmental problems, economic growth is usually given the highest priority.

27. In many publications the terms post-modernity and post-modernism are often used interchangeably. For an attempt to distinguish these terms (as well as 'modernity' and 'modernism') see Boyne and Rattansi (1990: chapter 1).

28. The 'representation crisis' is a central notion in post-modernism. An interesting expansion is Derrida's concept of logocentrism. This concept suggests that people tend to think in binomial categories, where one of the categories (usually the first) is seen as homogeneous and unproblematic in contrast to the second category. Examples of logocentric categorisations are: North and South, Man and Woman, White and Black. In connection with this it is important to point to the importance of post-colonialism, a 'school' connected to post-modernism. While post-modernism generally points to a misrepresentation of 'the Other', post-colonialism specifically expands on this for the history of Western ethnocentric representations of 'the Other' in the Third World; see Edward Said (1978).

29. Thus Riccardo Petrella (1989) mockingly talks of 'Japan Inc.' and 'L'Enterprise France'.

30. For criticism of post-industrialism and post-Fordism, see (among others) Albertsen (1988), Rose (1991), Callinicos (1989 and in Boyne and Rattansi 1990) and Clarke (1991).

31. See Christopher Norris, 'Lost in the Funhouse: Baudrillard and the Politics of Post-modernism', in Boyne and Rattansi (1990, pp. 119–53).

32. For further arguments see Schuurman in this volume.

33. In the remainder of his article Lummis tries to support his thesis that 'economic development' is a fraudulent, ethnocentric and anti-democratic concept.

34. For a general discussion of development theories and post-modernism see

Slater (1991). For a post-modern interpretation of the neighbourhood organisations in Latin America, see Friedmann (1989).

35. In Latin America many social movements find their origin in the military dictatorships of the 1970s and the start of the 1980s, a period in which governments left low-income groups to their own devices.

36. For an introduction to Giddens's structuration theory see Cohen (1989) and McLennan (1989). A sharp attack on Laclau and Mouffe's post-Marxism has been delivered by Norman Geras in *New Left Review* (1987, 1988).

37. Buttel and McMichael employ the notions of *explanandum* and *explanans* to indicate, respectively, the material and formal object.

38. Michael Edwards (this volume) adopts a radically opposite view.

Relevant Literature

Albertini, R. von. 1980. 'Colonialism and Underdevelopment: Critical Remarks on the Theory of Dependency'. In L. Blussé *et al.* (eds.), *History and Underdevelopment*, pp. 42–52. Leiden, Centre for the History of European Expansion.

Aglietta, M. 1976. *Regulation et Crises du Capitalisme*. Paris, Calmann-Levy.

— 1982. 'World Capitalism in the Eighties'. *New Left Review* 137, pp. 5–41.

Albertsen, N. 1988. 'Postmodernism, Post-Fordism, and Critical Social Theory'. *Environment and Planning* D 6, pp. 339–65.

Amin, S. 1974. *Accumulation on a World Scale*. London, Monthly Review Press (two vols).

— 1976. *Unequal Development*. Sussex, Harvester Press.

Apter, D. 1987. *Rethinking Development: Modernization, Dependency and Postmodern Politics*. London, Sage Publications.

Bairoch, P. 1980. 'Le Bilan Économique du Colonialisme: Mythes et Réalités'. In L. Blussé *et al.* (eds.), *History and Underdevelopment*, pp. 29–41. Leiden, Centre for the History of European Expansion.

Balassa, B. *et al.* 1982. *Development Strategies in Semi-Industrial Countries*. Baltimore, Johns Hopkins University Press.

Banaji, J. 1972. 'For a Theory of Colonial Modes of Production'. *Economic and Political Weekly* 7, pp. 2,498–502.

Baran, P. 1957. *The Political Economy of Growth*. New York, Monthly Review Press.

Bartra, R. 1975. 'La Teoría de Valor y la Economía Campesina: Invitación a la Lectura de Chayanov'. *Comercio Exterior* 25 (5), pp. 517–24.

Baudrillard, J. 1975. *The Mirror of Production*. St Louis, Telos Press.

Bauer, P. 1981. *Equality, the Third World and Economic Delusion*. London, Methuen.

— 1984. *Reality and Rhetoric: Studies in the Economics of Development*. London, Weidenfeld & Nicholson.

Becker, D., & R. Sklar (eds.). 1987. *Postimperialism: International Capitalism and Development in the Late Twentieth Century*. London, Lynne Rienner Publications.

Belden Fields, A. 1988. 'In Defense of Political Economy and Systemic Analysis: A Critique of Prevailing Theoretical Approaches to the New Social Movements'. In Nelson & Grossberg (eds.), *Marxism and the Interpretation of Culture*, pp. 141–56. Illinois.

Bell, D. 1973. *The Coming of Post-Industrial Society*. London, Basic Books.

Benton, T. 1989. 'Marxism and Natural Limits: An Ecological Critique and Reconstruction'. *New Left Review* 178, pp. 51–86.

Berman, M. 1982. *The Experience of Modernity: All that is Solid Melts into Air*. New York, Simon & Schuster.

Bernstein, H. 1979. 'Sociology of Underdevelopment vs. Sociology of Development?' In D. Lehmann (ed.), *Development Theory*, pp. 77–106. London, Frank Cass.

Bina, C., & B. Yaghmaian. 1991. 'Post-war Global Accumulation and the Transnationalisation of Capital'. *Capital & Class* 43, pp. 107–30.

Bondi, L. 1990. 'Feminism, Postmodernism, and Geography: Space for Women?' *Antipode* 22 (2), pp. 156–67.

Booth, D. 1985. 'Marxism and Development Sociology: Interpreting the Impasse'. *World Development*, vol. 13, no. 7, pp. 761–87.

Boulding, E. 1989. 'Cultural Perspectives on Development: The Relevance of Sociology and Anthropology'. *Alternatives* XIV, pp. 107–22.

Bourdieu, P. 1977. *Outline of a Theory of Practice*. Cambridge, Cambridge University Press.

Boyne, R., & A. Rattansi. 1990. *Postmodernism and Society*. London, Mac-Millan.

Brass, T. 1991. 'Moral Economists, Subalterns, New Social Movements, and the (Re)emergence of a (Post)modernised (Middle) Peasant'. *Journal of Peasant Studies* 18 (2), pp. 173–205.

Brenner, R. 1977. 'The Origins pf Capitalist Development: A Critique of Neo-Smithian Marxism'. *New Left Review* 104, pp. 25–92.

Brewer, A. 1980. *Marxist Theories of Imperialism: A Critical Survey*. London, Routledge & Kegan Paul.

Bromley, S. 1991. 'The Politics of Postmodernism – A Review Article on Harvey, Callinicos, Giddens and Sayer'. *Capital & Class* 45, pp. 129–50.

Burnham, P. 1991. 'Neo-Gramscian Hegemony and the International Order'. *Capital & Class* 43, pp. 73–93.

Buttel, F., & P. McMichael. 1991. 'Reconsidering the Explanandum and Scope of Development Studies: Toward a Comparative Sociology of State-Economy Relations'. Paper for the Hull Workshop on 'Relevance, Realism and Choice in Social Development Research', Centre for Developing Area Studies, University of Hull, 10–12 January 1991.

Calderón, F., & A. Piscitelli. 1990. 'Paradigm Crisis and Social Movements: a Latin American Perspective'. In Oyen (ed.), *Comparative Methodology*, pp. 81–96. London, Sage Publications.

Callinicos, A. 1989. *Against Postmodernism: A Marxist Critique*. Cambridge, Polity Press.

— 1990. 'Reactionary Postmodernism?' In R. Boyne & A. Rattansi, pp. 97–119.

Cardoso, F., & E. Faletto. 1970. *Dependencia e Desenvolvimento na America Latina*. Rio de Janeiro, Zahar. (English translation: *Dependency and Development in Latin America*. University of California Press, 1979.)

Cavarozzi, M., & M. Garretón. 1989. *Muerte y Resurrección. Los Partidos Políticos en el Autoritarismo y las Transiciones del Cono Sur*. Santiago, FLACSO.

Chossudovsky, M. 1991. 'Global Poverty and New World Economic Order'. *Economic and Political Weekly*, 2 November 1991, pp. 2,527–37.

Clarke, S. 1991. 'New Utopias for Old: Fordist Dreams and Post-Fordist Fantasies'. *Capital & Class* 43, pp. 131–55.

Cohen, I. 1989. *Structuration Theory: Anthony Giddens and the Constitution of Social Life*. London, MacMillan.

Cooke, P. 1987. 'Individuals, Localities and Postmodernism'. *Environment and Planning* D (Society and Space) (5), pp. 408–12.

Coquery-Vidrovitch, C. 1969. 'Recherches sur une Mode de Production Africaine'. *La Pensée*, April 1969.

Corbridge, S. 1986. *Capitalist World Development: A Critique of Radical Development Geography*. London, MacMillan.

— 1988. 'Deconstructing Determinism: A Reply to Michael Watts'. *Antipode* 20 (3), pp. 239–59.

— 1989. 'Marxism, Post-Marxism and the Geography of Development'. In R. Peet & N. Thrift (eds.), *New Models in Geography* (vol. 1), pp. 224–54. London, Unwin Hyman.

— 1990. 'Post-Marxism and Development Studies: Beyond the Impasse'. *World Development* 18, pp. 623–39.

Crocker, D. 1991. 'Towards Development Ethics'. *World Development* 19 (5), 457–83.

Davis, K. 1991. 'Critical Sociology and Gender Relations'. In K. Davis *et al.*, *The Gender of Power*, pp. 65–86. London, Sage Publications.

Dear, M. 1986. 'Postmodernism and Planning'. *Environment and Planning* D 4, 367–84.

Deleuze, G., & F. Guattari. 1983. *Anti-Oedipus*. Minneapolis, University of Minnesota Press.

— 1987. *A Thousand Plateaus*. Minneapolis, University of Minnesota Press.

Delsing, R. 1991. 'Sovereign and Disciplinary Power: A Foucaultian Analysis of the Chilean Women's Movement'. In K. Davis *et al.*, *The Gender of Power*, pp. 129–53. London, Sage Publications.

Derrida, J. 1973. *Speech and Phenomena, and Other Essays on Husserl's Theory of Signs*. Evanston, Northwestern University Press.

— 1976. *Of Grammatology*. Baltimore, Johns Hopkins University Press.

Dubois, M. 1991. 'The Governance of the Third World: A Foucauldian Perspective on Power Relations in Development'. *Alternatives* 16, pp. 1–30.

Edwards, M. 1989. 'The Irrelevance of Development Studies'. *Third World Quarterly* 11 (1), pp. 116–36.

Emmanuel, A. 1972. *Unequal Exchange: A Study of the Imperialism of Trade*. London, Monthly Review Press.

Evers, H., & T. Schiel. 1988. *Strategische Gruppen: Vergleichende Studien zu Staat, Bürokratie und Klassenbildung in der Dritten Welt*. Berlin, Dietrich Reimer Verlag.

Foster-Carter, A. 1978. 'The Modes of Production Controversy'. *New Left Review* 107, pp. 47–77.

Foucault, M. 1980. *Power/Knowledge*. New York, Pantheon Books.

— 1984. *The Foucault Reader* (ed. P. Rabinow). Harmondsworth, Penguin.

Frank, A. 1967. *Capitalism and Underdevelopment in Latin America*. London, Monthly Review Press.

— 1969. *Latin America: Underdevelopment or Revolution*. London, Monthly Review Press.

— 1991. 'Latin American Development Theories Revisited: A Participant Review Essay'. *Scandinavian Journal of Development Alternatives* vol. X, no. 3, pp. 133–50.

Frieden, J. 1987. 'International Capital and National Development: Comments in Postimperialism'. In D. Becker & R. Sklar, pp. 179–93.

Friedmann, J. 1989. 'La Dialéctica de la Razón'. *Revista EURE* 15 (46), pp. 29–46.

Fukuyama, F. 1989. 'The End of History'. *National Interest* (summer issue).

Geras, N. 1987. 'Post-Marxism?' *New Left Review* 163, pp. 40–82.

— 1988. 'Ex-Marxism Without Substance: Being a Real Reply to Laclau and Mouffe'. *New Left Review* 169, pp. 34–61.

Giddens, A. 1976. *New Rules of Sociological Method: A Positive Critique of Interpretative Sociologies*. London, Hutchinson.

— 1981. *A Contemporary Critique of Historical Materialism*. Berkeley, University of California Press.

— 1984. *The Constitution of Society*. Berkeley, University of California Press.

Gordon, D. 1989. 'The Global Economy: New Edifice or Crumbling Foundations?' *New Left Review* 178, pp. 24–64.

Habermas, J. 1990. 'What Does Socialism Mean Today? The Rectifying Revolution and the Need for New Thinking on the Left'. *New Left Review* 183, pp. 3–21.

Harrison, M. 1977. 'The Peasant Mode of Production in the Work of A.V. Chayanov'. *Journal of Peasant Studies* 4 (4), pp. 323–36.

Hettne, B. 1990. *Development Theory and the Three Worlds*. Harlow, Longman.

Hindess, B. 1986. 'Actors and Social Relations'. In M. Wardell & S. Turner (eds.), *Sociological Theory in Transition*. Boston, Allen & Unwin.

Hoffman. M. 1991. 'Restructuring, Reconstruction, Reinscription, Rearticulation: Four Voices in Critical International Theory'. *Millennium – Journal of International Studies* 20 (2), pp. 169–85.

Hoogvelt, A. 1982. *The Third World in Global Development*. London, MacMillan.

Hunt, D. 1989. *Economic Theories of Development: An Analysis of Competing Paradigms*. New York, Harvester Wheatsheaf.

Jenkins, R. 1991. 'The Political Economy of Industrialization: A Comparison of Latin American and East Asian Newly Industrializing Countries'. *Development and Change* 22, pp. 197–231.

Kahn, A. 1991. 'The Collapse of Actually Prevailing Socialism: Some Lessons'. *Social Scientist* 19 (7), pp. 3–17.

Kahn, H. 1979. *World Economic Development, 1979 and Beyond*. Boulder, Westview Press.

— & A. Wiener. 1967. *The Year 2000*. London, MacMillan.

Kay, C. 1989. *Latin American Theories of Development and Underdevelopment*. London, Routledge.

Komter, A. 1991. 'Gender, Power and Feminist Theory'. In K. Davis *et al.*, *The Gender of Power*, pp. 42–62. London, Sage Publications.

Laclau, E. 1971. 'Feudalism and Capitalism in Latin America'. *New Left Review*, pp. 19–38.

— & C. Mouffe. 1985. *Hegemony and Socialist Strategy: Towards a Radical Democratic Politics*. London, Verso.

— & C. Mouffe. 1987. 'Post-Marxism Without Apologies'. *New Left Review* 166, pp. 79–106.

Lal, D. 1983. *The Poverty of 'Development Economics'*. London, Institute of Economic Affairs.

Larrain, J. 1989. *Theories of Development: Capitalism, Colonialism and Dependency*. Cambridge, Polity Press.

Lazreg, M. 1988. 'Feminism and Difference: The Perils of Writing as a Woman on Women in Algeria'. *Feminist Studies* 14 (1), pp. 81–105.

Lechner, N. 1991. 'The Search for Lost Community: Challenges to Democracy in Latin America'. *International Social Science Journal* 129, pp. 541–53.

Lehmann, D. 1990. *Democracy and Development in Latin America*. Cambridge, Polity Press.

Lenin, V. 1917. *Imperialism, the Highest Stage of Capitalism*. Moscow, Progress Publishers, 1975.

Levine, D. 1988. 'Paradigm Lost: Dependence to Democracy'. *World Politics* XI (3), pp. 377–94.

Lipietz, A. 1984. 'Imperialism or the Beast of the Apocalypse'. *Capital & Class* 22, pp. 81–109.

Little, I. 1982. *Economic Development: Theory, Policies and International Relations*. New York, Basic Books.

— & J. Mirrlees. 1974. *Project Appraisal and Planning for Developing Countries*. London, Heinemann Educational.

Long, N. 1990. 'From Paradigm Lost to Paradigm Regained? The Case for an Actor-Oriented Sociology of Development'. *European Review of Latin American and Caribbean Studies* 49, pp. 3–24.

— & B. Roberts. 1978. *Peasant Cooperation and Capitalist Expansion in the Central Highlands of Peru*. Austin, University of Texas Press.

Lummis, C. 1991. 'Development Against Democracy'. *Alternatives* 16 (1), pp. 31–66.

Lyotard, J. 1984. *The Postmodern Condition: A Report on Knowledge*. Minneapolis, University of Minnesota Press.

— 1985. 'Defining the Postmodern'. *ICA Documents* 4/5, pp. 6–7.

Manzo, K. 1991. 'Modernist Discourse and the Crisis of Development Theory'. *Studies in Comparative International Development* 26 (2), pp. 3–36.

Mathur, G. 1989. 'The Current Impasse in Development Thinking: The Metaphysic of Power'. *Alternatives* XIV, pp. 463–79.

McLennan, G. 1989. *Marxism, Pluralism and Beyond: Classic Debates and New Departures*. Cambridge, Polity Press.

McMichael, P., & D. Myhre. 1991. 'Global Regulations vs. the Nation-State: Agro-Food Systems and the New Politics of Capital'. *Capital & Class* 43, pp. 83–105.

Meillassoux, C. 1971. *The Development of Indigenous Trades and Markets in Western Africa*. Oxford, Oxford University Press.

— 1972. 'From Reproduction to Production'. *Economy and Society* 1, pp. 93–105.

— 1981. *Maidens, Meal and Money: Capitalism and the Domestic Community*. Cambridge, Cambridge University Press.

Mies, M. 1986. *Patriarchy and Accumulation on a World Scale: Women in the International Division of Labour*. London, Zed Books.

Moore, B. 1966. *Social Origins of Dictatorship and Democracy: Lord and Peasant in the Making of the Modern World*. Boston, Beacon Press.

Mouzelis, N. 1988. 'Sociology of Development: Reflections on the Present Crisis'. *Sociology* 22 (1), pp. 23–44.

— 1988. 'Marxism or Post-Marxism?' *New Left Review* 167, pp. 107–23.

Nederveen Pieterse, J. 1991. 'Dilemmas of Development Discourse: The Crisis of Developmentalism and the Comparative Method'. *Development and Change* 22, pp. 5–29.

Norris, C. 1990. 'Lost in the Funhouse: Baudrillard and the Politics of Postmodernism'. In R. Boyne & A. Rattansi, pp. 119–53.

Offe, C. 1985. *Disorganized Capitalism*. Cambridge Massachusetts, Massachusetts Institute of Technology Press.

Parajuli, P. 1991. 'Power and Knowledge in Development Discourse: New Social Movements and the State in India'. *International Social Science Journal* 127, pp. 173–90.

Parsons, T. 1937. *The Structure of Social Action*. Glencoe, Free Press.

Peet, R. (ed.) 1980. *An Introduction to Marxist Theories of Underdevelopment*. Canberra, The Australian National University.

Petrella, R. 1989. 'Un Nouveau Partage du Monde entre les Entreprises'. *Le Monde Diplomatique*, August 1989.

Poulantzas, N. 1975. *Classes in Contemporary Capitalism*. London, New Left Books.

Rawls, J. 1972. *A Theory of Justice*. Oxford, Oxford University Press.

Ray, D. 1973. 'The Dependency Model of Latin American Underdevelopment: Three Basic Fallacies'. *Journal of Inter-American Studies and World Affairs* 15, pp. 4–21.

Rey, P. 1971. *Colonialisme, Neo-colonialisme et Transition au Capitalisme*. Paris, Maspero.

— 1973. *Les Alliances de Classes*. Paris, Maspero.

Risseeuw, C. 1991. 'Bourdieu, Power and Resistance: Gender Transformation in Sri Lanka'. In K. Davis *et al.*, *The Gender of Power*, pp. 154–79. London, Sage.

Rose, M. 1991. *The Post-Modern and the Post-Industrial: A Critical Analysis*. Cambridge, Cambridge University Press.

Rostow, W. 1960. *The Stages of Economic Growth*. Cambridge, CUP.

— 1978. *Getting from Here to There*. London, MacMillan.

Sadik, N. 1991. 'Rethinking Modernism: Towards Human-Centred Development'. *Development* (2), pp. 15–20.

Said, E. 1978. *Orientalism*. Harmondsworth, Penguin.

Scott, A. 1990. *Ideology and the New Social Movements*. London, Unwin Hyman.

Sheth, D. 1987. 'Alternative Development as Political Practice'. In Mendlovitz & Walker (eds.), *Towards a Just World Peace*, pp. 235–52. London, Butterworths.

Shiva, V. 1988. *Staying Alive: Women, Ecology and Development*. London, Zed Books.

Sklair, L. 1988. 'Transcending the Impasse: Metatheory, Theory, and Empirical Research in the Sociology of Development and Underdevelopment'. *World Development* 16 (6), pp. 697–709.

Slater, D. 1987. 'On Development Theory and the Warren Thesis: Arguments Against the Predominance of Economism'. *Environment and Planning* D (Society and Space) 5, pp. 263–82.

— 1991. 'Theories of Development and Politics of the Post-Modern: Exploring a Border Zone'. Paper for the ISS workshop on 'Rethinking Emancipation'. The Hague, 30 January–1 February 1991.

— 1990. 'Fading Paradigms and New Agendas – Crisis and Controversy in Development Studies'. *European Review of Latin American and Caribbean Studies* 49, pp. 25–32.

Soja, E. 1989. *Postmodern Geographies: The Reassertion of Space in Critical Social Theory*. London, Verso.

Stander, H., & D. Becker. 1990. 'Postimperialism Revisited: The Venezuelan Wheat Import Controversy of 1986'. *World Development* 18 (2), pp. 197–213.

Stauffer, B. 1990. 'After Socialism: Capitalism, Development, and the Search for Critical Alternatives'. *Alternatives* XV, pp. 401–30.

Taylor, J. 1979. *From Modernization to Modes of Production: A Critique of the Sociologies of Development and Underdevelopment*. London, MacMillan.

Tilly, C. 1984. *Big Structures, Large Processes, Huge Comparisons*. New York, Russell Sage Foundation.

Touraine, A. 1974. *The Post-Industrial Society, Tomorrow's Social History: Classes, Conflicts and Culture in the Programmed Society*. London, Leonard Mayhew.

Toye, J. 1987. *Dilemmas of Development: Reflections on the Counter-Revolution in Development Theory and Policy*. Oxford, Blackwell.

Trainer, F. 1989. 'Reconstructing Radical Development Theory'. *Alternatives* XIV, pp. 481–515.

Vandergeest, P., & F. Buttel. 1988. 'Marx, Weber, and Development Sociology: Beyond the Impasse'. *World Development* 16 (6), pp. 683–95.

Wallerstein, I. 1974. *The Modern World System*. New York, Academic Press.

— 1979. *The Capitalist World Economy*. Cambridge, Massachusetts, Cambridge University Press.

Warren, B. 1980. *Imperialism: Pioneer of Capitalism*. London, Verso.

Watts, M. 1988. 'Deconstructing Determinism: Marxisms, Development Theory and a Comradely Critique of Capitalist World Development'. *Antipode* 20 (2), pp. 142–68.

Wolffensperger, J. 1991. 'Engendered Structure: Giddens and the Conceptualization of Gender'. In K. Davis *et al.*, *The Gender of Power*, pp. 87–108. London, Sage Publications.

World Bank. 1991. *World Development Report*, 'The Challenge of Development'. Oxford, Oxford University Press.

2

Development Research:
From Impasse to a New Agenda

by David Booth

Introduction

Ten years ago it was widely accepted that social research and theorising about development had reached some kind of impasse. Interesting and valuable work was still being done but in many areas of enquiry there had been disappointingly little cumulative advance along the lines mapped out during the 1970s. Initially stimulating theoretical debates, most of them originating within or on the fringes of the Marxist tradition, had run into the sand, bequeathing few if any guidelines for a continuing research programme. Crucial real-world questions were not being addressed and the gulf between academic enquiry and the various spheres of development policy and practice seemed to have widened. Some practitioners were beginning to express serious doubts about the 'relevance' of academic development studies.

Today, the state of the social development field by no means justifies complacency; yet the heavy atmosphere of intellectual stagnation and self-imposed insulation from practical issues that was so prevalent in the early 1980s does seem to have cleared. Not only is fresh and exciting work being carried out at a variety of levels and on a host of different topics, but the convergences of style and perspective are sufficiently striking to justify the notion of a new research agenda.

Identifying what it is that effectively distinguishes that agenda is no easy matter, given the variety of substantive concerns and cross-cutting intellectual influences that have played a role in its emergence. One thing, however, is obviously and importantly new: the interest shown at all levels, and in relation to the whole gamut of substantive problems, in the investigation of diversity – and hence the illumination of choice – in development. Whereas formerly influential theories ignored – more or less deliberately – the complex diversity of the real world of development, the styles of research that have come into prominence since the early 1980s take as their central task explaining significant variations in patterns of development in different local, national and regional settings.

The range and substance of what we might now dare call 'post-impasse'[1] research on social (and political and spatial) aspects of development is a cause for celebration. However, both the variety of the contributing perspectives and the *ad hoc* manner in which the new agenda has arisen raise issues which merit some systematic consideration. I believe it is time to take stock; time to consider not just whether it is true that some progress has been made along the lines suggested, but also where precisely it gets us and what steps, if any, need to be taken to guarantee the renewed sense of collective direction that has been achieved.

This chapter has two purposes: to set out some of the evidence supporting the idea of a new research agenda, and to provide an initial overview of its problems and possibilities. I begin by characterising briefly the sense of impasse that provides the starting point for the whole discussion. I then point to the recent emergence of a new intellectual style among social development researchers, going on to indicate some of the differences in outlook that might seem to cast doubt upon its coherence. The remainder of the chapter provides a brief conspectus of the conceptual and methodological issues confronting these new tendencies in research.

Out of the Impasse?
The malaise of the 1980s appeared differently to different people, but among those who thought seriously about it there was wide agreement on at least some of its major features and immediate causes. Many of the most significant gaps and weaknesses in research seemed to be connected with the highly generalised and economistic explanatory frameworks of Marxist and neo-Marxist origin that dominated social development theory in the West during the 1970s. These theories aspired to excessive explanatory power. They failed to reflect and were incapable of explaining the diversity and complexity of the real world of development. By refusing to make diversity a focus of particular attention, moreover, they contributed little or nothing to illuminating the alternatives facing responsible actors in less developed countries. Also, whether as a cause or as a consequence of their generality, these theories seemed to neglect or even deny much of what is specifically human about human societies: action and interaction, history, culture and the 'social construction of reality'.[2] Disagreement centred on the degree to which these difficulties were intrinsic in and peculiar to the Marxist project.

In an article that seems to have helped re-focus the debate among development sociologists (Booth 1985), I argued that metatheoretical influences within Marxism had forced discussion into grand simplifications which were either simply wrong (untenable empirically, conceptually unstable or redundant) or else pitched at a level of generality that made them irrelevant to the most important practical issues facing developing countries. At one level, my argument was that the impasse in Marxist-influenced development sociology was indeed a general one: not the product of the weaknesses of one particular perspective (neo-Marxist dependency theory), or even of a mutually contradictory pair of approaches (dependency theory vs the 'classical' Marxism of Bill Warren), but the result of a generalised theoretical disorientation. There was no viable 'middle position' between the polarised paradigms of the 1970s; basic Marxist concepts such as mode of production had proved incapable of consistent application to the subject matter of development studies.

The second level of argument concerned the deeper reasons for the impasse in theory. The paper suggested that behind the distinctive preoccupations, blind spots and contradictions of Marxist-influenced development sociology there lay the metatheoretical commitment to demonstrating that the structures and processes of less developed societies are not only explicable but necessary under capitalism. This general formula was intended to cover two forms of necessitist commitment in Marxism: the notion that the salient features of capitalist national economies and social formations can be derived or 'read off' from the concept of the capitalist mode of production and its 'laws of motion', and the various forms of Marxist system-teleology or functionalism. Along with a revitalised interest in the real-world problems of development policy and practice, an enhanced sensitivity to metatheoretical issues of this type was an essential first step in any attempt to deal with the impasse in social development theory.

The suggestion, also made by Corbridge (1986, 1990), that Marxism is intrinsically inclined towards 'essentialism' and system-teleology proved controversial. A series of commentators on the impasse debate (e.g., Larrain 1989, Peet 1990) have argued not merely that not all interpretations of Marxism have suffered from these tendencies (a view I would accept[3]) but also that Booth and Corbridge had been misled into a peculiarly narrow understanding of the core of Marxism by Hindess and Hirst – a point usually made with more innuendo than argument. Sklair (1988) thought that while Booth's critique of Marxism might have substance, its particular formulation confused theoretical and meta-theoretical issues.

Several of the more sympathetic rejoinders to Booth were concerned, instead, about the limited scope of the critique. Both Vandergeest and Buttel (1988) and Corbridge (1990) drew attention to Booth's concentration on the functionalism and essentialism of the Marxist tradition to the exclusion of mainstream sociological functionalism, neo-liberal economic theory and other non-Marxist sources of these ills. Mouzelis maintained separately (1988a, 1988b) that Marxism compared favourably with mainstream sociological functionalism in its handling of the structure/agency issue, and would be an entirely suitable basis for a comparative enquiry into development trajectories but for one 'pervasive flaw', that of reductionism in handling politics.

A number of the foregoing points are of continuing interest. But a more widespread and enduring reaction to my article was to accept most of what it said while deploring its largely negative thrust. If these things were true, what was the way forward? Were there not any examples of theoretical ideas and empirical research that pointed the way out of the impasse? All of the more welcoming comments on the impasse paper drew attention to these issues, and several (especially Vandergeest and Buttel 1988, and Corbridge 1990) went on to provide more or less convincing examples of recent work that was breaking new ground in the required direction, both theoretically and, indeed, metatheoretically. Others (e.g., Long 1984, 1988, Mouzelis 1986, 1988a) could claim with some reason that they had been doing such work for some years.

In retrospect, it seems that the lacunae left by the dominant research trends of the 1970s formed patterns that were sufficiently distinct by themselves to define the outline of an alternative research agenda. Furthermore, without waiting for a definitive resolution of the meta-theoretical issues or in blameless ignorance of that debate, researchers working on various kinds of development topics had already started posing new sorts of research questions applicable to their particular corners of the social development field.

Rediscovering Diversity

During the last 10 years or so, I wish to argue, social, political and spatial research concerned with development issues has been substantially transformed as various groups of scholars, unannounced but decisively, have assumed the task of exploring systematic variation and, hence, illuminating choice in development. This has happened on at least three different levels.

From Macro-diversity to Responsible Politics

To begin with, macro work on the development of national economies and societies has become increasingly concerned with the differences beneath the commonalities derived from structural location or developmental stages. Sociologists and political scientists whose previous work had helped to establish generalising constructs about Third World change began to converge with those emphasising distinctive national trajectories on the need for systematic comparative studies.

The lead was taken by students of Latin American politics and development (notably Collier 1979, Roxborough 1984, Mouzelis 1986, Sheahan 1987). Having pioneered comparative studies within a dependency framework in the 1960s (Cardoso and Faletto 1979) and essayed a plausible hypothesis about economically-rooted developmental tendencies in the 1970s (O'Donnell 1978), Latin Americanists became increasingly disenchanted with the former's class reductionism and with the latter's over-simple economism. In the the 1980s writers such as Sheahan – a polymath economist in the tradition of Albert Hirschman – placed the study of Latin American development on the explicit basis of illuminating policy alternatives through systematic work on the diversity of national experiences.

As the full weight of the East Asian NIC phenomenon began to bear on the consciousness of social scientists in the West around the turn of the 1980s, a cartload of premature generalisation about the Third World had to be dumped (Buttel and McMichael 1991). There followed a flurry of interest in the national or perhaps regional specificities accounting for the remarkable achievements of South Korea, Taiwan and, to a lesser extent, Hong Kong and Singapore (e.g., Ruggie 1983, Evans *et al.* 1985, Deyo 1987, White 1988, Amsden 1989, 1990). As the growing gulf between the NICs' performance and that of sub-Saharan Africa helped to announce 'the end of the Third World' as a minimally uniform and coherent entity (Harris 1986), studies of the politics of economic decline and structural adjustment in Africa moved rapidly from generalities about 'the African state' (Hyden 1983, Chabal 1986, Ergas 1987) towards comparative national studies (Rothchild and Chazan 1988, Lofchie 1989, Bates 1989, Nelson 1990, Grindle and Thomas 1991).

Investigations such as these have enhanced enormously our sensitivity to historically-grounded variations in national political economies. In addition to demonstrating the non-viability of particular attempts to schematise the role of external economic relations and other economic factors in national development, they provide ample support for the theses of Skocpol (1979, 1985) and Mouzelis (1984, 1988a, 1990, 1991) on the specificity of the political and the role of the state. Variations in state structures or 'modes of domination', as distinct from societal structures and modes of production, are now established as worthwhile objects of enquiry in a way that they were not 15 years ago.

By privileging diversity at the macro level, such studies as those referred to in this section do more than illuminate the past. While they are not perhaps policy-relevant in the usual sense, it is not too much to hope that they may have a significant practical impact in the longer term, contributing in some small way to the demise of political cultures based on appeals to spurious necessity and the the denial of choice by leaders and political movements (cf. Unger 1987a, 1987b).

Meso-diversity: Gender and Class

At an intermediate analytical level, research on class and gender relations has experienced an analogous change. *Pace* Sklair (1988: 702–4), the 'discovery' of gender relations as a central topic for development research did not by itself provide a line of advance out of the impasse in development sociology. What is relevant in the present context is the way the study of gender in relation to class has successfully disentangled itself over the last 10 years from the universalist and functionalist pretensions with which it was initially encumbered. As compared with earlier attempts to set out a Marxist–feminist approach to Third World studies, recent research has uncovered previously unimagined variety and subtlety in the transformations of gender relations through economic change (Wilson 1985, Scott 1986) and in the socio-economic implications of patterns of gender (Mackintosh 1989, Sender and Smith 1990, Simo 1991, Townsend and Momsen 1987). Our understanding of development options and of the possibilities and limits of productive intervention has been deepened in striking ways by this progressive liberation of gender studies from the paradigms of the 1970s.

Much more hesitantly, students of class formation began over the same period to abandon their previous preoccupation with the fit or lack of fit between Third World social conditions and essentialist imagery of one kind and another (is there a genuine national bourgeoisie in Chile, in Kenya? etc.). In my view, this tendency is in its early infancy. Nevertheless, we are beginning to see case studies in class formation which offer raw material not only for systematic comparisions between different locations and countries (Becker 1983, Harriss 1980, 1987, MacGaffey 1987), but also for analyses that treat class structure and other aspects of group formation and interest-articulation, without reductionism, as variables in relation to critical issues of public policy such as agricultural pricing and policy reform (Moore 1985, Bates 1989, Lofchie 1989, Boone 1990).[4]

From Meso-diversity to Micro-diversity:
Room for Manoeuvre in Rural Development

Marxist rural development studies were, and to some extent still are, defined by a dialogue between 'Leninist' agrarian transition analysis (commoditisation leading to depeasantisation) and various more or less functionalist accounts of the persistence of peasant economy or simple commodity production. As I argued in 1985, the often excellent research done under the influence of these ideas quite quickly came up against two difficulties: first, the unexpected diversity of empirically documented patterns and trends of Third World agrarian change, and, second, the relative poverty of the prescribed explanatory frameworks ('reading off' from a universal transition model, reference to the 'needs of capital', etc.). Despite widespread acceptance of the reality of these difficulties, essentialist, functionalist and economically reductionist formulas do linger on in both militant and shamefaced forms.[5]

At the same time, the last 10 years have seen a multiplication of efforts to redefine rural development studies in terms of 'taking diversity seriously'. Without losing sight of the growing forces of global integration, rural social studies have been drawn towards the investigation of differential responses to, and different outcomes from, the central 'tendencies' of agrarian change. At the sectoral level of analysis, internationally comparative rural studies have made significant progress with empirical and analytical work spanning the former 'First', 'Second' and 'Third' Worlds (Buttel and Goodman 1989, Marsden *et al.* 1990, Goodman and Redclift 1991). As Aidan Foster-Carter writes in a different connection, the best of this work 'avoids any false opposition or one-way determinism between the global and the local – but rather insists on studying *both* the specificities of particular places *and* the broader forces which shape *and are shaped by* particular local circumstances and histories' (1991: 11, author's emphasis). At the sub-sectoral level, a recurrent theme is the heterogeneity of existing agrarian structures and farming systems, and the resulting insufficiency of previously standard analytical categories (Long and van der Ploeg 1991, Buttel and Mc-Michael 1991, Dalling 1991). Although not immune to the temptations of premature aggregation and the reification/organicisation of socio-economic structures, this work represents a distinct advance on previous approaches to the study of Third World rural formations.

Placing emphasis on the actual workings, as distinct from the formal objectives or abstract representation, of key development processes, recent rural development research has done much to demystify not only the excessively aggregative formulas of neo-Marxist development sociology – peripheral capitalism, agrarian transition, etc. – but also the official ideologies and institutions of rural 'planning' and agricultural 'modernisation' (Elwert and Bierschenk 1988, Long and van der Ploeg 1991). Social scientists whose research entails working 'downwards' from the national level to particular sectoral institutions and programmes (e.g., Apthorpe 1987, Grindle 1980, 1986, Clay and Schaffer 1984) have found common ground with those working 'upwards' from the micro-level of the individual household (e.g., Arce 1987, Long 1988, 1989), in focusing on the 'space for change' or 'room for manoeuvre' in rural development situations. Others, probing the limits of human creativity and resistance, have explored the technological resources of rural people and the scope for indigenous alternatives to state-sponsored rural development (Chambers 1983, Scott 1985, Richards 1985). To a greater or lesser extent 'actor-oriented', these new directions in rural development research have revealed the important extent to which changes in the well-being of rural people are the result of complex interactions between individuals and groups endowed with different and changing amounts of knowledge and power. Potentially at least, this is 'relevant' research in the most obvious sense; its findings relate directly to the means of empowering and improving the lives the poor and the downtrodden of the world here and now.

The Problem of Theoretical Coherence

In 1985 I expressed the hope that the excursion into metatheoretical issues that I proposed would only be brief, and I stand by that preference. Nonetheless, the most obvious question begged by the kind of rapid survey I have just conducted is whether there is really much of any great substance that unifies the work alluded to. To what extent does an interest in the variety of things, even when combined with a general aspiration to improve the scope for rational decision-making by real-world actors, amount to a single 'approach', let alone a coherent theoretical or methodological framework? Are we in a position to answer the charge that what I have called post-impasse research is not only varied in terms of subject matter and the product of people with enormously diverse intellectual biographies, but also quite simply a mish-mash?

The revival of interest in the diversity of development is, certainly, both child and parent of a rather heterogeneous set of related intellectual developments, with different perspectives and priorities. At one level, the new directions in social development research are the expression of more or less explicit and self-conscious 'post-Marxist' critiques or neo-Weberian revivals. In this context, interest in diversity (comparative studies) is bound up with limited theoretical assertions about the independent variability and causal significance of such 'partial structures' or contextual factors as modes of political domination, patterns of gender, ethnic and cultural differences and a society's relations with its natural environment. Such claims are meant to qualify the substance, but in a sense continue to occupy the terrain, of classical social theory. The approach is conceptually innovative but structural (if not perhaps structural-*ist*); it is critical of the epistemological basis of particular sorts of classical claims, while accepting others.

A second broad tendency takes a 'constructivist' view of the social reality of development, drawing on a long tradition of social phenomenology (Schutz) and interactionist anthropology (Barth) as well as, to a greater or lesser extent, the critical techniques of such writers as Foucault (discourse analysis) and Derrida (deconstruction). Interest here is not only in the the multiple forms of social knowledge and their relations with power, but also in the diversity of outcomes of social processes that becomes visible once the constructedness and interactive character of such processes are given their due. Criticism is directed towards those forms of structural analysis which either by their explanatory procedures (e.g., essentialism or teleology) deny the possibility of such differences, or by sheer aggregation and abstraction effectively suppress them as objects of analytical attention (cf. Long 1988: 108–18). In this limited sense, but not necessarily in any others, the approach is *anti*-structuralist.

It cannot be assumed that those who borrow analytical methods from post-structuralist or 'post-modernist' sources necessarily share any of the wider views about the state of the world and the nature of social science expressed by such theorists of post-modernism as Lyotard (1984). In any case, there seem to be good grounds for doubting whether post-modernism in the social sciences amounts to anything more precise than a 'relatively widespread mood', broadly analogous, but no more, with the similarly named movements in the arts (Boyne and Rattansi 1990: 9-13). The recent interest in diversity and difference, and in the multiplicity of perspectives, in development is nonetheless at least broadly consonant with the characterisation of post-modernity given by Lyotard and others. To the extent that this is more than a casual connection, it is relevant to note the radicalism of Lyotard's claim, as summarised by Boyne and Rattansi, that 'all of the grand discourses of Western society, which is to say all of the legitimating narratives which purport to provide valid and definitive principles, in any sphere, across all societies, can now be seen to be defunct' (*ibid*.: 16).

Occupying what appears, at least superficially, to be an intermediate position between post-Marxism/neo-Weberianism and constructivism (with or without post-modernist coda) is a third important collection of influences on recent social development research. In one form this is the sort of 'actor-oriented' work that aspires not so much to explore the limits of structural constraint as to uncover through interactionist investigations the very processes that produce and reproduce particular structural forms; the micro foundations of the macro framework. The other manifestation of this tendency is the 'new political economy' of the rational-choice school of Robert Bates. Though the general idea of seeking to explain institutional outcomes by reference to the choices of individual or collective actors scarcely counts as a new theme in the social sciences, the recent convergence on this point between the anthropological interactionism of the 'Manchester' school (Kapferer, Long) and Bates's notably non-neoclassical applications of rational-choice analysis in the field of development studies (1981, 1983, 1988) adds up to a significant trend.

The multiplicity of the theoretical influences that have played a part in (and been advanced by) the rethinking of the basis of social development research is potentially a great source of strength. It is also potentially destructive of the limited sense of renewed direction that those doing research in this area now feel. This being the case, there is much to be gained from a constructive dialogue designed to map out areas of agreement and disagreement on at least a few of the major analytical and methodological issues that arise at this point.

The issues that we may hope to address effectively would seem to belong to three broad categories:
1) questions about *theory and method*, especially the desirability and methodological implications of translating the gains from recent research into consolidated theoretical advances;
2) new and perennial issues, or perennial issues in new guises, concerning the relationships between *agency, structure and explanation*;
3) the ramifactions of the proposal that social development research can and should be assessed in terms of its *relevance*.

In this paper there is space only for a few preliminary words on each of these topics.

Theory and Method

The issues to be considered here revolve around the charge, lurking in the background if not explicitly formulated by anyone, that the 'post-impasse' tendency in social development research is simply glorified empiricism. It is a suggestion that gains plausibility from the seeming inconsistency of views about the role and importance of theory between the different strands of post-Marxist and post-modernist critique. Not only are currently influential ideas on this subject varied, but in certain instances they are apparently contradictory. Contrasting assessments of the role of theory are related closely to divergent understandings of what is entailed by 'the rediscovery of diversity'.

On the one hand, the latter refers above all to an increased sensitivity to systematic variation, that is to say diversity about which it is possible to *generalise* at a certain level. At the other extreme lies the position of those for whom the rediscovery of diversity refers more to variety rather than variability, more to the *celebration of difference* than to the recognition of patterns of diversity. According to the explicitly post-modernist variant of this position, all generalities are suspect, linked as they are to one or other of the grand discourses or 'metanarratives' of modern Western thought. These in turn are vitiated by their 'foundation-alism': their adherence to theories of knowledge that 'seek to guarantee the validity of substantive enquiries in *a priori* formulae' (Crook 1990: 51). Those who take this view are unclear and thus far divided about where exactly it leads, but it commonly generates ambivalence towards the whole idea of a generalising social science.

The affinities are real between the 'incredulity towards metanarratives' that typifies the post-modernism of Lyotard and others and the critiques of Marxist and neo-Marxist grand theories that were the stuff of the impasse debate. Lyotard's attack on foundationalist social theory is broadly consistent at least in respect of Marxism with the 'post-Marxist' views of Hindess and Hirst, which are cited by Booth and Corbridge. As Corbridge (1991) has shown, however, post-modernism goes some way beyond post-Marxism in the sweep of its condemnation of the concepts and methods of modern social science. Its careless espousal of relativistic and nihilistic positions, and its illogical extension of the critique of a prioristic notions of progress to cover all general enquiries about process, render it singularly unsuited to the task of reconstituting the basis of social development research.

The challenge to the theoretical ambitions of post-impasse thinking comes, however, not merely in the highly articulated form of post-modernist particularism. It also comes in more mundane guises. Together with pressures that are beyond our control, such as the limited budgets of research funding agencies and the practical difficulties of doing fieldwork in more than one location, the 'innate' intellectual proclivities of those working at the micro, or more actor-oriented, end of the social research spectrum may also weaken the thrust towards systematic comparative work and the development of new strands of substantive theory.

In a number of sub-fields of social development research today synthetic and comparative work is lagging well behind the production of detailed empirical studies. We face the danger that social researchers, disillusioned with the old theoretical certainties and perhaps also a little intoxicated by their renewed immersion in an ever-surprising empirical reality, will become very good at producing detailed case studies but rather bad at communicating the general implications of their work to a wider academic audience, not to speak of a wider public of development practitioners. Accelerating the rate at which empirical findings are translated into 'theoretical' formulations is important not just because doing theory is intellectually more satisfying, but because it is only at the theoretical level that research findings achieve a sufficient level of generality to be of interest and relevance to those wider audiences. If we fail to produce new theories, our claims to relevance and responsibility will begin to appear hollow.

In what form are new theories of development likely to emerge? The question may well be unanswerable at this stage. Even to establish the kinds of answer we might give, it is necessary to consider the several issues raised in the next section regarding the different and possibly competing claims of structural, 'constructivist' and actor-oriented research and analysis.

Agency, Structure and Explanation

There are three topics that need specific attention here:
- how to reconcile insights about indigenous alternatives and room-for-manoeuvre in local settings with the kinds of understandings of larger structures without which they will lack realism;
- the potential role of 'actor' or social choice analysis in the reconstitution of structural analysis or 'political economy';
- how to reconcile the analytical requirements of comparison and theory-building with the 'constructed' and multi-dimensional character of social processes, and vice-versa.

Action and Social Context

As we have seen, post-impasse social research on development topics includes a significant body of work whose distinguishing feature is an analytical emphasis on agency, the social contruction of development situations and the sorts of opportunities for alternative approaches to development that remain obscure so long as the variety of development experience is treated in purely structural terms. Interest in such issues need not imply a blanket refusal of conventional methods of structural analysis (e.g., cross-country comparisons). Moreover, most practitioners of actor-oriented research acknowledge in principle the interdependence of action and structure. It is, however, one thing to recognise what is the case in principle and another to build it effectively into the design of one's research. A specific problem of this sort arises from the fact that most actor-oriented studies are not only 'micro' in the sense of being concerned with face-to-face processes, but also highly localised spatially. It is legitimate to ask how we are to ensure that the findings of local-action studies reflect not only local realities and room-for-manoeuvre, but also the constraints upon action that may only emerge at the regional or national level (or over longer time-periods).

If I am not mistaken, post-impasse research trends have led, not by design but by default, to a reopening (or at any rate a continued lack of closure) of the gulf between localised micro studies and the kinds of understanding of larger structures that are needed to place them in their proper context. For those engaged in local studies, disillusionment with neo-Marxist structural theories has tended to lead in practice to abandonment of the terrain of 'political economy'. To be sure, those doing participatory research or conducting case studies in particular regions of

developing countries invariably concede that to be realistic their interpretations and recommendations need to draw on an understanding of
the wider social, economic and political context. Long and van der Ploeg
(1991: 17, 20) vigorously refute the suggestion that their approach
implies a neglect of the contexts of action. Nevertheless, today as in the
past most local studies remain determinedly micro in both senses, the
wider context being allowed to escape from view in a way that is
disturbingly reminiscent of the bad old days of functionalist anthropology.

What is worse, we seem to have slipped backward since the 1970s.
Twenty years ago Norman Long and Bryan Roberts pioneered the idea
that collaborative projects with a regional (that is to say relatively
inclusive) focus could be an effective vehicle for integrating micro-action
studies with the exploration of political-economic issues. The results of
their work (1978, 1984) generally vindicated the claim. Yet to my
knowledge the experiment has not been repeated, either by Long and
Roberts or by anyone else.

Practical difficulties undoubtedly weigh very heavily where such
ambitious collaborations are involved, but the problem also has an
intellectual dimension. A recent paper by Anthony Bebbington (1991)
illustrates one way of bridging the gap between local action studies and
macro-structural analysis. Commenting on the strongly polarised debate
between students of indigenous technological change (Richards 1985,
Chambers *et al.* 1989) and some of those interested in the political-
economic context of such change in West Africa (Watts 1989), Bebbington argues that such a degree of polarisation is unnecessary; neither
approach is as comprehensive and self-sufficient as its advocates
maintain. Moreover, certain topics, such as the role of peasant organisations and the evolution of rural civil society, are equally ignored by
both. Using such bridging themes it is possible within the limitations of
existing fieldwork methods to do research that both takes peasant agency
seriously and gives proper attention to structural constraint.

Reconstituting a Political Economy?
Even if, as this suggests, we are in a position to achieve better linkages
upwards from the micro to the meso and the macro, there remains the
whole question of the conceptual language and forms of explanation that
are appropriate to analysing these latter, wider structures. Addressing
this issue, Buttel and McMichael (1991) wish to reclaim major parts of
the classical tradition of social theory, while Corbridge (1991) insists on
the continuing intellectual vitality of important aspects of Marxism.
Bebbington (1991) is not alone in seeing contemporary relevance in such
classical concepts as 'civil society'. But under what conditions is it

productive to detach concepts from the wider theoretical nexus to which they belong, and to put them to purposes other than those for which they were intended? By what means are we to go about reconstructing the political economy of development along non-essentialist, non-functionalist lines? Do micro studies and actor-oriented research have a role to play here? The answer seems to be yes, in at least two different senses, to be discussed in this section and the next.

A persistent suggestion, coming now from at least two distinct quarters, is that actor studies hold the key to a better understanding of the structures that constrain developmental possibilities, because of the way they may illuminate the micro-foundations of macro-processes. As Long and van der Ploeg have argued (Long 1989: 226-31, Long and van der Ploeg 1991), the use of micro-action studies to illuminate structures does not imply radically individualist or reductionist assumptions. Emphasising that the focus of such studies is not so much individual decision-making as interactional processes embedded in systems of belief and both local and intermediate social relationships or networks, Long commends Randall Collins's (1981) proposal for a 'reconstitution of macro-sociology on the basis of its necessary micro-foundations', involving a systematic programme for the ' "unpacking" of macro-sociological metaphors'. The promise of micro studies to macro understanding lies not in the reduction of the latter to the former, but in the disentangling of the invariably complex web of unintended consequences and feedback effects that form the link between action and structure.

Long and his collaborators are not alone in seeing in all this a fascinating challenge to sociological explanation in the development studies field and beyond. The 'collective choice' approach pioneered in its application to African development issues by Bates (1981, 1989) involves a similar conception. Regrettably, the reception of Bates's most widely-read book (1981) has been coloured by the close coincidence of his opening account of the proximate economic causes of the decline of African agricultures with that of the World Bank's somewhat notorious 'Berg Report' (1981). As Mick Moore (1987, 1990) has shown, however, the originality of Bates lies in his persistence in seeking not economic but political explanations for economic failure. The stuff of his analysis is an unravelling of various macro mysteries by reference to the unanticipated consequences of the interlocking preferences of relevant groups of actors – peasants, bureaucrats and politicians. It is worth noting that Bates's actors are more often collective than individual, and that their choices are not assumed to be reducible to the neo-classical paradigm of rational decision-making – i.e., abstracted from their social and cultural context.[6]

Reconstituting political economy on a non-essentialist and non-teleological basis is not going to be the work of a single day. Nor, in spite of Long's claims for interface analysis or those of Bates for collective choice (1983, 1988), is it likely to rest on the achievements of a single school of thought. Nevertheless, a rather wide range of central topics in the contemporary political economy of development does seem to be amenable to a style of analysis that moves back and forth between the macro and the micro. Are there, indeed, any areas in which we can say with confidence that there is no scope for realising these kinds of analytical potentialities?

Deconstruction and Concepts of Structure

Whatever answer is given to the above question, it seems unreasonable to suppose that explaining structures and structural diversity by reference to other structural variables will ever cease to be an important sort of analytical activity for social development researchers. Nor, despite Long and van der Ploeg's (1991: 21) wish to say a 'definite *adieu* to structure understood as explanans', should we regard this as in any way undesirable – provided appropriate concepts and explanatory procedures can be found. On the other hand, arriving at a suitable body of de-essentialised, non-teleological and non-reductionist concepts for structural analysis may be easier said than done; and here lies another important role for the action-oriented strand of recent thinking.

Thinking about structures in a new way requires new structural concepts. As the past and recent work of Nicos Mouzelis (1986, 1990, 1991) shows, it may be possible to arrive at such concepts by judicious adjustments to classical concepts from Marxism and elsewhere. Mouzelis's elaboration of the concept of 'mode of domination' is a case in point. This is modelled in some but not all respects on Marx's 'mode of production' (in Mouzelis, there are forces and relations but no 'laws of motion' or structures that secure their own conditions of existence), and it serves well enough to direct comparative analytical attention to a range of vital issues that have been neglected by previous work. Parallel use has been made by Skocpol and her collaborators (Evans *et al.* 1985) and by such writers as Grindle (1986) and Migdal (1988) of concepts extracted critically from the tradition of Max Weber.

Such concepts should of course be subject to critical deconstruction, and in particular they need to withstand the test that they have indeed shed their skins of pre-impasse essentialism and functionalism. But this is different from saying that structural concepts are out of order *per se* or need to be replaced wholesale and regardless of the purpose in hand by descriptions of interactional processes and their outcomes. Particular social scientists in particular contexts may be guilty of premature aggregation and structuralisation of interactional events; but there will also always be occasions when it is legitimate and illuminating to place the 'micro foundations' on one side or 'between brackets'.

That having been said, there is a level of structural concept formation where in the future it is going to be necessary to promote a more direct dialogue between structural and actor-oriented or constructivist work than has occurred until now. I have in mind the level at which the researcher attempts to characterise the mode of domination or the class structure, or the gender relations, at a specific place and time. At present there is a large gulf between the more structural and the more actor-oriented approaches to these issues.

Currently, actor-oriented rural researchers tend to substitute for the old Marxist and Weberian analytical categories – agrarian capitalism, simple commodity production, rural proletariat, etc. – not alternative analytical categories but actors' self-descriptions: 'entrepreneur', 'small producer', 'campesino', etc. This stems from a worthwhile effort to incorporate the lived experience of rural development, to penetrate the 'life-worlds' of the participants. With good reason it is argued that not only the 'hard' Marxist concepts but even such seemingly innocent terms as 'village', 'peasantry' and 'working class' have been rendered prob- lematic; that 'our categories have been so essentialised that even using common terms tends to pitch us back into the use of a discourse replete with transcendant entities' (Hobart 1990: 15). But this, it may be argued, deals only with the most obvious and least plausible alternative to actors' categories and falls short of providing a convincing rationale for *exclusive* reliance on life-world descriptions.

The challenge to structural concept formation today is, surely, to arrive at ways of using life-world categories to inform 'objective' statements about the structural locations of individuals and groups, *and vice versa*. It is a truism in social anthropology that while accounts of actors' culturally informed definitions of activities and institutions are invariably an essential ingredient of any explanation, they are often insufficient on their own, if only because what people say they do commonly differs from what they really do. Observers need also to draw on their own observations, which need in turn to be disciplined not only by sensitivity to cultural differences but also by a conscious reflexivity. The mutual indispensability of the 'emic' (description of cultural meanings) and the 'etic' (observation of behaviour) is well trodden terrain in this context (e.g., Pelto and Pelto 1978). In my submission, there are tasks arising from these observations that need to be tackled urgently by sociologists, human geographers and political scientists concerned with the meso and macro structures of development.

In a recent paper, John Harriss (1991) argues the case for a reanalysis of the class structure of rural India in terms which recognise the 'constructed' character of class relations and the role of cultural defin- itions of what it is to belong to a particular group. The combination of emic and etic concerns in a single analytical process is also one of the benefits of the 'theoretically informed empiricism' exemplified in the recent paper by Barnett and Blaikie (1991). This is ground-breaking work and correspondingly difficult, but it holds out the promise of the sort of thoroughgoing critical regeneration of the lower-order concepts of the Marx-Weber tradition that is an essential condition for the reconstitution of the political economy of development.

Relevance, Realism and Choice

From the beginning of the discussion about the impasse in development sociology, a major concern of many of us was not just that the established theoretical controversies were getting nowhere, but that the subject was failing to respond creatively to the great public issues of the day in the 'real world' of development. This plea for social research in and about the developing world to be more responsive to the concerns of those who formulate, execute, benefit or suffer from development policies, prog- rammes and projects, has become more pointed in recent years as the range of different sorts of 'development practitioners' and intermediary organisations has multiplied. In particular, the expansion of the roles of Non-Government Organisations (NGOs) throughout much of Africa, South and Southeast Asia and Latin America in the 1980s, brought with it new sources of dissatisfaction with the orientation of academic development research. To date the most radical and articulate statement of this latter kind of concern is Michael Edwards's angry declamation on 'The Irrelevance of Development Studies' (1989).

Despite the memorable title, Edwards's argument was directed against ' "development studies of a particular form" ' (1989: 131) rather than against the entire output of the subject. Nevertheless the scope of his critique is quite broad, and it is by no means clear that much of the research that has been characterised here as post-impasse escapes its strictures. Edwards's general concern in looking at the relationship between research and development is about 'the absence of strong links between understanding and action' (117). His particular *bêtes noires* include the cult of the expert and the devaluation of local knowledge, the tendency for research to be guided by the professional interests of the researcher rather than the needs of those being researched, the concent- ration of knowledge and hence power by elites, and the lack of an ongoing relationship between research and appropriate forms of involvement in development processes. Since increasingly ' "popular participation" is accepted as the only real basis for successful development', Edwards argued, the key to a better model for the future is the spread and consolidation of 'participatory research' or 'action research', understood as research linked to projects which aim at 'facilitating people's own development efforts' (123, 129). Not all useful research can or should be directly participatory, but 'higher-level work must grow out of and be based upon participatory research at lower levels' (130).

Our response to the 'NGO view' (if that is what it is) needs to take the form of a dialogue, a consideration not just of how well current research efforts measure up in terms of practical criteria, but also of what those criteria ought to be. There are also a number of preliminary issues than cannot be skipped over entirely. To what extent is there agreement on the meaning, desirability and attainability of 'relevance'? Are moral concerns the essential driving force, or to the contrary the bane, of development studies? Having settled these points, we can go on to ask: Do NGOs know what research they want, and is this what they need? Is relevant research the same as applied research? Is macro work less relevant than micro work? And when it comes to applied research and practical intervention, how much and in what ways does 'theory' matter?

The meaning and desirability of 'relevance' in social development research turns out, somewhat surprisingly, to be one of the *most* controversial issues among social development researchers. Differences on this issue, moreover, do not correspond at all closely to disagreements on the other dimensions reviewed here. Buttel and McMichael (1991), writing from the perspective of development sociology conceived as comparative structural enquiry, make a strong appeal for a greater separation than has existed in the past between the mainstream of the discipline and 'applied development studies'. In their view, the search for generalisable recipes for development problems was one of the main sources of the over-generalised and one-dimensional theorising of the 1960s and 1970s.

From a position which on the face of it is no less structuralist, Corbridge (1991) makes the sharply different plea that our relations with 'distant strangers' are an undeniable moral issue, and that the study of development is correspondingly imbued with ethical as well as scientific concern. This view, which by no means implies a reduction of development studies to an 'applied' field (Bebbington 1991: 1), seems to be widely shared, especially by those such as Barnett whose own work has spanned the 'pure' and 'applied' (Barnett and Blaikie 1991). It is not, however, a universal view, even among researchers whose findings seem to be redolent with practical implications at the grass-roots level.

Edwards's appeals are directed at everyone, but they have a special significance for those who have been doing research among poor people and of a kind that is or could in principle be directly participatory. Proponents of actor-oriented 'interface' (Long 1989) and other research on local movements and power structures do claim that their work has a payoff in the form of understandings which make possible improvements in rural programmes and/or direct measures to empower the powerless and the poor. This, however, is not the same as offering a recipe for 'getting development right' (Long and van der Ploeg 1991: 26). It is certainly a different matter from holding that research should be invariably linked to empowerment schemes or participatory projects. Actor-oriented research is not the kind of 'participant observation' in the service of improved top-down planning upon which Edwards heaps scorn, but neither is it to be equated with 'action research'. It should not be 'embraced as a kind of new panacea for ameliorating the poverty, uncertainties and vulnerabilities of disadvantaged groups ... but it can afford various social actors a useful conceptual framework for analysing their own life circumstances and for assessing possible strategies for action' (*ibid.*).

One of the implicit concerns here is the issue of 'who decides?'. One of the worries that academic social researchers often feel in the face of demands for greater relevance is that the necessary question 'relevant to whom and for what purpose?' has not been properly answered or its implications pursued. It is for this reason rather than for a lack of concern about practical issues that they prefer to let their work 'stand or fall by its analytical results' (*ibid.*). For related reasons, research on NGOs and NGO projects may be done best if it is the fruit of a collaborative relationship between NGOs and academic researchers, rather than defined and controlled by the former from the outset (Hulme 1991).

There is also another set of questions about what relevant research is supposed to be relevant to. Although as we have seen Edwards does not restrict the characterisation 'relevant' to local participatory projects to the exclusion of all other forms of development research, the criterion that the entire field should 'grow out of and be based upon' such projects is very restrictive indeed, particularly when accompanied by references from which one infers that other criteria of a more political sort may also be involved (1989: 130). The underlying proposition that popular participation has been shown to be the only real basis for successful development seems to me to be problematic, not because I doubt the achievements of the better NGO projects and of the new 'grassroots' movements as a whole, but because especially outside Africa there is a good deal of developmental success that has nothing to do with this sort of activity.

Should local studies enjoy a special privilege when we are talking about relevance to practice, or even relevance to people? Given the capacity of an unfavourable macro or meso context to dissipate the gains from merely local efforts, is not research on the regional, national and international levels potentially the most 'relevant' of all – provided it is good research (cf. Bebbington 1991)? As Barnett and Blaikie show (1991), even directly applied work which perforce 'ignores the wider picture' may nevertheless need to draw on a good 'toolbox' of theoretical issues and concepts. Perhaps, after all, this is what it means to say that macro research should 'grow out of' participatory work, but in that case the formula is ambiguous and we should give our minds to how it might be sharpened up.

Beyond a certain rather general level of discussion, it seems to me undesirable to enter into discussions about which sorts of research are 'relevant' and which not. What does seem clear and worth reaffirming is the general interdependence that seems to have been established between the triplet relevance, realism and choice. By adopting a research agenda centred on diversity, social development studies may not have fully attended to the 'irrelevance of development studies' in the eyes of the new NGO activists. But because of the association of diversity with choice, an agenda constituted in this way is relevant to the world of practical concerns in a way that previous agendas were not, and this is surely a good thing. True relevance also depends on the realism of the findings of research, which means attempting to resolve the difficult dilemmas outlined in the middle sections of this paper – between theory and empirical work, between action and its structural contexts, between emic and etic methods – few of which are likely to be satisfied by a single pattern of localised and participatory research. While much remains to be done in these respects, there is much promise in the recent trends to which it has been possible to refer.

Conclusion

The echoes of the 'impasse debate' are still with us and will no doubt continue to be heard for some time yet. But in important ways, I have argued, the field of social development research has already been reconstituted on new, more productive and more challenging lines. What is common to the new directions in which research is moving is the attention being given – at macro, meso and micro levels – to the investigation and explanation of diversity.

To put the matter in this way, it has been conceded, does give a misleading impression of intellectual coherence, belied by the observation that interest in developmental diversity is the child and parent of three or four distinct strands of theoretical critique. Diversity means different things in different contexts, and different sorts of contributors to 'post-impasse' thinking are not of one mind on such issues as the proper place of theoretical work, the relationship between 'actor-oriented' and structural analysis, and the desirability of judging research by the criterion of relevance.

As this chapter has tried to show, however, the tendency of recent discussions has been to bring forward more evidence of agreement, and fewer signs of fundamental disagreement, than many would have expected. I have no brief to present a consensus and the paper has not attempted to construct one. Nevertheless, I believe there is a good measure of agreement behind a number of the propositions advanced here. Diversity can and should be the subject of generalisations and theoretical work. While both action-based and structural explanations are permissible, there are limits to the productive pursuit of either on its own – the gulf between local action studies and 'political economy' must be bridged, and deconstruction and social choice brought to bear on the reconstitution of the latter. And, lastly, it is both desirable and possible for post-impasse research to achieve a 'relevance' that was denied to or rejected by earlier work on the social, political and spatial dimensions of development.

Notes

1. The expression has the advantage of allowing us to sidestep the issue of whether labels like 'post-Marxist' are applicable or make good sense (cf. Corbridge 1990, Mouzelis 1988b, Geras 1987). Although I have some sympathy for Corbridge's handling of the question, there is no doubt it is a can of worms.

2. These, at least, were the more or less shared and more or less elaborated contentions of what became a longish series of articles and books appearing in print from around the middle of the decade (Long 1984, Booth 1985, Corbridge 1986, Richards 1986, Mouzelis 1988, Vandergeest and Buttel 1988, Hall and Midgley 1988, Edwards 1989, Hulme and Turner 1990, Arce and Mitra 1991).

3. Several contributors to a recent *Socialist Register* (especially Geras 1990, Cammack 1990) are concerned – in some part no doubt rightly – about a general trend towards casual misrepresentations of the Marxist tradition, including some authors referred to favourably in this chapter.

4. Relevant points about theory and method are made by Corbridge (1982), Kitching (1985), Booth (1987), Hindess (1987, 1989) and Moore (1990).

5. E.g., respectively, Brass (1990, 1991) and Bernstein (1990).

6. Sandiland (1985) provides an excellent demonstration of the superiority in practice of this substantially modified rational choice approach over other applications of the doctrine in the development field.

Relevant Literature

Amsden, Alice H. 1989. *Asia's Next Giant: South Korea and Late Industrialisation*. New York, Oxford University Press.

— 1990. 'Third World Industrialization: "Global Fordism" or New Model?' *New Left Review*, no. 182, July/Aug.

Apthorpe, Raymond (ed.). 1987. 'Institutions and Policies'. Special issue, *Public Administration and Development*, vol. 6, no. 4.

Arce, Alberto. 1987. 'Bureaucratic Conflict and Public Policy: Rainfed Agriculture in Mexico'. *Boletin de Estudios Latinoamericanos y del Caribe*, no. 42, June.

— 1989. 'The Social Construction of Agrarian Development: A Case Study of Producer-Bureaucrat Relations in an Irrigation Unit in Western Mexico'. In N. Long (1989).

— & Norman Long. 1987. 'The Dynamics of Knowledge Interfaces between Mexican Agricultural Bureaucrats and Peasants: A Case Study from Jalisco'. *Boletin de Estudios Latinoamericanos y del Caribe*, no. 43, Dec.

— & Subrata Mitra. 1991. 'Making Development Relevant: Beyond the Impasse in Development Studies'. University of Hull, Department of Sociology & Social Anthropology, Occasional Paper 7.

Barnett, Tony & Piers Blaikie. 1991. 'On Ignoring the Wider Picture: AIDS Research and the Jobbing Social Scientist'. Paper presented to Workshop on Relevance, Realism and Choice in Social Development Research, University of Hull, Jan.

Barth, F. 1966. 'Models of Social Organization'. *Occasional Paper* 23. London, Royal Anthropological Institute.

Bates, Robert. 1981. *Markets and States in Tropical Africa: The Political Basis of Agricultural Policies*. Berkeley, University of California Press.

— 1983. 'Conclusion' in R. Bates, *Essays in the Political Economy of Rural Africa*. Cambridge, Cambridge University Press.

— (ed.). 1988. *Toward a Political Economy of Development: A Rational Choice Perspective*. Berkeley, University of California Press.

— 1989. *Beyond the Miracle of the Market: The Political Economy of Agrarian Development in Kenya*. Cambridge, Cambridge University Press.

Bebbington, Anthony. 1991. 'Theory and Relevance in Indigenous Agriculture: Knowledge, Agency and Organisation'. Paper prepared for publication in David Booth (ed.), *New Directions in Social Development Research*.

Becker, David G. 1983. *The New Bourgeoisie and the Limits of Dependency: Mining, Class, and Power in 'Revolutionary' Peru*. Princeton, Princeton University Press.

Bernstein, Henry. 1990. 'Agricultural "Modernisation" and the Era of Structural Adjustment: Observations on Sub-Saharan Africa'. *Journal of Peasant Studies*, vol. 18, no. 1, Oct.

Boone, Catherine. 1990. 'The Making of a Rentier Class: Wealth Accumulation and Political Control in Senegal'. *Journal of Development Studies*, vol. 26, no. 3, Apr.

Booth, David. 1985. 'Marxism and Development Sociology: Interpreting the Impasse'. *World Development*, vol. 13, no. 7, July.

— 1987. 'Alternatives in the Restructuring of State-Society Relations: Research Issues for Tropical Africa'. *IDS Bulletin*, vol. 18, no. 4, Oct.

Boyne, Roy & Ali Rattansi. 1990. 'The Theory and Politics of Postmodernism:

By Way of an Introduction'. In R. Boyne & A. Rattansi (eds.), *Postmodernism and Society*, London, Macmillan.

Brass, Tom. 1990. 'Peasant Essentialism and the Agrarian Question in the Colombian Andes'. (Review article), *Journal of Peasant Studies*, vol. 17, no. 3, Apr.

— 1991. 'Moral Economists, Subalterns, New Social Movements, and the (Re-)Emergence of a (Post-)Modernised (Middle) Peasant'. *Journal of Peasant Studies*, vol. 18, no. 2, Jan.

Buttel, Frederick H. & David Goodman (eds.). 1989. 'Class, State, Technology and International Food Regimes'. Special issue, *Sociologia Ruralis*, vol. 29, no. 2.

— & Philip McMichael. 1991. 'Reconsidering the Explanandum and Scope of Development Studies: Toward a Comparative Sociology of State-Economy Relations'. Paper presented to Workshop on Relevance, Realism and Choice in Social Development Research, University of Hull, Jan.

Cammack, Paul. 1990. 'Statism, New Institutionalism, and Marxism'. In Ralph Miliband *et al.* (eds.), *Socialist Register 1990*, London, Merlin Press.

Cardoso, Fernando Henrique & Enzo Faletto. 1979. *Dependency and Development in Latin America*. Berkeley, University of California Press.

Chabal, Patrick (ed.). 1986. *Political Domination in Africa*. Cambridge, Cambridge University Press.

Chambers, Robert. 1983. *Rural Development: Putting the Last First*. Harlow, Longman.

—, Arnold Pacey & Lori Ann Thrupp (eds.). 1989. *Farmer First: Farmer Innovation and Agricultural Research*. London, Intermediate Technology Publications.

Clay, Edward & Bernard Schaffer (eds.). 1984. *Room for Manoeuvre: An Exploration of Public Policy in Agriculture and Rural Development*. London, Heinemann.

Collier, David (ed.). 1979. *The New Authoritarianism in Latin America*. Princeton, Princeton University Press.

Collins, Randall. 1981. 'Micro-translation as a Theory-building Strategy'. In K. Knorr-Cetina & A.V. Cicourel (eds.), *Advances in Social Theory and Methodology: Towards an Integration of Micro- and Macro-sociologies*, Boston, Routledge & Kegan Paul.

Corbridge, Stuart. 1982. 'Urban Bias, Rural Bias, and Industrialization: An Appraisal of the Work of Michael Lipton and Terry Byres'. In John Harriss (ed.), *Rural Development: Theories of Peasant Economy and Agrarian Change*, London, Hutchinson.

— 1986. *Capitalist World Development: A Critique of Radical Development Geography*. London, Macmillan.

— 1990. 'Post-Marxism and Development Studies: Beyond the Impasse'. *World Development*, vol. 18, no. 5, May.

— 1991. 'Marxisms, Modernities and Moralities: Development Praxis and the

Claims of Distant Strangers'. Paper prepared for publication in David Booth (ed.), *New Directions in Social Development Research*.

Crook, Stephen. 1990. 'The End of Radical Social Theory? Notes on Radicalism, Modernism and Postmodernism'. In R. Boyne & A. Rattansi (eds.), *Post-modernism and Society*, London, Macmillan.

Dalling, Michael. 1991. 'Representations of Farming in Britain'. University of Hull, Department of Sociology & Social Anthropology, ms.

Derrida, Jacques. 1967. *L'écriture et la Différence*. Paris, Editions du Seuil.

Deyo, Frederic (ed.). 1987. *The Political Economy of the New Asian Industrialism*. Ithaca, Cornell University Press.

Edwards, Michael. 1989. 'The Irrelevance of Development Studies'. *Third World Quarterly*, vol. 11, no. 1, Jan.

Elwert, Georg & Thomas Bierschenk (eds.). 1988. 'Development Aid as an Intervention in Dynamic Systems'. Special issue, *Sociologia Ruralis*, vol. 28, no. 2/3.

Ergas, Zaki (ed.). 1987. *The African State in Transition*. London, Macmillan.

Evans, Peter B. *et al.* (eds.). 1985. *Bringing the State Back In*. Cambridge, Cambridge University Press.

Foster-Carter, Aidan. 1991. 'Development Sociology, Whither Now?'. *Sociology Review*, vol 1, no. 2, Nov.

Foucault, Michel. 1972. *The Archaeology of Knowledge*. London, Tavistock.

Geras, Norman. 1987. 'Post-Marxism?' *New Left Review*, no. 163, May/June.

— 1990. 'Seven Types of Obloquy: Travesties of Marxism'. In Ralph Miliband *et al.* (eds.), *Socialist Register 1990*, London, Merlin Press.

Goodman, David & Michael Redclift. 1991. *Refashioning Nature: Food, Ecology and Culture*. London, Routledge.

Grindle, Merilee S. (ed.). 1980. *Politics and Policy Implementation in the Third World*. Princeton, Princeton University Press.

— 1986. *State and Countryside: Development Policy and Agrarian Politics in Latin America*. Baltimore, Johns Hopkins University Press.

— & John W. Thomas. 1991. *Public Choices and Policy Change: The Political Economy of Reform in Developing Countries*. Baltimore, Johns Hopkins University Press.

Hall, Anthony & James Midgley (eds.). 1988. *Development Policies: Sociological Perspectives*. Manchester, Manchester University Press.

Harris, Nigel. 1986. *The End of the Third World: Newly Industrializing Countries and the Decline of an Ideology*. London, I.B. Tauris

Harriss, John. 1980. 'Why Poor People Stay Poor in Rural South India'. *Development and Change*, vol. 11, no. 1, Jan.

— 1987. 'Capitalism and Peasant Production: The Green Revolution in India'. In Teodor Shanin (ed.), *Peasants and Peasant Societies*, 2nd edn., Oxford, Basil Blackwell.

— 1991. 'Between Economism and Post-Modernism: Reflections on the Study of "Agrarian Change" in India'. Paper prepared for publication in David Booth (ed.), *New Directions in Social Development Research*.

— & Mick Moore (eds.). 1984. *Development and the Rural-Urban Divide.* London, Frank Cass.

Hindess, Barry. 1987. *Politics and Class Analysis.* Oxford, Basil Blackwell.

— 1989. *Political Choice and Social Structure: An Analysis of Actors, Interests and Rationality.* Aldershot, Edward Elgar.

— & Paul Hirst. 1975. *Pre-capitalist Modes of Production.* London, Routledge & Kegan Paul.

— & Paul Hirst. 1977. *Mode of Production and Social Formation: An Auto-critique of Pre-capitalist Modes of Production.* London, Macmillan.

Hobart, Mark. 1990. 'Discerning Disorder: Is It Really There?' Paper presented to EIDOS Erasmus Summer School, Free University of Amsterdam, June.

Hulme, David. 1991. 'Social Development Research and the Third Sector'. Paper presented to Workshop on Relevance, Realism and Choice in Social Development Research, University of Hull, Jan.

— & Mark Turner. 1990. *Sociology and Development: Theories, Policies and Practices.* New York, Harvester Wheatsheaf.

Hyden, Goran. 1983. *No Shortcuts to Progress: African Development Management in Perspective.* London, Heinemann.

IPEALT. 1990. *Agricultures et Paysanneries en Amérique Latine: Mutations et Recompositions.* Proceedings of international colloquium held at Université de Toulouse-Le Mirail, 13–14 Dec.

Kapferer, B. 1972. *Strategy and Transaction in an African Society.* Manchester, Manchester University Press.

Kitching, Gavin. 1985. 'Politics, Method and Evidence in the "Kenya Debate" '. In Henry Bernstein & Bonnie K. Campbell (eds.), *Contradictions of Accumulation in Africa,* London, Sage.

Larrain, Jorge. 1989. *Theories of Development: Capitalism, Colonialism and Dependency.* Cambridge, Polity Press.

Lofchie, Michael F. 1989. *The Policy Factor: Agricultural Performance in Kenya and Tanzania.* Boulder, Lynne Rienner.

Long, Norman. 1984. 'Creating Space for Change: A Perspective on the Sociology of Development'. Inaugural lecture, Agricultural University of Wageningen.

— 1988. 'Sociological Perspectives on Agrarian Development and State Intervention'. In A. Hall and J. Midgley (1988).

— (ed.). 1989. *Encounters at the Interface: A Perspective on Social Discontinuities in Rural Development.* Wageningen, Wageningen University Press.

— & Jan Douwe van der Ploeg. 1991. 'Heterogeneity, Actor and Structure: Towards a Reconstitution of the Concept of Structure'. Paper presented to Workshop on Relevance, Realism and Choice in Social Development Research, University of Hull, Jan.

— & Bryan Roberts (eds.). 1978. *Peasant Cooperation and Capitalist Expansion in Central Peru.* Austin, University of Texas Press.

— & Bryan Roberts. 1984. *Miners, Peasants and Entrepreneurs: Regional*

Development in the Central Highlands of Peru. Cambridge, Cambridge University Press.

Lyotard, Jean-Francois. 1984. *The Postmodern Condition.* Manchester, Manchester University Press.

MacGaffey, Janet. 1987. *Entrepreneurs and Parasites: The Struggle for Indigenous Capitalism in Zaire.* Cambridge, Cambridge University Press.

Mackintosh, Maureen. 1989. *Gender, Class and Rural Transition: Agribusiness and the Food Crisis in Senegal.* London, Zed Books Ltd.

Marsden, Terry, Philip Lowe & Sarah Whatmore (eds.). 1990. *Rural Restructuring: Global Processes and their Responses.* London, David Fulton.

Midgley, James *et al.* (eds.). 1986. *Community Participation, Social Development and the State.* London, Methuen.

Migdal, Joel. 1988. *Strong Societies and Weak States: State-Society Relations and State Capabilities in the Third World.* Princeton, Princeton University Press.

Moore, Mick. 1985. *The State and Peasant Politics in Sri Lanka.* Cambridge, Cambridge University Press.

— 1987. 'Interpreting Africa's Crisis: Political Science versus Political Economy'. *IDS Bulletin*, vol. 18, no. 4, Oct.

— 1988. 'Economic Growth and the Rise of Civil Society: Agriculture in Taiwan and South Korea'. In G. White (1988).

— 1989. 'What and Where is Political Economy?' (Review article), *Journal of Development Studies*, vol. 25, no. 4, July.

— 1990. 'The Rational Choice Paradigm and the Allocation of Agricultural Development Resources'. *Development and Change*, vol. 21, no. 2, Apr.

Mouzelis, Nicos. 1984. 'On the Crisis of Marxist Theory'. (Review article), *British Journal of Sociology*, vol. 35, no. 1, Mar.

— 1986. *Politics on the Semi-Periphery: Early Parliamentarism and Late Industrialisation in the Balkans and Latin America.* London, Macmillan.

— 1988a. 'Sociology of Development: Reflections on the Present Crisis'. *Sociology*, vol. 22, no. 1, Feb.

— 1988b. 'Marxism or Post-Marxism?' *New Left Review*, no. 167, Jan–Feb.

— 1990. *Post-Marxist Alternatives: The Construction of Social Orders.* London, Macmillan.

— 1991. 'The State in Late Development: Historical and Comparative Perspectives'. Paper prepared for publication in David Booth (ed.), *New Directions in Social Development Research.*

Nelson, Joan (ed.). 1990. *Economic Crisis and Policy Choice: The Politics of Adjustment in the Third World.* Princeton, Princeton University Press.

O'Donnell, Guillermo. 1978. 'Reflections on the Patterns of Change in the Bureaucratic-Authoritarian State'. *Latin American Research Review*, vol. 12, no. 1.

Peet, Richard. 1990. *Global Capitalism: Theories of Societal Development.* Boston, Routledge.

Pelto, Pertti J. & Gretel H. Pelto. 1978. *Anthropological Research: The Structure of Inquiry*. 2nd edn., Cambridge, Cambridge University Press.

Richards, Alan. 1986. *Development and Modes of Production in Marxian Economics: A Critical Evaluation*. Chur, Harwood Academic Publishers.

Richards, Paul. 1985. *Indigenous Agricultural Revolution: Ecology and Food Production in West Africa*. London, Hutchinson.

Rothchild, Donald & Naomi Chazan (eds.). 1988. *The Precarious Balance: State and Society in Africa*. Boulder, Westview Press.

Roxborough, Ian. 1984. 'Unity and Diversity in Latin American History'. *Journal of Latin American Studies*, vol. 16, no. 1.

Ruggie, John G. (ed.). 1983. *The Antinomies of Interdependence: National Welfare and the International Division of Labor*. New York, Columbia University Press.

Sandiland, Martin. 1985. *What is Political Economy? A Study of Social Theory and Underdevelopment*. New Haven, Yale University Press.

Schutz, A. 1962. *The Problem of Social Reality*. The Hague, Martinus Nijhoff.

— 1967. *The Phenomenology of the Social World*. Evanston, Illinois, Northwestern University Press.

Scott, Alison MacEwan. 1986. 'Women and Industrialisation: Examining the "Female Marginalisation" Thesis'. *Journal of Development Studies*, vol. 22, no. 4, July.

Scott, James C. 1985. *Weapons of the Weak: Everyday Forms of Peasant Resistance*. New Haven, Yale University Press.

Sender, John & Sheila Smith. 1990. *Poverty, Class and Gender in Rural Africa: A Tanzanian Case Study*. London, Routledge.

Sheahan, John. 1987. *Patterns of Development in Latin America: Poverty, Repression, and Economic Strategy*. Princeton, Princeton University Press.

Simo, John A. Mope. 1991. 'Gender, Agro-Pastoral Production and Class Formation in Bamunka, North-Western Cameroon'. University of East Anglia, Ph.D. thesis.

Sklair, Leslie. 1988. 'Transcending the Impasse: Metatheory, Theory, and Empirical Research in the Sociology of Development and Underdevelopment'. *World Development*, vol. 16, no. 6, June.

Skocpol, Theda. 1979. *States and Social Revolutions*. Cambridge, Cambridge University Press.

— 1985. 'Bringing the State Back In: Strategies of Analysis in Current Research'. In P.B. Evans *et al.* (1985).

Townsend, Janet & Janet H. Momsen. 1987. 'Towards a Geography of Gender in Developing Market Economies'. In J.H. Momsen and J. Townsend (eds.), *Geography of Gender in the Third World*, London, Hutchinson.

Unger, Roberto Mangabeira. 1987a. *Social Theory: Its Situation and Tasks*. Cambridge, Cambridge University Press.

— 1987b. *False Necessity: Anti-Necessitarian Social Theory in the Service of Radical Democracy*. Cambridge, Cambridge University Press.

Vandergeest, Peter & Frederick H. Buttel. 1988. 'Marx, Weber, and Development Sociology: Beyond the Impasse'. *World Development*, vol. 16, no. 6, June.

Watts, Michael. 1989. 'The Agrarian Crisis in Africa: Debating the Crisis'. *Progress in Human Geography*, vol. 13, no. 1.

White, Gordon (ed.). 1988. *Developmental States in East Asia*. London, Macmillan.

Wilson, Fiona. 1985. 'Women and Agricultural Change in Latin America: Some Concepts Guiding Research'. *World Development*, vol. 13, no. 9, Sept.

World Bank. 1981. *Accelerated Development in Sub-Saharan Africa: An Agenda for Action*. Washington, DC.

3

How Relevant is Development Studies?

by Michael Edwards[1]

'Why is so much that is said, written and spent on development having so little effect on the problems it seeks to address?' This was the question I posed in an article written four years ago entitled 'The Irrelevance of Development Studies'.[2] This article was unashamedly polemical, born out of years of frustration at the way in which many academics had taken information and ideas from those whom they were 'researching', without contributing to the lives of these people either directly (by enabling them to improve their situation on the ground), or indirectly (by changing attitudes and policies at the national and international levels). As a fieldworker for a number of development agencies, I also knew that much of this research was inaccurate because it failed to incorporate the views, aspirations, wisdom and imperfections of real, living people. Research and practice were 'two parallel lines that never met', and both suffered accordingly. 'Practitioners do not write, and theoreticians remain in the abstraction of their theories'.[3] This amply summarised the prevailing situation.

My article on 'Irrelevance' has helped to stimulate a good deal of discussion over the last two years about the relationship between research and practice, and has provoked a number of critical questions. Rightly, I have been pressed to explain parts of my argument which are seen as unclear, and taken to task for over-generalisation. In this contribution, therefore, I attempt to answer these criticisms, update my arguments, and explore in more depth some of the issues touched on only briefly in the original.

The chapter begins by summarising the major points raised in my original article in order to provide enough context for the discussion that follows. The next section attempts to answer four major questions posed about my arguments by David Booth at a conference in 1991 at the University of Hull.[4] The final section of the paper looks in some detail at recent attempts to bring research and practice closer together in a variety of ways, and assesses what promise these initiatives hold out for the future.

NOTE: *The views expressed in this chapter are the author's own and not necessarily those of Save the Children Fund.*

The Irrelevance of Development Studies

My original article began by juxtaposing the continued existence (and in many cases, the worsening) of poverty and exploitation in the Third World with the ever-increasing amount of development research, advice and funding being undertaken, supposedly to counteract these trends. 'The fact that this immense outpouring of information and advice is having little demonstrable effect on the problems it seeks to address should at least give us cause for concern'.[5] I sought to explain this apparent contradiction through a critique of conventional approaches to the creation and use of knowledge, which are based on the separation of theory from practice, understanding from action, subject from object, and researcher from 'researched'. As Nigel Maxwell has written, 'Insofar as academic enquiry does try to promote human welfare, it does so ... by seeking to improve knowledge of various aspects of the world.' In contrast, 'for the philosophy of wisdom, the fundamental kind of rational learning is learning how to live, how to see, to experience, to participate in and create what is of value in existence'.[6]

Conventional approaches to development research and practice value the technical knowledge of the 'outside expert' over the indigenous knowledge of the people being 'studied' or 'helped'. In consequence, 'general solutions manufactured from the outside are offered to problems which are highly localised. The practice of development work teaches us that problems are usually specific in their complexity to a particular time and place'.[7] In addition, 'it is impossible to understand real-life problems unless we grasp the multitude of constraints, imperfections and emotions which shape the actions of real people. Conventional research cannot do this because it divorces itself from the everyday context within which an understanding of these emotions can develop'.[8] Researchers think they perceive the reality of what is going on, but do so through a series of biases which they carry with them from their training and cultural experiences.

'Being for the satisfaction of the researcher rather than the re-searched',[9] such an approach is also selfish: it relies on the extraction of information from people who do not benefit from the use to which this information is put. These centralising and extractive tendencies are directly 'anti-developmental' because they prevent poor people from thinking and acting for themselves.

This is not to say that the *process* of research – of understanding the forces which affect the development of people – is irrelevant. 'We cannot change the world successfully unless we understand the way it works; neither can we understand it fully unless we are involved in some way in the processes that change it'.[10] To this extent, 'development cannot be studied at all: we can participate in the processes that underlie development and observe, record and analyse what we see, but we can never be relevant to problems in the abstract'.[11] The key to being relevant lies in the participation of poor people in constructing our understanding of how their world operates. 'We cannot be relevant to people unless we understand their problems, but we cannot understand these problems unless people tell us about them'.[12]

Reversing traditional attitudes to development research therefore means uniting research and practice, understanding and action, researcher and researched, into a single, unitary process. And this in turn implies that researchers must accept being changed by the results of their research, must be accountable to the subjects of their work, and must be prepared to see the value of their work judged according to its relevance in improving the lives of the people concerned. This does *not* mean that all research that is relevant also has to be 'directly participatory'. Research which analyses similarities and differences over time and space can be extremely 'relevant', but the usefulness of such 'secondary' research will be a function of its effectiveness in changing attitudes among the powerful in a direction which will ultimately enable the less powerful to think and act for themselves.

In conclusion, 'we need consciously to adopt a position of humility with respect to our own limitations and the limitations of our kind of education and training. We must learn to appreciate the value of indigenous knowledge and the importance of popular participation in showing us what is relevant and what is not. In this way, we will begin to move from practice based on the philosophy of knowledge, to practice based on the philosophy of wisdom, to a form of enquiry in which what we do and what we are matter more than what we know'.[13] Although the arguments for such changes are complex in their details, it is important to remember that they are based on only two fundamental assertions, one concerning *ethics*, the other concerning *methods*.

First, the purpose of research is to promote the development of poor and powerless people around the world. Second, in order to be relevant and useful in this task, research must involve its subjects in some way and at some stage in constructing both process and output. These two underlying questions – the purpose of intellectual enquiry and ways of knowing reality – need to be kept in mind throughout the discussion that follows. In this way, we will be able to explore both questions in more depth without becoming lost in detail.

Criticisms

In his introductory paper for a workshop on 'Relevance, Realism and Choice in Social Development Research' held at the University of Hull early in 1991, David Booth[14] posed a series of questions relating to my

article on 'Irrelevance' which provide a useful structure for exploring my arguments in more depth. The most important of these questions are:
- To what is relevant research supposed to be relevant?
- Does this apply only to local participatory projects or to other forms of research also?
- Should local studies of this kind be privileged, especially given the capacity of the macro-context to dissipate gains from purely local efforts?
- Is it possible to determine in advance the sorts of knowledge that will be useful to the causes of which we approve but not those of which we disapprove?

I will try to address each of these questions in turn.

To What is Relevant Research Supposed to be Relevant?
Ethics are ever-present in debates about development, because development is about things which *ought* to take place.[15] As Kant stressed, 'ought implies can', so that the development debate is as much about *practice* (or how to bring about what 'ought to be') as about *principle* (or what 'ought to be' in the abstract). Relevant research must help us to develop both good practice and good principle. However, this does not free us from defining what 'ought to be' in the first place: in other words, from defining what we mean by 'development'.

In my original article, I defined development in terms of 'empowerment' – increasing the control which poor and powerless people (and specifically the poorest and most powerless) are able to exert over aspects of their lives which they consider to be important to them. Not unnaturally, therefore, research which was not 'participatory' – which did not increase people's control in this way – was taken to be 'anti-developmental'. In his workshop paper, Booth pointed out that development and participation are neither synonymous nor necessarily associated with each other, citing as an example the case of rapid economic development in Southeast Asia over the last two decades, which has taken place with minimal participation by the poor in decision-making and the political process in these countries.

It is difficult not to fall into tautologies here – since if development is defined as empowerment, cases which are not empowerment cannot be defined as development. More seriously, economic growth may bring material benefits to people, but development is about much more than this, being a process of enrichment in every aspect of life. No-one would deny that material benefits are an essential part of development, but the underlying principle of control is much more important. Rising incomes are one result of this process, as well as being a contributory factor in increasing control in other areas of life (such as health and education).

But if incomes rise for only some people, or if people value other changes as much as or more than rising incomes, then clearly 'development' in its fullest sense is not occurring. There are clear moral and intellectual choices here which have to be made before one can progress to the next stage of the argument. No doubt different people will make different choices about what is and is not 'developmental'.

Whatever one's choice of definitions, it seems axiomatic to me that the purpose of intellectual enquiry *in this field* is to promote 'development'. In contrast to 'pure' science or art history (for example), development studies concern real, living people and cannot therefore be conducted in the abstract. This is particularly true for Non-Governmental Organisations (NGOs) such as my own, for which there is no role in a world without moral discourse. At the very least, we need to be clear about the implications of our work for people's lives, and to declare our beliefs and allegiances openly instead of sheltering behind a spurious 'objectivity'. While there is always a danger that well-meaning outsiders will determine local agendas by imposing their own moral choices, this danger is reduced if these outsiders are open and honest about their values right from the word go. At least in theory, moral stances can then be negotiated and, if appropriate, rejected. This is the only legitimate answer to a question which worries many academics, namely 'who decides' what is 'relevant' and what is not? As John Harriss once put it to me, 'Should outsiders' respect for indigenous knowledge and values lead to the acceptance of indigenous injustice because the powerful in another society have a different system of ethics?'[16] The answer, at least for an NGO, must be 'no', because the NGO must have and declare its own underlying values – what, in other words, is *not* negotiable – before offering any assistance at all. Research about the forces which can impoverish, exploit or liberate people can never be neutral, but it can play a crucial role in helping to bring about progressive change. Good research (relevant research) helps us to make informed choices about alternative ways of doing things, enabling a selection to be made between more and less effective strategies to reach our goals. Whether it is possible to conduct good, relevant research without the active participation of the subjects of study is a question which is taken up in the next two sections of this paper.

It is important to clarify here, however, that 'relevant' research does not simply mean 'research to be used by development agencies'. NGOs and other agencies have their own agendas which also need to be openly declared. They are often protective, defensive and resistant to criticism, and because of these characteristics there must, within the broad range of development research being undertaken, remain a large area which is independent of institutional practitioners.

In summary, 'relevant' development research should be 'relevant' to those whose lives it embraces. It should contribute to their self-development by opening up new and better ways of doing things and clarifying the lessons of experience. It should, in my own conception of 'development', contribute to the ability of poor and powerless people to increase the control they can exert over their own lives. It should also make explicit *how* it intends to accomplish these goals, and this brings us to David Booth's second question, which concerns the structure and methodology which make research more, or less, relevant.

Does This Apply Only to Local Participatory Projects?

A good deal of confusion seems to have been caused by references in my original paper to the primacy of 'participatory research' in development studies. As the above question implies, this has been taken to mean that the only research which is relevant is research which takes place directly in the context of development practice at micro- (or project) level. What I was trying to say here was that, to be relevant, research must *in some way* be linked to the real experience and concerns of people at grassroots level. Quite rightly, I have been taken to task for failing to specify precisely what this might mean in practice.

The key sentences here in my original paper read as follows: 'The important distinction to be made is that such "higher-level" work must grow out of and be based upon participatory research at lower levels ... If the link with people's real concerns and experiences is sufficiently strong, then even "higher-level" research can be genuinely developmental'.[17] In other words, it is the link with people's experience that is crucial and not the link to a particular development 'project'. This link can be made in a variety of ways, some of which do not (and cannot) involve the direct participation of the subjects of the research.

For example, much of the most useful research work carried out over the last few years in areas such as gender relations, environmental concerns ('sustainable development'), empowerment and participation, and the impact and efficacy of 'structural and macro-economic adjustment', has been developed through comparison and synthesis over a long timescale and a broad geographical area. These comparative experiences have yielded powerful evidence of both positive and negative trends at grassroots level, and have stimulated important policy changes among development practitioners (including the most powerful institutions of all, such as the World Bank). But equally important is the fact that all this work was built upon careful research at micro-level which, while not necessarily 'participatory' in methodology, did highlight what was actually happening to people in their daily lives. Because of this, it was 'relevant' both in the sense of accuracy (demolishing some of the myths created by those who were ignorant of grassroots realities) and in terms of people's development (changing policy and practice in ways which ultimately enabled people to gain more control over their incomes, resources and relationships with each other).

Hence, both the micro- and the macro-levels are crucial to relevance in development research: the important thing is to ensure that they are explicitly related to one another, a theme which is taken up in the next section. Major problems inevitably arise whenever one or the other level is considered in isolation.

Then, higher-level research quickly becomes inaccurate or irrelevant, while lower-level research and practice may become ineffective in the face of more powerful forces which can crush or distort it. There are many ways of linking the two together: the crucial thing is always to build from the 'bottom upwards'. In other words, always to ensure that people's real experiences and concerns provide the raw material for higher-level analysis and synthesis. Any higher-level research which fails to do this may misinterpret what is actually happening and will therefore fail to inform development policy and practice at higher levels in a responsible way.

Should Local Studies of This Kind be Privileged?

Naturally, the answer to this question follows much the same lines as the previous section. If what matters in research is the *linkage* between micro- and macro-levels, then it follows that neither local nor global studies 'should be privileged'. Both have an important role to play. The impact of wider economic, political and environmental forces on development at community level is increasingly being recognised by practitioners, particularly by NGOs whose traditional focus has been more or less exclusively on small-scale projects. Village cooperatives are often undermined by deficiencies in the wider agricultural extension and marketing systems within which they have to operate, while social action groups can be frustrated by more powerful political forces at higher levels of the system. No development project can be successful in the longer term unless it takes account of these wider forces. This is why structural change at national level is a vital precondition for the successful development of people. For this reason, both academics (who call this the 'micro-macro interface') and NGOs (who call it 'scaling-up' their impact) are taking an increasing interest in finding better ways of linking different levels of research and practice together.

This is a very helpful development because it moves all of us away from an unhealthy concentration on one level to the exclusion of the others. As the previous section made clear, micro- and macro-levels exist in symbiosis and have no meaning in isolation from each other. It would help both researchers and practitioners if they also dispensed with similarly simplistic dichotomies such as 'indigenous and modern knowledge', 'individual and structural explanations', and 'projects and processes.' In reality, it is impossible to dichotomise any of these things. They all have meaning only in relation to the other. Relevant research is research which understands this and illuminates the complex and everchanging relationships between people and the environment in which they live and work.

It is perhaps true that practitioners have in the past focused too much on site-specific detail and have ignored the importance of wider economic and political frameworks. Equally, there is truth in the charge that academics have focused too much on wider forces in their search for grand theory, while neglecting the infinite variation of the real world. One of the achievements of bringing research and practice closer together (analysed in detail in the next section) is that each can enrich the other, leaving behind the notion that they are somehow exclusive categories or occupations. At the same time, I would argue (as throughout this chapter) that we should always examine wider forces and trends *through the eyes of those who experience and act in them*, for it is their perceptions and actions which give meaning to these forces. This is the same as 'building from the bottom upwards' in development research, or, to put it simply, generalising from the particular. For, if we are not learning by comparison from one real-life situation to another, how *are* we learning?

This brings me to one of the most difficult questions in this whole debate, which concerns the *nature of theory* in 'relevant' development research (something which a practitioner should, perhaps, steer well clear of!). Theory is important as a tool for understanding and explaining the world (and, therefore, as a necessary precondition for changing it), but if every situation is unique and every person different, how is theory to be constructed?

It seems to me that it is perfectly possible to be 'systematic about diversity' without falling into 'glorified empiricism', to use Norman Long's terminology. Micro-level studies do suggest that there are wider trends in development which affect people in similar ways across time and space. For example, the commercialisation of markets in urban and rural areas has enriched some groups at the expense of others: given inter-household differences in the distribution of land, labour and other resources, inequality will increase over time. We know this to be true from empirical observation, and we can therefore predict what will happen in similar circumstances elsewhere (though never with complete accuracy or reliability). When the universe under study is circumscribed in some way (geographically, culturally or sectorally, for example), these patterns become clearer. Indeed, when used in this more limited way, many concepts from past 'metatheories' remain very useful – as in the case of ownership of the 'means of production' cited above. This sort of theory is as useful to development practice as it is essential to development studies, since it helps those involved to understand what is happening to them, and to choose between alternative options for the future.

In the 'post-modernist void' which faces development studies today, it is important to have some convincing theory to act as a counterweight to conventional economics. Otherwise, as is obvious even from a cursory examination of the policy and practice of the ruling institutions of our world, classical economics will continue to rule the day, and we shall all be the worse for it. However, what is this alternative theory to be? Is there in fact any alternative to an eclectic approach which examines everyday experience from a number of different points of view and then synthesises the results into higher-level explanation? This combination of economics, sociology, political science, psychology and other disciplines, theories and paradigms is precisely what follows from the 'bottom-up' approach I have been recommending. To practitioners this approach is second nature because this is how we live our lives anyway. So long as theory is constructed from real experience it will have explanatory power. But it will never be 'grand theory' in the sense implied in the classical tradition. This may be a disappointment to academics, but is scarcely relevant to practitioners.

Can One Pre-determine Knowledge Which Will Only be of Value to the Causes of Which We Approve?

The answer to this 'old chestnut', as David Booth calls it, is obviously 'no'. In the nature of things, knowledge can be used for good or ill, because it is created and used by human beings. Progress in nuclear physics can be used to develop alternative energy sources or weapons of mass destruction; research in microbiology to create new vaccines or germ warfare, and so on. While development research is rarely involved in such stark alternatives, its findings remain open to abuse in much the same way. Imperfect human beings will use knowledge to advance themselves in relation to their neighbours, as is demonstrated countless times in communities across the world. Technological advances in agriculture, for example, are never neutral, because different people are more or less able to use them according to circumstance. The consequences of the Green Revolution for rural inequality show this to be true. Anyone involved in the creation and dissemination of knowledge must therefore be conscious of the potential abuses, as well as uses, of this knowledge, and act accordingly.

Where, then, does this leave the participatory approach to development studies? Although certain social, economic and environmental goals are implicit in participatory development (such as equality, sustainability and respect for human rights), none of these ideals is or should be enforced over and above participation in decision-making – individuals' ability to share in decisions which affect them, and hence increase the control they can exert over aspects of their lives which concern them. Indeed, the real goal of participatory development is to equip people with the skills, confidence, information and opportunities they need to make their own choices. Once so-equipped, the rest is up to them. By its very nature, the process of empowerment is uncertain: although it is possible to initiate the journey in a structured way (using particular techniques and methods, for example), the ultimate destination is always unknown.

The way in which individuals use their increasing confidence, knowledge, skills and resources (their power, in other words) is absolutely crucial, but it cannot be pre-determined (however much outsiders might want to do so). However, evidence from many communities around the world shows that (except in situations of acute inequality and competition for scarce resources) people do cooperate and help each other, if they are given the resources and opportunities to do so. I would claim, therefore, that participation *does* increase the likelihood that people will act responsibly, and that they will use their own knowledge and the knowledge that others can bring for mutual benefit. Likewise, if people are involved in the creation and use of their own knowledge, there is more of a chance that this knowledge will be used for causes of which *they* approve, to paraphrase Booth's words. Whether they use it to advance causes of which 'we' approve is, in a sense, irrelevant.

In this respect, the role of research should be to maximise the range of ideas and information to which people have access, so that they can make their own decisions on the strongest possible foundation. By reducing complex situations to a series of answerable questions, good research can help people to find a way through the daunting constraints imposed on them by poverty, inadequate resources, lousy infrastructure and an unresponsive government. It is in this sense that participatory research (or more accurately, bearing in mind the conclusions of the previous two sections, research which builds on people's real experience) can generate knowledge which is likely to be used progressively. However, to imagine that this can ever be guaranteed is clearly un-realistic.

Knowledge and Action: Hope for the Future

A constant refrain in both my earlier article on 'Irrelevance' and the present paper is that knowledge and action, theory and practice, understanding and change, must always go together. In this synthesis and symbiosis lies the key to relevance in both research and practice. When people are fully involved in development programmes or in research which affects them, there is a much greater chance that these programmes will be relevant to their real concerns, accurate, usable and empowering. In the same way, higher-level research or action which attempts to be developmental (in the sense in which I defined this word above) must also grow out of grassroots experience.

This is not, of course, an uncontroversial view of things. Indeed, in a paper presented to the same workshop on 'Relevance, Realism and Choice in Social Development Research', Frederick Buttel and Philip McMichael state categorically that 'development sociology and development practice should be (formally) separated'.[18] They go on to qualify this statement by saying that these two activities should be seen as 'related, but distinct areas of work, mainly on account of their different levels of analysis and different problematics'.[19] Despite this qualification, I feel this view is fundamentally wrong. Such a separation can lead only to research which is irrelevant and practice which is deficient. It imposes a divide between those who 'do' development work, and those who 'think' about development. It encourages competition within development academia on terms which have nothing to do with the usefulness of research to its subjects (and everything to do with the quantity of papers published). And it perpetuates the historic dependence of those without access to knowledge and power on those who have monopolised these things for hundreds of years. For all these reasons, such a separation is therefore 'directly anti-developmental', as I put it in my earlier paper.

Thankfully, there is increasing evidence that academics and practitioners are realising this, and are making strenuous efforts to work more closely together. They have seen that in the integration of research and practice lies one of the most fruitful directions for the future. At the recent Annual Conference of the United Kingdom Development Studies Association in Swansea, for example, papers on various aspects of NGO work occupied an unprecedented one-and-a-half out of the three days on offer. The conference established an 'NGO Study Group' to bring academics and practitioners together on a regular basis in order to explore issues of common concern. Indeed, it is difficult to keep up with the number of links currently being forged between NGOs and academics in the UK. University departments seem to be falling over themselves to initiate research and training programmes on and for NGOs and other development practitioners.[20] The Institute for Development Policy and Management at Manchester University co-sponsored with Save the Children Fund a workshop on 'Scaling-Up NGO Impact: Learning From

Experience' in January 1992, while Britain's Overseas Development Institute in London has recently completed a huge study of NGO effectiveness in the alleviation of poverty in Africa and Asia.[21]

NGOs around the world are becoming much more serious about evaluating the impact of their work and feeding the lessons of their experience back into policy and practice. Indeed, INTRAC, the 'International Training and Research Centre' (to be based in Oxford) is one of four or five other initiatives from within the NGO community itself, which aim to encourage NGOs to reflect critically on their experience and to improve training for NGO staff in the techniques of project appraisal, monitoring and evaluation, planning and management.[22] All these initiatives have in common the desire to bring understanding and action together so that development practitioners are better equipped to play their role effectively, and development academics are better able to appreciate the reality they are studying. In the process, we are at last beginning to produce the kind of 'organic intellectual' beloved of Gramsci and others, the combination of theory and praxis in the same individual which enables them to 'interpret' and to 'change' the world simultaneously.

One of the most interesting of these new areas of joint work is what Norman Long has called 'demythologising' or 'deconstructing planned intervention' – the critical analysis of development practice which takes into account the different and sometimes conflicting perceptions of the same issue or action among practitioners and the subjects of the project in question.[23] For, as Long has written, practice is 'an ongoing, socially-constructed and negotiated process, not simply the execution of an already-specified plan of action with expected outcomes'.[24] This is the logical corollary of the participatory approach to development *studies*. NGOs and other practitioners can hardly recommend the virtues of popular participation and then deny a role for those they serve in evaluating and contributing to the policy and practice of the agency in question. If, as made clear above, we must start to consider the 'ethics of ends' in development research and practice (i.e., a justification of what we are trying to achieve), we must also consider the 'ethics of means' – which methods of development practice are ethically superior to others? [25] This is an extremely challenging question for development practitioners, and one which, in my view, will provide fruitful territory for collaboration with researchers in the future.

Despite these encouraging developments, there is sometimes a tendency for people to use these new relationships between research and practice for what are essentially selfish ends. There is a danger that NGOs and development projects will become an *object* for academic study, in much the same way as poor people themselves were treated as objects in the conventional approach to development studies. It was this approach which I criticised so strongly in my original article on 'Irrelevance', both on the grounds that it was exploitative, and on the grounds that it was bound to produce results which were inaccurate. The point is to work *together* in a joint search for better practice and better theory, and this requires an acceptance of each other as equals.

Another encouraging set of initiatives are the new methodologies of 'participatory' research, appraisal and evaluation which have undergone rapid development over the last five years. I would also include in this category the 'actor-oriented approach' of the Wageningen School, though the members of this school (such as Norman Long) might disagree! As Long has pointed out many times, 'actor-orientation' is *not* a tool for improving development intervention, but it shares with these other methodologies an explicit attempt to involve the subjects of development in understanding and changing their own lives. Indeed, it makes clear that there can be no successful understanding *without* an appreciation of what is happening through the eyes of those concerned.

Similarly, what was initially 'Rapid Rural Appraisal' has metamorphosed into 'Participatory Rapid Appraisal' and now into 'Participatory Relaxed Appraisal'! A wide range of new techniques have been developed to facilitate joint action among agencies and the people with whom they are working, to enable them to understand social structure and development issues within a given location. These techniques include 'wealth-ranking', 'profiles', maps of various kinds, and semi-structured discussions such as 'focus groups'. Participatory monitoring and evaluation are also developing quickly, particularly in the area of social development and the evaluation of development *processes*.[26] Participatory research itself (a term which covers a very wide range of research methods) is now almost taken for granted in development work.

Even here, however, there is a temptation to use such techniques and methods to extract more information for outside use, rather than using it to facilitate the development of the community concerned. It is the ends to which such methods are used that are important, not the methods themselves. The acid test is whether the subjects of the research, evaluation, programme or whatever become more able to develop themselves as a result of participating in the exercise. At the same time, of course, the lessons learned can quite legitimately be fed 'upwards' into development theory, as discussed above. However, as I put it three years ago, we have to guard against using participatory techniques in a way which becomes 'merely another form of exploitation, serving the purposes of outsiders who have their own agenda but who know they cannot gain a complete picture of the problems that interest them through conventional methods alone'.[27]

In summary, there are signs that academics and practitioners are developing a fruitful collaboration in an increasing number of areas. In addition, techniques of combining research and practice, or understanding and action, into the same process are gaining ground all the time, and are being used to improve both development practice and development theory in ways which directly empower the subjects of this work. What is clear is that there is no one, single or universally-agreed way of doing this successfully. The evaluation of these different methods and techniques will be another fruitful area of collaboration among researchers and practitioners over the next few years. Our priority must be to bring more people together around these issues, and others which are of both practical and theoretical significance (such as 'scaling-up', 'sustainable development', gender relations, and development evaluation), in a joint search for progress, undertaken as equal partners.

Conclusion

As I hope to have shown in this contribution, there are encouraging signs that development research and development practice are moving closer together in ways which do empower poor people to control their own development. While it is a useful discipline to review one's own arguments at regular intervals, I see no reason to change the broad thrust of what I wrote three years ago in 'The Irrelevance of Development Studies'. While the details of my argument require further elaboration (much more than I have been able to do in this paper), I would like to finish by re-emphasising the two core elements of that article:

First, that the purpose of intellectual enquiry in this field of study is to promote the development of people denied access to knowledge, resources and power for hundreds of years.

Second, that the most effective way of doing this is to unite understanding and action, or theory and practice, into a single process which puts people at the very centre of both. This is the real task for development theories in the 1990s.

In essence, these are both moral stands rather than intellectual positions, and this, I believe, is inevitable given the normative nature of development itself. What is important for all of us who are involved in this endeavour is to make our own values and objectives explicit, so that they can also be criticised and 'deconstructed'. Under the Western empirical tradition, even knowledge and information have become commodities which we must 'possess', competing with each other to amass more of these commodities but rarely questioning the purpose of the enterprise itself. Now, at last, this is beginning to change. In Erich Fromm's words, we are learning to *be* more instead of to *have* more.[28] This is the real goal of intellectual enquiry.

Notes and References

1. The author is grateful to John Harriss, Peter Oakley and David Booth for their comments on the original draft.
2. M. Edwards. 1989. 'The Irrelevance of Development Studies'. *Third World Quarterly*, vol. 11 (1), pp. 116–36.
3. Edgar Stoesz. Quoted in R. Bunch, *Two Ears of Corn: A Guide to People-centred Agricultural Improvement,* p. iii, Oklahoma City, World Neighbours.
4. 'Relevance, Realism and Choice in Social Development Research', a workshop held at the Centre of Developing Area Studies, Hull University, 10–12 January 1991 (convened by David Booth).
5. M. Edwards, *op. cit.,* p. 116.
6. N. Maxwell. 1984. *From Knowledge to Wisdom.* Oxford, Basil Blackwell, pp. 2, 66.
7. M. Edwards, *op. cit.,* p. 120.
8. *Ibid.,* p. 121.
9. *Ibid.,* p. 122.
10. *Ibid.,* p. 125.
11. *Ibid.,* p. 125.
12. *Ibid.,* p. 126.
13. *Ibid.,* p. 134.
14. D. Booth. 1991. 'Relevance, Realism and Choice: An Introduction to the Workshop'. Paper presented to the Workshop on Relevance, Realism and Choice in Social Development Research, Hull University, Jan., p. 11.
15. See D. Crocker, 1991, 'Toward Development Ethics', *World Development,* vol. 19 (5), pp. 457–83.
16. Personal communication, John Harriss, London School of Economics.
17. M. Edwards, *op. cit.,* pp. 130-131.
18. F. Buttel & P. McMichael. 1991. 'Reconsidering the Explanandum and Scope of Development Studies: Toward a Comparative Sociology of State-Economy Relations'. Paper presented to the Workshop on Relevance, Realism and Choice in Social Development Research, Hull University, Jan., p. 3.
19. *Ibid.,* p. 17.
20. For example, the London School of Economics, the Institute for Development Studies at Sussex University, and the Development Administration Group at Birmingham.
21. Contact Mark Robinson at the Overseas Development Institute, Regents College, London, for details.
22. For example, the 'El Taller Centre' in Barcelona.
23. See N. Long & J.D. van der Ploeg, 1989, 'Demythologizing Planned Intervention: an Actor Perspective', *Sociologia Ruralis,* vol. 29 (314), pp. 226–49.
24. N. Long. 1990. 'From Paradigm Lost to Paradigm Regained? The Case for an Actor-Oriented Sociology of Development'. *European Review of Latin American and Caribbean Studies,* vol. 49, Dec., pp. 3–24.

25. See D. Crocker, *op. cit.*
26. See P. Oakley & D. Marsden, 1990, *Social Development Evaluation*, Oxford, Oxfam.
27. M. Edwards, *op. cit.*, p. 129.
28. E. Fromm. 1976. *To Have or To Be?* New York, Bantam New Age Books.

4

The Political Meanings of Development: In Search of New Horizons

by David Slater

Not only is it possible to analyse the continuing existence of a crisis in Third World development – a crisis which has become so chronic in many parts of the periphery that the concept of 'crisis' is itself in question – but also we can draw attention to the continuation of a crisis in development theory and in our attempts to represent the meaning of development. In particular, critical interpretations have been undergoing a period of rethinking; ideas of a so-called 'impasse' in the framing of theoretical questions and concern over the breaking-up of an erstwhile neo-Marxist consensus, reflect a sense of doubt and in some cases a pervasive feeling of disenchantment. Meanwhile, under the sign of a 'universalisation of the drive to affluence' (Connolly 1991: 172), the imperatives of neo-liberalism continue to propel forward new waves of capitalist modernisation.

Development in a Time of Disenchantment

For the poor, in many countries of the South, the 1980s have been described as a 'lost decade' (World Bank 1990: iii). In Latin America and Africa, declining GDP per capita, the growing burden of debt, negative trends in the level of real wages, a growth in urban unemployment and underemployment, increases in income inequalities, and the urbanisation as well as the feminisation of poverty, are just some of the more well-known features of the socio-economic crisis (Ghai and Hewitt de Alcántara 1990). This partial list could be greatly expanded; for Latin America, for instance, one can add the new problems of drugs, AIDS, emigration and the intensification of new forms of violence; for many regions of the South, environmental degradation and devastation are becoming increasingly acute; and in a growing number of areas the psychological scars of poverty and destitution continue to erode the potential for human emancipation. Couched within a certain tradition, one might even suggest that we are living the 'end of development'. But are we? What meanings can we attribute to 'development' in the 1990s?

Before discussing these and related questions, I want to examine some aspects of the dominant neo-liberal discourse on development.

The 1980s has been a decade of 'structural adjustments', of the imposition of a new round of 'financial discipline', and of the 'streamlining of the state' (Fishlow 1990). The contents of 'structural adjustment' packages are well-known; one finds, *inter alia*, devaluation, increased producer prices and reduced wage bills, wage freeze, decline in real wages and salaries, elimination of subsidies, and privatisation. The strategic concepts are: to cut, to differentiate, to dismiss and to discipline. 'Adjusting the structure' is far more than an exercise in economics. To illustrate this suggestion, we may refer to the case of Bolivia.

In 1985 a newly-elected government proclaimed a New Economic Policy (NEP), which was founded on the belief that the cause of the country's crisis was the State, and its solution was the Market. The NEP was implemented more as a political plan than a strictly economic programme. Following enactment of the governmental decree of August 1985, a 'state of siege' was declared whereby hundreds of COB (Central Obrera Boliviana) leaders were sent into 'internal exile' (Conaghan *et al.* 1990: 25). Suspension of constitutional guarantees and rights for political and trade union leaders was accompanied by the violent repression of demonstrations. Along a parallel route, the government launched a programme of creating unemployment through closing factories and dismissing more than 23,000 workers from the State Mining Corporation. The informalisation of the economy proceeded apace, and urban unemployment rose from 5.8 per cent in 1985 to 10.2 per cent in 1989 (ECLAC 1989: 18). Key elements of the government's discourse were to link the idea of saving '*la Patria*' with the need for private accumulation, of connecting the 'rational necessity' of 'administering scarce resources' to the policies of monetarism, and of stressing the imperative of competitiveness in the context of the 'self-regulation' of the market. Finally, as Torrico (1990) expresses it, the government combined simulation with dissimulation; it simulated the idea of a 'Bolivian miracle', based on the fall of inflation, but ignoring the financial incorporation of cocadollars,[1] and dissimulated the real social costs by projecting an image of societal acceptance of state policies.[2]

In Latin America, the Bolivian case has been one of the most transparent examples of the coming of age of neo-liberalism, but there are many others.[3] In the African context, Hoogvelt (1987) provides a brief but incisive commentary on the devastating effects of 'conditionality' in Sierra Leone, and for the Philippines, Broad (1990) dissects the impact of World Bank and IMF policies, criticising the orthodox equation of growth with development. In a wider-based exploration, Biersteker

(1990) argues that IMF and World Bank prescriptions undermine the fiscal basis of the peripheral state, and in the process endanger its long-term legitimacy. Finally, Payer (1991) has examined aspects of the politics of debt, emphasising the fact that since 1982 the Third World has been a net exporter of hard currency to the developed countries.[4]

The 1980s began with the World Bank stressing the centrality of economic growth. Indeed it was argued, for example, that there was sufficient evidence to indicate that 'economic growth generally contributes to the alleviation of poverty', and that, in a more general sense, 'human development depends on economic growth to provide the resources for expanding productive employment and basic services' (World Bank 1981: 67, 97). By the beginning of the 1990s, it was suggested that development was only likely to be successful if it was 'market-friendly'. After a decade of 'structural adjustment', the World Bank sees the most appropriate role for government as one of supporting rather than supplanting competitive markets (World Bank 1991: 11). This role is defined in relation to a number of functions. Governments ought to invest in education, health, nutrition, family planning and poverty alleviation; in addition, investing in infrastructure (e.g., social, administrative, physical, regulatory and legal), mobilising resources to finance public expenditures, intervening to protect the environment and providing a stable macro-economic foundation are given as further key functions.

It is of course symptomatic of the current orthodoxy that much attention and analytical consideration are given to rethinking the state, and to retuning precepts of privatisation and deregulation. As I shall indicate subsequently, in considering aspects of the Marxist approach to development, a rethinking of the state in relation to civil society and the economy must be a key element of our analysis. The point here, however, is that within the official discourse of the World Bank, IMF and a broad range of related international organisations, one rarely if ever encounters a discussion around the need to *rethink the private sector*; in other words, the market, free trade and investment, the functioning of capitalist enterprises, the politics of accumulation and so on are predominantly protected from any questioning critique. Furthermore, it is not only the absence of a critical consideration of the economic system that needs to be mentioned but also the nature of the underlying political philosophy that governs the conceptualisation of the economic, breathing life into an often hidden but crucial definition of the individual and of 'human development'. Briefly, I want to trace some aspects of the continuity of the contemporary neo-liberal discourse on development. This is necessary because not infrequently the impression is conveyed that today's capitalist modernisation is almost as it were *ab initio*.

In the context of Latin America, Nun (1991) draws our attention to the tendency for idealised versions of modernisation to be disseminated across the continent. In this sense, the continuity of the modernisation process tends to be obscured. For example, over 20 years ago Sunkel referred to the combined reality of transnational integration and national disintegration, and Nun himself referred to the idea of a 'marginal mass', stressing the particular nature of the development of a relative surplus population in peripheral societies. Today, however, we are presented with what Nun appropriately refers to as 'imaginary discontinuities', as if Latin America had never experienced capitalist penetration, as if its economies have never been open to the world market, as if the early 1960s doctrine of modernisation had never existed. In addition, there is also a tendency to invert the relationship with democracy; now political democratisation is viewed as an obligatory and preliminary step to economic and social modernisation. But how meaningful, or even secure, is that democracy when the new wave of capitalist modernisation is accompanied by full-scale privatisation, and the withering away of the social and economic functions of the peripheral state – this in societies already severely corroded by earlier waves of capitalist modernisation?

The historical connection in this passage takes us back to the 1950s and early 1960s, to that period when the first wave of modernisation theory gave discursive credibility to the expansion of United States investments, and more importantly to the diffusion of American geo-political power.[5] However, the possible genealogy of current notions of the self-regulation of the market, of the sanctity of property, of the cultural superiority of the West, of a minimal role for the state, of the celebration of the individual as possessor, and of the centrality of acquisitiveness, can take us back much further.

Writing in the early 1940s, Laski (1943) noted that some would find our salvation in the famous maxim *ne pas trop gouverner*; let government restore once again freedom of enterprise to businessmen, and we could enter upon a new era of creativeness from which war and insecurity would be abolished. Behind this maxim there were a number of assumptions which Laski listed as follows: 'that private property in the instruments of production is sacred, that whatever is done by government agency must be less well done than if attempted by private enterprise, that the law-making power operates in the common interest, that each man knows his own interest best, and is in the best position to advance it' (Laski 1943: 13). For Laski, not only were these assumptions untenable, but moreover, looking back in time he suggests that although the businessmen had a 'century's space in which to prove the social validity of their philosophy ... at the end, it could be written down, for all its early conquests, only as a grim failure which enslaved whole continents to the rapacious service of private profit' (*op. cit.*: 15).[6]

At about the same time as Laski was elaborating his reflections on the world during a period of war, Polanyi outlined a similar position on the notion of a self-regulating market. He argued then, in a statement which survives the patina of time, that the 'true criticism of market society is not that it was based on economics – in a sense, every and any society must be based on it – but that its economy was based on self-interest' (Polanyi 1957: 249). For 19th-century thinkers, it was assumed that in his economic activity man strove for profit, and that nothing could be more normal than an economic system consisting of markets; further, the goal of all progress was seen as the development of a society based on the market. As Polanyi reminded us, however, contrary to the myth of the natural emergence of a self-regulating market, the market was the outcome of a 'conscious and often violent intervention on the part of government which imposed the market organisation on society for non-economic ends' (*op. cit.*: 250).

Market relations ought not to be seen as separate from conceptions of the individual. Going further back, it is clear that in the work of Hobbes and Locke, and especially the former, one can locate the roots of much modern thinking on the relations between the market and the individual. In Hobbes and Locke the image of the individual was created in the image of market man. If society was a series of relations between proprietors, political society was a contractual device for the protection of proprietors and the orderly regulation of their relations. Macpherson (1988), in his fascinating study of the roots of liberal-democratic theory, convincingly argues that the original 17th-century individualism had an essentially possessive quality. This possessive quality is found in its conception of the individual as basically the proprietor of his own person or capacities, owing nothing to society for them. As Macpherson (1988: 3) expresses it, 'the human essence is freedom from dependence on the wills of others, and freedom is a function of possession'. In the vision of Hobbes, society was envisaged as a series of competitive relations between naturally dissociated and independently self-moving individuals, with no natural order of subordination.

The centrality of the possessive individual, of the sanctity of property, and of the sovereignty of the market, continued through to the 19th century and beyond, but not of course without opposition, nor, especially in the 20th century, without major modification with, for example, the development of a stronger socio-economic role for the state. Hirschman (1981), in his eloquent examination of the political arguments for capitalism before its triumph, points to the ways in which interests, money-making, accumulation and the creation of wealth were seen as a

healthy and innocuous path away from the potentially disastrous un-
leashing of the self-destructive and violent passions of human nature.
The pursuit of gain and the self-improvement of the individual were
bestowed with a quality of virtuousness that Hirschman traces through a
wide variety of writers from Adam Smith to Keynes.[7]

But the association of the pursuit of material interests with rationality
and virtue, and the posited separation of such a pursuit from the
recklessness of passion, did not go uncriticised, as the works of Adam
Ferguson and Tocqueville demonstrated. Obviously however, the idea
that men pursuing their interests would be forever harmless was aban-
doned when as Hirschman (1981: 126) puts it, 'the reality of capitalist
development was in full view'. As the expansion of capital accumulation
through the 19th and 20th centuries uprooted millions of people,
generated increasing social polarisation and created large-scale unemployment, it became clear that those caught in these violent transformations would 'on occasion become passionate – passionately angry,
fearful, resentful' (Hirschman, *ibid.*).

If the dominant spirit of our age invests the market with the sign of the
sacred, and projects an image of the individual embedded in the imperative of possession, we ought not to assume that this spirit has no history.
The current of possessive individualism that Macpherson has traced back
to the 17th century has certainly not evaporated. Castoriadis, in replying
to questions on democracy and politics, argues that the fundamental drive
of contemporary society is the maximisation of production and of
consumption. This maximisation has become the almost exclusive,
imaginary signification of late 20th-century society. For Castoriadis
(1990: 137), 'as long as it remains the sole passion of the modern
individual, there can be no question of a slow accretion of democratic
contents and liberties'; he goes on, 'democracy is impossible without a
democratic passion, a passion for the freedom of each and of all, a passion
for common affairs which become ... the personal affairs of each'.

Castoriadis sees modern society as being characterised by the emergence of a type of individual that is centred on consumption, apathetic
towards public matters, and cynical in its relation to politics. He links
this with the process of privatisation and the development of a depolit-
icisation of the social, of growing apathy and conformity. His conception
of democracy is related to political reflectiveness, which he sees as
largely absent from the contemporary world. Whilst I would argue that
Castoriadis is far too sombre, neglecting other more optimistic and
emancipatory trends,[8] his portrayal of individualism and the political
significance given to passion could not be more relevant. In today's
world, liberal individualism presupposes a model of the normal or
rational individual against which the behaviour and inner reality of each

self are measured and evaluated. In this mode of theorisation the complex politics of identity and subjectivity are left out of account; and instead there is a strong tendency to consent to a 'politics of normal individualisation' (Connolly 1991: 75).

Overall, what I am arguing here is this: first, the current orthodoxy of neo-liberalism, with its normative ensemble of market, democracy and the individual, has a continuity which needs to be continually analysed;[9] second, that when criticising the policies of structural adjustment, of monetarism, and in a more general framework the discourse of neo-liberalism, it is essential to remember that the theoretical constitution of the economic also insinuates a conception of the individual;[10] and third, that this conception of possessive individualism is encapsulated in a political philosophy that aspires to be universal and everlasting – Fukuyama's (1989) belief in the 'universalisation of Western liberal democracy as the final form of human government' represents one example of such a projection.

These three points are interwoven and connected to a further consideration that now requires some introduction. The current orthodoxy on development carries within it a particular interpretation of the West, and of the non-West, which is pivotal in the construction of its meaning. What Mohanty (1988), in the sphere of feminist studies, has appropriately referred to as ethnocentric universalism receives its deepest and most pervasive expression in the domain of mainstream development theory.[11]

It will be recalled that one of the primary thrusts of the dependency perspective was to call into question two central tenets of modernisation theory. First, the notion that the Third World had no meaningful history prior to its 'discovery' and inscription into the Western project was effectively exploded. Second, the contention that the relations between the First and Third Worlds were beneficial for the Third was inverted; in contradistinction to the conventional doctrine it was most frequently argued that the periphery suffered from these relations; they were characterised by the creation of underdevelopment, the extraction of surplus, the bringing into being of the domination/dependence syndrome. Flowing out of this thesis came the idea that development could only be effected through radical, revolutionary breaks with international capitalism. These two components formed the core of the critique, but there is a third and missing component. What was and still is needed, probably now more than ever, is the deconstruction of that imaginary edifice called the Western world.

One approach to this discussion is to view the First World as other; to think of its peculiarities, to investigate the 'savage' and 'primitive' in the 'sophisticated' and 'modern'; to disturb and subvert the conventional sedimentation of meaning that gives the West its apparent normalcy and certitude of superiority. In the evaluation of societies, one could think of a series of factors that would make a Tanzania or a Tunisia more developed than the United States: violent crime rates, levels of drug abuse, treatment of the elderly, the value of community, etc. From the advent of slavery, through the 'modernising innovation' of colonialism to the barbarism of Fascism and the machine-like violence of today's serial killer, who may fabricate items of furniture from the remains of his victims, the dark side of the Occident can be brought into focus. Such a project would not be aimed at the politics of a simple reversal, where, paraphrasing Stuart Hall, we would replace the essential, bad, white (First World) social subject with the essential, good, black (Third World) social subject.[12] Rather the complex diversity and heterogeneity of the periphery with its rich plurality of political experience needs to be stressed as a counter to the ethnocentric flattening of Third World reality into a series of stale stereotypes.[13]

Equally, and especially for those of and in the West, the constructed images of the West itself need to be split open and juxtaposed to other images which destabilise the oft-sanctimonious representation of what we are supposed to be. When a Fukuyama (1989: 9) calls our attention to the posited 'egalitarianism of modern America', which is seen as representing the 'essential achievement of the classless society envisioned by Marx', even the least critical reader will undoubtedly pause. Although it is admitted that there is economic inequality, and that the gap between the rich and poor has grown in recent years,[14] it is still maintained that the underlying legal and social structure of the United States is 'fundamentally egalitarian and moderately redistributionist' in nature, so that the root causes of economic inequality are traced back to the legacy of pre-modern times, as is also the condition of 'black poverty'.

At the same time, and in a somewhat Hegelian mould, the reader is informed that when considering the 'common ideological heritage of mankind ... it matters very little what strange thoughts occur to people in Albania or Burkina Faso' (*ibid.*); in any case, the 'vast bulk of the Third World remains very much mired in history', since it is still pursuing its own misguided uniqueness, rather than embracing the universalism of the liberal-democratic project.

The idea of such an unfortunate fate, to remain stuck in history, trapped in a backward uniqueness, recalls one Third World writer's remark that it would seem that 'to join the West in its quest for progress is an imperative, an advancement, an almost necessary condition of being human'.[15] In a related fashion, traditional notions of underdevelopment, or the state of 'developing', capture a sense of lack, and a lack, as DuBois (1991: 2) observes, that 'stands out in relief against the backdrop of a "complete" Western society'. But this idea of completion, of being in a state that is already 'developed', that holds out to those willing 'to develop' the image of their potential future, is an idea based on an ethnocentric idealisation of the 'modern society'.[16]

Finally, in this regard, and remembering the second component of the radical *dependencia* critique, the celebration of a certain version of the liberal-democratic project fails to take account of the long history of Western penetration and subordination of peripheral societies.

The attempts to discipline the Third World, to 'police the development process', and to punish those governments or movements that have opposed the will to global power – all these modes of intervention and subjection have continuously raised questions of resistance, of rebellion and of revolution. How, in the aftermath of the withering away of what was the Second World, do we approach these other questions?

The Eclipse of the Revolutionary Rupture

In his interesting essay on the 'crisis of socialism' and the Third World, Hinkelammert (1991) argues that today the Third World in its conflict with the central capitalist countries of the First World can no longer count on the support of another bloc of countries. The solidarity that the Second World once showed to the countries of the periphery is no more. In a similar vein, Galeano (1991) reminds his readers that the Soviet system helped to 'fund justice in Cuba, Nicaragua and many other countries'. He goes on, 'I suspect that in the not very distant future this will be remembered with nostalgia'.

The crumbling of past certitudes relates not only to the crisis of socialism in its practical, geopolitical sense, but also to the general waning of Marxist thought. In this section, I want to outline some of the problems with the traditional Marxist perspective, as it has informed much of the content of radical development analysis, and I shall conclude this component of my discussion with a few remarks on revolution.

I would argue that the primary thrust of the Marxist position has been characterised by three interrelated problems. In the first place, there has been a strong tendency to view the economy as determinant in the last instance. This has meant that the accumulation, valorisation and devalorisation of capital have been granted a logic which determines the pattern of social and political processes. The accumulation of capital, as a theoretical abstraction, has been allocated a determining, causative power over social action and political outcomes. Moreover, within this particular setting, classes, the state, mobilisation, etc., have been interpreted as the reflections or epiphenomena of the economic. In this sense the structure has absorbed the subject.

Second, when there has been an analysis of socio-political change, the key subject is always a class subject, and class struggle has always been defined as *the* struggle. Here we have two major difficulties: i) the constitution or formation of the subjectivity of social agents is short-circuited, that is, the process through which an individual is constituted as a social subject, in all its complexity and potential volatility, and in some instances as an eventual class subject, is by-passed – instead, the class category, as one possible point of arrival, is taken as a pre-given analytical point of departure; and ii) in a related manner, it has been assumed that in the construction of social consciousness, the point of production is central.

This has meant that subjectivity has been frequently reduced to class as emanating from the process of production, and class consciousness has been seen as central to the project of radical change and the struggle against capitalism. Feminist theory, despite the different currents within it, has, of course, been crucial in undermining and displacing such a traditional view of social and political subjectivity (Flax 1991, Weedon 1987). However, this does not mean that all the work of women social scientists on Third World development is free of class reductionism; not infrequently there has been a tendency to add gender to class, rather than using the rich literature on psychoanalysis and feminism to reconstruct the whole discussion of subjectivity and action in peripheral societies.[17]

Finally, there has always been a strong inclination to pre-suppose that there is a pre-given, privileged social subject, cast in the role of the historical bearer of the revolutionary break from capitalism – I refer of course to the working class. But history has shown something else. Looking at the Cuban or Nicaraguan revolutions, it is clear that at a certain historical moment, a variety of social subjects, unified around a certain vision, a particular political horizon, which combined a range of attitudes, feelings, objectives, hopes and ideas around questions of the nation, of the fight against dictatorship, of social justice, of the struggle against imperialism, came together and took a series of actions that culminated in the moment of revolution. These revolutions were not made by an insurgent working class, but by an amalgamation or coalition of forces sharing a common political imagery in a given historical moment. The determinism of class has never served our analysis, and neither has it engendered the practice of radical change.

In the radical literature on Third World development there has always been a strong tendency to defend the achievements of post-revolutionary societies. Conversely, in the mainstream of development studies, the emphasis on the authoritarian nature of the one-party state has not infrequently been used to erase the possible relevance of the welfare achievements of revolutionary projects in countries such as Cuba and Nicaragua. In addition, the effects of United States hostility to such projects and the destabilising role of the United States in a whole range of other Third World cases have very often been left unanalysed. Looking back on the experience of post-revolutionary societies, and restricting myself in this case to the Cuban example, what would be the main points of a post-Marxist critique?

The presence of a totalising imperative in socialist thought has a long history. In the Cuban case, it was concisely expressed by Fidel Castro in his speech to the 1975 Congress of the PCC (Cuban Communist Party), when he declared that the Party was the 'synthesis of everything', embodying the 'Soul of the Revolution' (Castro 1976: 231–2). But, in the Cuban example, the attempt to encompass the whole is not only found in the speeches of the leader of an institutionalised revolution but also in the writings of its foremost guerrilla leader. Che Guevara, in his celebrated essay on man and socialism in Cuba, where he stressed the significance of moral incentives, also wrote that 'we are looking for something new that will permit a complete identification between the government and the community in its entirety' (Guevara 1988: 7). This notion of a complete identification does away with the need to maintain a distinction between civil society and the state, and further still the force of the mechanism of identification implies that nothing will escape state power; as Guevara put it: 'Society as a whole must be converted into a gigantic school.' It is within the sphere of this discourse that the prosecution of economic and social development comes to be equated with socialism.[18]

With the institutionalisation of revolution, as occurred in the Cuba of the 1970s and 1980s, it is possible to identify three broad tendencies. First, there is a trend towards the continual displacement and then transcendence of the divisions between the state and civil society, political and administrative power, and the state bureaucracy and the party. As an eventual condensation, power comes to be materialised in one organ (or in extreme cases in one individual) that has the supposed capacity of concentrating and representing in itself all the forces of society ('the Party is the synthesis of everything').

Second, the problem of antagonisms internal to society is denied. There are no longer any contradictions within the organisation of production or the general structure of society. We have arrived on the plateau of a classless society.

Finally, the notion of social heterogeneity, as far as it radically contradicts the image of a society in harmony with itself, is rejected. The negation of heterogeneity, and of difference, the exigency of societal harmony and the fortification of a Marxist-Leninist conformity foreclose the development of political culture, of alternative socialist as well as democratic thought. When the paralysis of official doctrine is publicly recognised, and when the need for structural reform is accepted, the radical sources of alternative thought and vision have already been terminally crippled, if not erased. The political landscape is so riven by the official contours of 'scientific socialism' that a move to its perceived opposite, capitalism, is starkly reinforced. As Lowy has observed, Marxism can only develop in an atmosphere of ideological and cultural pluralism. If an attempt is made to impose an ideological monopoly of Marxism, or worse still one of its particular variants, this can only lead to 'the degeneration of Marxism itself and its transformation into a state's official doctrine or religion' (Lowy 1986: 272).

In the case of Cuba, it is clear that the revolution carried forward remarkable improvements in the welfare of the population, the reduction of inequalities, and in the satisfaction of basic material needs. However, even leaving aside the issue of what constitutes a material need in a rapidly changing world, there is still the problem of political needs, which may be connected to the question of individual and civic rights. In this kind of society, where a certain standard of living has been guaranteed, the individual, in exchange for the minimum amount of goods, which ensure a certain physical and cultural self-reproduction, renounces the possibility of a political alternative. Rather than seeing the evolution of a self-governing society, in which the critical use of the intellect and a general release from social tutelage are the hallmarks of political development, the omniscient Party develops through absorbing society.

Along a different axis, the Nicaraguan experiment pointed to the possibilities of combining revolution with plurality and democracy. As an objective, the political construction of new social identities traversed both the popular organisations operating in an emerging civil society and the organs of the post-revolutionary state. Such a phenomenon developed from a situation where an original popular-democratic insurgency had led to the seizure of state power; but that capture, in contrast to the Cuban case, did not usher in a period of political closure. In fact, the co-existence of both representative and direct forms of democracy provided a key facet of the originality of the Sandinista project. Nonetheless, as became very clear, geopolitical circumscription, with the continuing disruption of war and socio-economic destabilisation, coupled with a growing dislocation between the party in power and the grassroots organisations (exacerbated by a show of over-confidence by some leaders of the government) brought to a halt this innovative experiment in post-revolutionary democracy.

In the context of the contemporary trend to attach notions of violence to the experience of revolution, and to guerrilla movements, it is essential to emphasise the violence used by the United States to undermine the Nicaraguan experiment. This does not mean to imply that we want to convey a romanticised picture of that particular experiment in combining revolution with democracy, but it does mean that we still live in an era of imperialist intervention. It is symptomatic of a certain genre that in a study of 'development wars' the strategic violence deployed by the 'world's policeman' is not only not examined – it is simply ignored (Elguea 1991).

With the fading away of the Second World, and the global predominance of neo-liberal discourse, the feasibility of future revolutionary breaks of the kind that punctuated the course of Third World political development in the post-war epoch has been severely impaired, if not entirely foreclosed. It is in this sense that I have suggested the idea of the eclipse of revolutionary rupture. This does not mean that I would take the deterministic position that such ruptures are impossible in the future, but certainly their possibility, seen as the final condensation of armed struggle, is highly unlikely.

Within an orthodox current of Marxist politics, one had the idea that power had to be seized, taken hold of, wrenched away from repressive apparatuses and exploiting classes. In the violent climax of revolutionary insurrection, the steely instruments of the new society would be forged and put to immediate use. But if revolution, as a violent rupture, is in historical eclipse, does this mean that there is no other alternative?

Rethinking the Political in a Post-Marxist Direction

Writing 20 years ago, in a rather famous article, Dudley Seers (1972) argued that any discussion of the meaning of development could not realistically avoid the question of value judgements. For Seers development ought to be seen in the context of providing the necessary conditions for the universally acceptable aim of 'the realisation of the potential of human personality' (p. 23). Therefore, the questions to ask about a country's development were: what has been happening to poverty, to unemployment and to inequality? If all three of these had become less severe, then beyond doubt there had been a period of development in the country concerned; conversely, if one or two of these central problems had been growing worse, or especially if all three had, then, for Seers, it would have been strange indeed to call the result 'development', irrespective of what had happened to per capita income.

It is also interesting to note that Seers expressed a healthy scepticism about the First World; for example, he wrote that 'few if any of the rich countries now appear to the outside world as really desirable models ... some aspects, such as their consumption levels, seem enviable, but these are associated, perhaps inseparably, with evils such as urban sprawl, advertising pressures, air pollution and chronic tension' (Seers 1972: 22). In challenging the orthodoxy of that time, which made a fetish out of economic growth, Seers was putting on the agenda, in a measured way, a series of issues relating to the ethics of development.

In the World Bank's latest development report, equity and redistribution are given some emphasis. The reader is informed, however, that 'when markets work well, greater equity often comes naturally' (World Bank 1991: 138). In contrast, Seers informed his reader that market forces reflect a country's income distribution (*op. cit.*: 26). The World Bank's introduction of a discussion of equity and redistribution finds a parallel in a recent United Nations ECLA publication, which strongly argues for productive transformation with equity (CEPAL 1990). After a decade in which most countries of the South have experienced a process of increased poverty, inequality and underemployment, the 'social' is officially re-introduced in a time of increasing political fluidity.

For some writers it is necessary to counterpose democracy to development. For Lummis, for example, the ideology of development brings in its wake a series of changes that are hardly positive: 'Villagers are driven out and dams are built; forests are cut down and replaced by plantations; whole cultures are smashed and people recruited into quite different cultures; people's local means of subsistence are taken away and they are placed under the power of the world market' (Lummis 1991: 48). In this vision, the development metaphor is seen as promoting a colonisation of consciousness which is deeply anti-democratic.

In the heartlands of the West the project of modernity is itself in question. The melting away of fixed horizons for development and progress; the subversion and displacement of the universalist certitudes of the Enlightenment; and the growing porosity of the erstwhile solid domains of disciplinary knowledge (the 'counter-disciplinary' trend) – all express the characteristic features of what Vattimo (1991) has called 'the end of modernity'. In post-modern times, projects that carry the sign of universalism, of Emancipation in the singular, and a notion of the transparent, unitary social subject, can be the target of a radical deconstruction.

It needs to be said, of course, that the politics of the post-modern, as I have argued elsewhere, are radically ambiguous. In one exemplification of the post-modern, the universalist pretence of Western projects of 'development and progress' can be effectively cracked open; in another, centres and peripheries can be dissolved in a game of linguistic acrobatics. I would argue that the post-modern turn can be enabling in our analysis of the political meanings of development; its sense of irreverence and constant questioning can usefully feed into a continually reflexive and critical post-Marxist perspective. But, finally, how do we situate or interpret the 'political' in our studies of the meanings of 'development'?[19]

It is becoming increasingly evident that there can be no single-shot, fixed function for the political. The political is not a 'level', split off and granted a relative autonomy from other levels. Sometimes, the political is delimited as the domain of state power, against which civil society must organise its institutional and interactive mechanisms of defence. Often, a binary division is drawn between the realm of the political, bounded within the state, and political parties, and the space of the social, framed around the family, the school, religion, the individual, movements and so on. However, dissolving this binary split, just as the post-Marxist would transcend the base-superstructure division, or the post-structuralist would subvert any idea of a pre-supposed separation between 'institutions' and 'discourse', we can argue that the very genesis of society is itself political. Expressed differently, it can be argued that the political has a double nature, in the sense that it is both inscribed within the different spheres of the social whole, and at the same time it is constitutive of the terrain on which the fate of the social whole is decided. Hence, what is and is not political at any moment changes with the emergence of new questions, posed by new modes of subjectivity (e.g., 'the personal is political') and different kinds of social relations. But also the 'political' does not eliminate the social conditions from which its question was born; gender, religious belief, the environment, regionalism ... may become political but they are not *only* political.

A primary element in the erosion of the contours of an official discourse relates to the questioning of the given, of what appears to be socially obvious. When 'the given' is not accepted as such, but referred back to the initial act that led to its installation, the unstable sense of the given is revealed, reactivated. In this potentially never-ending process of the desedimentation of the social, the concealed nature of the political can be revealed. Thus, for example, tracing back dominant views on the 'beneficial essence of the market' to the origin of ideas on property and individualism can help to unearth and destabilise the settled nature of today's politically given. Similarly, investigating the historical tracks of what is now referred to as 'structural adjustment', can lead us back to another period in Latin American development, when the 'money doctor' from the United States dispensed very similar medicine (Drake 1989).

Progress and 'development' today no longer possess their original sense of a final destination; they have become a part of the routine of consumer society, which depends upon the constant production of 'new' items of consumption. Interestingly, over 60 years ago, Ortega y Gasset (1957, first published 1930) wrote that faith in modern culture was a gloomy one; this was so because it meant that progress consisted merely in advancing, for all time to be, along a road identical to the one already under our feet – such a road was 'rather a kind of elastic prison which stretches on without ever setting us free' (p. 33). But to escape from that road meant to come out once again under the stars into the world of reality, the world of the profound, the terrible, the unforeseeable, the inexhaustible. Not knowing what was going to happen tomorrow in the world in the year 1930 was for Ortega y Gasset cause for secret joy; 'that very impossibility of foresight, that horizon ever open to all contingencies, constitutes authentic life, the true fullness of our existence' (p. 34).

Ortega y Gasset's 'elastic prison' is the road to 'development' offered to the Third World by the money doctors of the contemporary West. The political meaning of that kind of development is antagonistic to the 'realisation of the potential of human personality'. At the same time it is inimical to the democratisation of society. Coming from another direction, we have seen that Marxist versions of the path to development through revolution and bureaucratisation do not guarantee the nurturing of a radical democracy.

Another meaning of development can be found in the context of movements of resistance and the creation within civil society of another kind of democratic innovation. Carried inside some of today's reverse discourses of emancipation there is an ethics of conviction in responsibility – for the environment, for human rights, for difference, for emancipation from oppression, exploitation and subjection. If development is seen as inscribed in these reverse discourses, then its meaning can be evocative of an emancipatory imagery. Rather than 'counteridentify' and dismiss development because of the specific way it is articulated in the orthodox discourses of the international system, we can think of ways in which development can be recast in a quite new kind of project. Whilst being a long way from Ortega y Gasset's world of 'hyperdemocracy' and the fear of plenitude, we might share with him that feeling of being on open ground, free from any iron laws of historical destiny.

Notes

1. According to a report of the Bolivian Chamber of Deputies in 1987, 'the illegal trafficking of coca leaves and its by-products has become the most dynamic sector in the economy ... over the past five years exports of cocaine and its derivatives were 300 per cent higher than all other export earnings put together ...' See *Latin American Regional Reports Andean Group*, RA 87 03, 9 April 1987, p. 7.

2. Societal acceptance of neo-liberalism has also been aided by a variety of prominent intellectuals; the historian, José Luis Roca, for example, has recently suggested that the 'democratisation of capital' can be partly achieved through the privatisation of state enterprises; see *Temas en la Crisis*, issue on *Privatización*, no. 39, April, p. 43, La Paz. These and related views have of course been the subject of much debate; for an alternative perspective which

challenges the connection between democracy and privatisation see Oporto (1991).

3. In December 1990, the Peruvian President, Fujimori, stated that 'we cannot overcome the economic and fiscal crisis without reducing the state machinery and making it more efficient'. Surplus bureaucrats would have to go, as would surplus workers (*Andean Group Report*, 31 January 1991). A more recent example is provided by Argentina, where in mid-November 1991, the Menem government announced a far-reaching programme of privatisation of state enterprises and liberalisation of the economy – see *El País*, jueves, 14 November 1991, p. 58.

4. Payer gives a number of clear examples of the effects of IMF/World Bank policies. On structural adjustment she lists the following four major objectives: a) opening a closed or protected economy to world market forces through import and exchange liberalisation; b) realigning domestic prices with world market prices; c) privatisation of state enterprises; and d) reducing labour's share of national income. With respect to the politics of debt servicing, she usefully draws our attention to the difference in US treatment of Zaire compared to Nicaragua during the early 1980s – see Payer (1991: 96, 110 respectively).

5. This does not mean to imply that the expansion of European and Japanese investments, especially the former during these years, had no role in the diffusion of Western modernisation, but in the context of the Cold War and the deployment of Western discourses of the Third World other, the United States, then as now, assumed a quite central position.

6. In an interesting and for today continually relevant remark, Laski noted that it was a sufficient commentary on the claims of the businessmen to rule unfettered in the economic domain to say that in the United States, the richest country in the world, 12 million citizens were in 1939 dependent upon relief for their means of life, and that in Great Britain, one out of every four children was undernourished – see Laski (1943: 15).

7. In a quote from Keynes, Hirschman gives us an acute exemplification of his thesis; Keynes wrote in the 1930s as follows: 'Dangerous human proclivities can be canalised into comparatively harmless channels by the existence of opportunity for money-making and private wealth, which, if they cannot be satisfied in this way, may find their outlet in cruelty, the reckless pursuit of personal power and authority, and other forms of self-aggrandisement ...' See Hirschman (1981: 134).

8. Elsewhere, in a discussion of social movements and power relations, I have tried to show that not everything has to be fitted into the constraining context of gloom and doom – see Slater (1991a, 1991b).

9. Since the maxim 'those who do not remember the past are condemned to repeat it' holds far more for the history of ideas than for the unfolding of actual events, the subversion and deconstruction of the dogma of 'structural adjustment', and of current notions of the individual, need their relevant historical context.

10. The critical economist Sen, in discussing the connections between concepts of the individual and concepts of the economy, noted that the purely economic man, the ruthless maximiser, in the neo-classical vision, is 'indeed close to being a social moron' (Sen 1979, quoted in Williams 1990: 66).

11. Nor am I implying that ethnocentric universalism is only found in this particular domain, as I illustrated in the case of my critique of the Warren thesis – see Slater (1987).

12. For this observation and many other relevant remarks see Julien and Mercer (1988).

13. Elsewhere, I have considered various aspects of this process of 'flattening' in relation to critical urban studies – see Slater (1992a).

14. For some recent data, Phillips (1991: xii) notes that the wealth share of the top 1 per cent of Americans had increased from 27 per cent in the 1970s to 36 per cent at the end of the 1980s. Further the net worth of the 400 richest Americans had trebled from $92 billion in 1982 to $270 billion in 1989.

15. Quoted in DuBois (1991: 3).

16. And, in a not entirely distinct manner, in some representations of the post-modern intervention, Western ethnocentrism lives on – for some further discussion, see Slater (1992b).

17. I have discussed this point in Slater 1991b and 1992b.

18. Lummis (1991), in his critical evaluation of Marxism-Leninism, reminds us of the commanding imperatives of Lenin's approach to development in the post-revolutionary situation. One quotation will suffice: 'We must learn to combine the "public meeting" democracy of the working people ... with *iron* discipline when at work, with *unquestioning obedience* to the will of a single person, the Soviet leader, while at work' (p. 40).

19. As Nederveen Pieterse (1991: 11) reminds us, the political is always close at hand in the conceptualisation of development; over 20 years ago, for instance, Walt Rostow declared that 'the glory of America has been not its relative material wealth but the sense of its transcendent political mission in reconciling liberty and order'.

Relevant Literature

Biersteker, T.J. 1990. 'Reducing the Role of the State in the Economy: A Conceptual Exploration of IMF and World Bank Prescriptions'. *International Studies Quarterly* 34, pp. 477–92.

Broad, R. 1990. *Unequal Alliance – The World Bank, The International Monetary Fund and the Philippines*. Berkeley and London, University of California Press.

Castoriadis, C. 1990. 'Does the Idea of Revolution Still Make Sense? – an Interview with Cornelius Castoriadis'. *Thesis Eleven* no. 26, pp. 123–38.

Castro, Fidel. 1976. *Report of the Central Committee of the Communist Party of Cuba to the First Congress, First Congress of the Communist Party of Cuba, December, 1975*. Moscow, Progress Publishers.

CEPAL. 1990. *Transformacion Productiva Con Equidad*. Santiago, Chile.

Conaghan, C.M., J.M. Malloy & L.A. Abugattas. 1990. 'Business and the "Boys": The Politics of Neoliberalism in the Central Andes'. *Latin American Research Review* vol. XXV, no. 2, pp. 3–30.

Connolly, W.E. 1991. *Identity\Difference – Democratic Negotiations of Political Paradox.* Ithaca, Cornell University Press.

Drake, P.W. 1989. *The Money Doctor in the Andes – The Kemmerer Missions, 1923-1933.* Durham and London, Duke University Press.

DuBois, M. 1991. 'The Governance of the Third World: A Foucauldian Perspective on Power Relations in Development'. *Alternatives* vol. 16, no. 1, Winter, pp. 1–30.

ECLAC. 1989. *Preliminary Overview of the Economy of Latin America and the Caribbean.* Santiago, Chile.

Elguea, J.A. 1991. 'El Sangriento Camino hacia la Utopía: las Guerras de Desarrollo en América Latina'. *Estudios Sociológicos* IX: 25, pp. 145–64.

Fishlow, A. 1990. 'Streamlining the State'. *Hemisfile*, Jan., pp. 1–2.

Flax, J. 1991. *Thinking Fragments – Psychoanalysis, Feminism and Postmodernism in the Contemporary West.* Berkeley and Los Angeles, University of California Press.

Fukuyama, F. 1989. 'The End of History?' *The National Interest,* Summer, pp. 3-18.

Galeano, E. 1991. 'In the Defence of the Right to Dream'. *New Statesman and Society* (South Supplement), 11 Oct., pp. 6–7.

Ghai, D. & C. Hewitt de Alcántara. 1990. 'The Crisis of the 1980s in Sub-Saharan Africa, Latin America and the Caribbean'. *Development and Change* vol. 21, no. 3, July, pp. 389–426.

Guevara, E. 1988. *Socialism and Man in Cuba.* Sydney, Pathfinder (originally published in 1965).

Hinkelammert, F.J. 1991. 'La Crisis del Socialismo y el Tercer Mundo'. *Páginas* vol. XVI, no. 109, pp. 60-72. Lima.

Hirschman, A.O. 1981. *The Passions and the Interests – Political Arguments for Capitalism before its Triumph.* Princeton, Princeton University Press.

Hoogvelt, A. 1987. 'The Crime of Conditionality: open letter to the IMF'. *Review of African Political Economy* no. 38, Apr., pp. 80–5.

Julien, I. & K. Mercer. 1988. 'Introduction – De Margin and De Centre'. *Screen* vol. 29, no. 4, Autumn, pp. 2–10.

Laski, H.J. 1943. *Reflections on the Revolution of our Time.* London, Allen and Unwin.

Lowy, M. 1986. 'Mass Organization, Party and State: Democracy in the Transition to Socialism'. In R.R. Fagen, C. Diana Deere & J.L. Coraggio (eds.), *Transition and Development – Problems of Third World Socialism,* pp. 264–79, New York, Monthly Review Press.

Lummis, C.D. 1991. 'Development Against Democracy'. *Alternatives* vol. 16, no. 1, Winter, pp. 31–66.

Macpherson, C.B. 1988. *The Political Theory of Possessive Individualism – Hobbes to Locke.* Oxford, Oxford University Press.

Mohanty, C. 1988. 'Under Western Eyes: Feminist Scholarship and Colonial Discourses'. *Feminist Review* no. 30, Autumn, pp. 61–88.

Nederveen Pieterse, J. 1991. 'Dilemmas of Development Discourse: The Crisis of Developmentalism and the Comparative Method'. *Development and Change* vol. 22, pp. 5–29.

Nun, J. 1991. 'Democracy and Modernization, Thirty Years After'. Paper presented at the Plenary Session on 'Democratic Theory Today: Empirical and Theoretical Issues', 15th World Congress, International Political Science Association, Buenos Aires, Jul. 21–6.

Oporto, H. 1991. *La Revolución Democratica – una Nueva Manera de Pensar Bolivia*. La Paz, Los Amigos del Libro.

Ortega y Gasset, J. 1957. *The Revolt of the Masses*. New York and London, W.W. Norton and Company (originally published in Spanish in 1930).

Payer, C. 1991. *Lent and Lost – Foreign Credit and Third World Development*. London, Zed Books.

Phillips, K. 1991. *The Politics of Rich and Poor – Wealth and the American Electorate in the Reagan Aftermath*. New York, Harper Perennial.

Polanyi, K. 1957. *The Great Transformation – the Political and Economic Origins of our Time*. Boston, Beacon Press.

Seers, D. 1972. 'What Are We Trying to Measure?' *Journal of Development Studies* vol. 8, no.3 , Apr., pp. 21–36.

Slater, D. 1987. 'On Development Theory and the Warren Thesis – Arguments Against the Predominance of Economism'. *Society and Space* (Environment and Planning D) vol. 5, no. 3, pp. 263–82.

— 1991a. 'New Social Movements and Old Political Questions: Rethinking State Society Relations in Latin American Development'. *International Journal of Political Economy* vol. 21, no. 1, Spring, pp. 32–65.

— 1991b. 'Power and Social Movements in the Other Occident: Latin America in an International Context'. Paper presented at the CEDLA/CERLAC Joint Workshop on 'Social Movements and Power Relations: the Latin American Experience', 13–15 November, Amsterdam.

— 1992a. 'On the Borders of Social Theory – Learning from Other Regions'. *Society and Space* (Environment and Planning D), vol. 10, July, pp. 307–27.

— 1992b. 'Theories of Development and Politics of the Post-Modern – Exploring a Border Zone'. *Development and Change*, vol. 23, no. 3, pp. 283–319.

Torrico, E.R. 1990. 'Bolivia: el Rediseño Violento de la Sociedad Global'. *Nueva Sociedad* 105, pp. 153–63.

Vattimo, G. 1991. *The End of Modernity*. Oxford, Polity Press.

Weedon, C. 1987. *Feminist Practice and Poststructuralist Theory*. Oxford, Blackwell.

Williams, D.E. 1990. 'Crisis and Renewal in the Social Sciences and the Colonies of Ourselves'. *International Political Science Review* vol. 11, no. 1, Jan., pp. 59–74.

World Bank. 1981, 1990, 1991. *World Development Report*. New York and Oxford, Oxford University Press.

5

Political Programmes and Development: The Transformative Potential of Social Democracy

by Ronaldo Munck

The debate on the relationship between social democracy and development has usually centred on the economic conditions necessary for the realisation of democracy. To my mind, two equally untenable positions have been put forward in this regard. On the one hand, Bill Warren has stated baldly that 'Capitalism and democracy are ... linked virtually as Siamese twins'.[1] This view quite simply ignores the authoritarian history of 'actually existing' capitalism, especially in the developing world we are concerned with. To this view we can counterpose that of Gunder Frank, for whom repression is 'not accidental or merely ideologically motivated. Rather it is a necessary concomitant of economic exploitation ...'[2] This perspective, on the other hand, ignores (or downgrades) the recent flourishing of democracy in the Third World and, in theoretical terms, makes a necessity of what is, in essence, a contingent relationship. To go beyond this impasse it may be useful to invert the usual terms of considering this relationship, to consider the development potentials of democracy. First, though, it is necessary to clarify some aspects of the recent debate on the crisis of development theory and the prospects for social democracy in (relative) isolation.

Concepts

Recent debate on the 'impasse' of development theory has focused on its theoretical aspects.[3] This is understandable and even necessary, but maybe it is not sufficient. From a Third World perspective, development is both more than and different from a theory which is an academic sub-field (where intellectuals make and unmake each other's reputations) and a mode of political intervention in the Third World. Development in the Third World is the overarching referent of all political discourse. It is hard to overestimate the political overdetermination of development theory. Modernisation theory was unambiguously and directly an expression and agent of the then-hegemonic US imperialism. For its part, dependency theory was, 'in the last instance', a justification and tool of a revolutionary strategy. The failure of both theories was, also, due less to their conceptual inconsistencies than to their collapse as political strategies.

Now that the political climate in many parts of the Third World has shifted from reaction (modernisation theory) to revolution (dependency theory) to social democracy, so development theory is seeking a new face. Dependency theory still permeates many studies, even when explicitly rejected; there is an uneasy, and often unacknowledged, borrowing from the modernisation arsenal, and there is a new-found concern with sustainable development, in a gesture towards the new ecology.[4]

In an era of uncertainty and ambiguity it may seem ludicrous and dogmatic to stress simple oppositions. Yet the development theory debate, referred to above, requires some definition. It appears to me that none of the 'ways out' of the development theory impasse are adequate to construct a new paradigm, be it post-imperialism, regulation theory, a gender focus or Michel Foucault. While not neglecting the contribution of any of these, I would argue that the underlying choice is still between modernisation and dependency theory. This is similar, I believe, to how the unfolding events in Eastern Europe show there is no 'middle way' between the conscious regulation of economic affairs and the unfettered operation of the market.

My argument for the continued relevance of the dependency approach is no nostalgic kick-back to the 1960s. Cristobal Kay, in a recent critical overview of Latin American theories of development, has similarly argued for the contemporary relevance of structuralism and dependency analysis.[5] The issue of foreign debt cannot be divorced from financial and technological dependence. Structural heterogeneity is still a fundamental issue: the debate on 'marginality' may have passed into history but not the people it referred to. The debates on stabilisation plans and on alternative development strategies are still operating within the field originally defined by the dependency theory critique of modernisation.

To reinforce this choice I would argue that none of the critics of the dependency framework of analysis have definitively overthrown the methodology of F.H. Cardoso and Guillermo O'Donnell, for example.[6] Of course O'Donnell may have committed the sin of economism in his pioneering analysis of the relationship between economic structures and political process in Latin America. Of course, Cardoso's socio-economic analysis of Latin American history was at times schematic. What critics, especially those engaged in the once-fashionable exercise of 'auto-critique', seldom recognise is that their own enterprise is about political choices. Neither Cardoso or O'Donnell shared the naive revolutionary optimism and 'immediatism' of those who popularised dependency theory. Thus they neither need to defend nor reject their earlier work.[7] An analysis centred around the concept of 'dependent development' has no necessary apocalyptic political implications. In fact, to shift continents, it is at the heart of establishment, as much as alternative economic debates in contemporary Ireland.[8] The point of this discussion, for the present paper, is that social democracy, as much as Cuban socialism, is compatible with the dependency approach. Whether social democracy is a viable vehicle for dependency reversal is, of course, another question.

Norbert Lechner has expressed a general feeling among Latin American intellectuals in stating that: 'If revolution was the articulating axis of the Latin American debate in the 1960s, in the 1980s the central theme is democracy'.[9] To be more specific, social democracy has become hegemonic in Latin American political discourse both of the state and the opposition. The long night of military dictatorship – for which the revolutionary project was held at least partly responsible – has led to the revalorisation of democracy. Social democracy is the intellectual common sense of the era, the framework in which debates take place and their inevitable horizon. I would argue, however, that the *objectives* of social democracy cannot be met by the *methods* of social democracy, at least outside of the advanced industrial societies. At the same time, the socialist project, as we have hitherto known it, is closed for the foreseeable future. Its objectives, likewise, cannot be met by traditional methods. This points us (or rather me) towards the project of radical democracy articulated in different forms by Ernesto Laclau and Roberto Mangabeira Unger. This is the political counterpart to maintaining 'dependent development' as a framework of analysis for developing Third World societies.

Whereas the classical emancipatory discourse was characterised by globality, today's diverse emancipatory demands are not unified in a global rupture with the old order. For Laclau it follows that 'socialism is no longer a blueprint for society, and comes to be part of a radical democratisation of social organisation'.[10] The radical democratic alternative differs from classical liberalism in its recognition of new antagonisms in post-modern society and the varieties of social arrangements compatible with democracy. Through engagement with the practical politics in the post-dictatorial Brazil, Roberto Mangabeira Unger made his own version of empowered democracy more specific. Its main objective is seen as the overcoming of the economic dualism and the political cycles typical of Brazil, and most of Latin America. It rejects both conservative reformism and a socialist project seen as a mirage whose inaccessibility serves as an alibi for immobility. Unger's own revolutionary reformism is premised on the belief that there is 'a specific path of cumulative institutional innovation which can reconcile the objectives of economic growth with the overcoming of the brutal inequalities which degrade and corrupt our collective life'.[11] Unger's anti-determinism rejects the notion that institutions are simply effects of laws of social evolution and denies that political projects have necessary class agents.

These as yet somewhat abstract debates are mirrored in the sharp ideological struggles around socialist renewal in the parties of the Latin American left.[12] Having rediscovered democracy, many currents are falling willingly into the arms of European social democracy. But there are other *renovador* currents who do not seek there a third way between US capitalism and failed Soviet communism. In fact, these political tendencies, with their watchword of radical democracy, are harking back to that space which once existed between the Second International of social democracy and the Third International of communism. Between the two world wars there was a brief flourishing of a Second-and-a-half International which failed to establish itself but which continued through Austro-Marxism to offer a revolutionary reformist perspective. The debates today on social pacts, class compromise and *concertacion* (democratic political pacts) have a clear link to what might appear to some a mere pre-history. Given the dominant mood of post-modernism with its free-floating, de-contextualised debates, this concrete reference point for current discussion on the possible outlines of a radical democratic project might not go amiss.

Practice

We need now to ask to what extent Mangabeira Unger's vision was matched by the actual democratisation process in Latin America of the 1980s. We can use Gramsci's concept of 'moments' to consider the various aspects of democratisation. The military moment – demilitarisation – has proceeded well in some countries but not in others (Argentina). The socio-economic moment of democratisation has, frankly, been bleak. The democratic regimes have turned to austerity policies which have deepened social and economic divisions and increased poverty and unemployment. Considering the political moment of democratisation we note the most significant changes and advances. As Cardoso writes, 'the new democratisation includes a reequilibrium of powers between the State, civil society movements and parties'.[13] Political parties look to social movements as much as the state now. At the level of everyday life democratisation has simply not proceeded very far. The main constraints on democratisation are, in the 'external' arena, the foreign debt, and, on the 'internal' front, the unequal distribution of wealth and power.

Dependent development remains, in brief, the main constraint on consistent democratisation in Latin America.

Much hope was pinned during the transition period on a 'democratic pact' in which the various parties agree to the procedural norms which will prevail in the new democracies, and commit themselves to an overriding allegiance to the framework of the new order. This does not preclude conflict, nor does it preach an impossible consensus; it simply sets the 'rules of the game'. The democratic pact, in theory, opens and maintains a space for democratic and socialist struggles, and creates a united front of democratic forces to rebuff threats from the old military regime. In some cases (Uruguay) this political pact was quite explicit and successful, in others less explicit (Brazil) but nevertheless fruitful, whereas in other cases (Argentina) it soon degenerated. In some cases democratisation led to a further 'social pact', or at least the attempt to construct one. These brought labour and capital together with the state in a bid to regulate wages and profits. Yet *concertacion* was (or wanted to be) more than a mere wages agreement. It sought the creation of a new legitimacy and social order. The underlying issue behind the debate in the socio-economic pact was whether class compromise was possible under conditions of (dependent) capitalism.

I would argue that the structural heterogeneity of dominated capitalist nations poses insuperable barriers to a durable class compromise. There is an essential contradiction between the transnational level at which the reproduction of capitalism is organised and the national level at which political consent is organised. However, this does not mean that we should reject the whole *concertacion* exercise as 'mere' reformism and 'class treachery' by labour leaders. In fact, the depth of social and economic problems makes a strategy of socio-economic reforms not only necessary but also viable. The democratic pacts may not produce a class compromise but they may create the conditions for an effective struggle for radical democratic reforms. Non-cooperation with the social pact runs the real risk of jeopardising the very existence of the national community. The pitfalls of populism and the subsequent horrors of military rule led many to see the pact as virtuous in and of itself, and all its critics as enemies of democracy. The apparent failure of most social pacts during the 1980s should not surprise us, but neither should it lead us to reject the social pact out of hand and go on to seek a new magic answer.

A major strand of the new democratic ideology in Latin America of the 1980s centred around human rights and the rule of law. For some Marxists the idea of human rights is largely a mystification because it counterposes individual social rights to social inequality. After the military regimes, such objections faded as human rights became a strategic component of the project for reinforcing civil society. Human rights were to become the ethical principle of the new democracies in Latin America, as never before in history. Apart from human rights, the other major component of the new democratic ideology concerned the so-called rule of law (*estado de derecho*). Against previous denunciations of the merely 'formal' mechanisms of parliamentary democracy, its institutions were now elevated into an unqualified good, especially against the 'corporatist' trade unions. Under the new democratic order, political parties were seen as the legitimate bodies to mediate and articulate the various social demands of the population. If the new democracies proclaimed many virtues as those examined above, in practice we saw many shabby compromises, back door deals and backsliding. This is not surprising if democracy is seen as a process rather than a one-off act of conception.

T.H. Marshall, well known theorist of the British welfare state, distinguished three elements of citizenship: i) *civil*, including freedom of speech, the right to justice, and other prerequisites for individual freedom; ii) *political*, involving the right to participate in the exercise of political power through local government and parliament; and iii) *social*, which ranged from 'the right to a modicum of economic welfare and security to the right to share to the full in the social heritage and to live the life of a civilised being according to the standards prevailing in the society'.[14] The relevance of this approach for Latin America is reflected in the current interest among progressives in the notion of 'civic culture', once the preserve of the conservative political modernisation discourse. The need to extend the concept of citizenship in Latin America from its civil and political connotations to a full social citizenship with all that implies is now firmly on the agenda. In that sense, amongst others, social democracy has radically affected development theory which, in its dependency guise, maintained a narrow and instrumentalist view of politics, focused almost exclusively on the state. Whether traditional social democracy can deliver on this issue is, of course, another question.

Debate

With socialism as we know it dead and buried, capitalism is resurgent and with it modernisation theory. The remaining opponents of this practical/political hegemony are in disarray. Any project to move 'beyond the fragments' of the opposition movements has long since collapsed. The watchwords, for those who can afford it, centre around the 'pleasure principle' and a lofty detachment from partisan commitments. Out of this morass, social democracy, once reviled for its containment effect on revolt and even its 'repressive tolerance', is now celebrated as not just an achievable second-best but, essentially, as what socialism was really all about from the start.

Our concern here, however, is more specifically whether social democracy offers a way out of the impasse in which development theory finds itself. The question is not as strange as it may appear at first sight if we recall that Leninism, beyond its political project, served as an effective ideology of development in many Third World countries. Richard Sklar has pointed in this direction, arguing that 'The current crisis in developmental thought ... requires, in addition to political theories of development, political theories for development. Development theory faces the challenge of democracy'.[15] Answering that challenge is now our theme.

In Latin America today, as Moises points out, 'not everyone has been fully convinced that democracy, as desirable as it may be, is the best alternative for solving these societies' serious economic and social problems'.[16] As we saw above, this is, if anything, an understatement. If one reason for the collapse of socialism in Eastern Europe was its perceived economic failure, something similar could happen (is happening) in Latin America with regard to social democracy. What Sklar has in mind in the project of a 'developmental democracy' is to show that this is not necessarily the case. He accepts that the idea that democracy may itself be a mainspring for development could appear to be 'putting the cart before the horse'. Nevertheless, he argues persuasively that 'increasing degrees of mass political participation will enhance constitutional liberty and foster the creation of political environments that, in turn, would be conducive to economic achievements by industrious persons ...'[17] Social democracy, with its corresponding attributes of political pluralism, constitutional liberties and democratic participation, can thus be seen as compatible with and even complementary to economic efficiency.

To my mind, however, we need to go further than merely showing that social democracy can be good for business. The real failure of the dependency approach was its inability/refusal to produce a viable/transitional economic strategy to counterpose to that of military monetarism. Because the perceived alternative was socialist revolution (pure and simple) there was no reformist macro-economic strategy to implement in the new democracies. In political terms, the new democracies were more inventive, even though the discourse was to some extent derivative. The notion of a class compromise was novel to an opposition discourse which took a zero sum conception of politics as given. Where violence and fraud were routine it was hard to accept that all might benefit from general democratic 'rules of the game'. A new way of conducting politics may not emerge overnight, especially when the economic conditions are not propitious, but it is a process which has begun. We are, however, in one of those uneasy transition periods which Gramsci referred to, in which the old is dead but the new has not yet been born, except that the old is only moribund and the new is struggling to live. It is a contest which will determine the future prospects of a democratic development project.

Francis Fukuyama proclaimed recently that 'liberal democracy is the final form of government' for the world as a whole.[18] Now, economic and political liberalism are, of course, in the ascendant. It does not mean that 'there is no alternative' (TINA) – as Mrs Thatcher, who often proclaimed this, found out to her cost. Within capitalism there are momentous debates such as that surrounding the Europe 1992 project. New and old social movements carry the seeds of a radical democracy even if on the fringes of society. Unequal and uneven development on a world scale continue to generate the tensions resulting in national liberation and socialist struggles, as in the past. In short, as Bob Stauffer has argued in a lucid essay, 'we can expect empirical conditions to continue to generate both opposition to capitalism and a search for alternatives'.[19] We have not reached 'the end of history', nor have the internal contradictions of the world system been eliminated – on the contrary they may well have been accentuated by the global spread of the market. The question is whether social democracy, any more than socialism 'as we knew it', represents an adequate alternative. It should be noted that we are now posing the issue in directly political terms rather than in relation to development theory.

It may seem harsh, but nevertheless accurate, to note that concern with the 'impasse' of development theory is largely a concern of what used to be known as the 'development industry'. The dependency approach, whatever its limitations, broke decisively with that whole discourse. We can no longer operate within the carefully compartmentalised arenas of theory (development theory) and politics (social democracy). We need to ask whether we actually need a globalising 'theory of development' anyway. It also seems ludicrous to try to separate the economic from the political, social or cultural aspects of democracy. Social democracy cannot become a new developmentalist ideology, a panacea for the post-socialist era. That is not to say that projects of radical democracy or 'revolutionary reformism' will not emerge to challenge oppression in all its forms, including unequal international economic relations. Social democracy, like Keynesianism, is inextricably bound up with the nation state. The project of radical democracy, on the other hand, has in its theory and practice an internationalist element which seems now more necessary than ever to counteract the 'maldevelopment'[20] produced by capitalist expansion on a world scale.

Notes and References

1. B. Warren, *Imperialism: Pioneer of Capitalism* (London, Verso, 1980), p. 28.
2. A.G. Frank, *Crisis in the Third World* (London, Heinemann, 1981), p. 188.
3. See amongst others D. Booth, 'Marxism and Development Sociology: Interpreting the Impasse', *World Development,* vol. 13, no. 7 (1985); L. Sklair, 'Transcending the Impasse: Metatheory, Theory and Empirical Research in the Sociology of Development and Underdevelopment', *World Development,* vol. 16, no. 6 (1988); S. Corbridge, 'Post-Marxism and Development Studies: Beyond the Impasse', *World Development,* vol. 18, no. 5 (1990); and A. Escobar, 'Discourse and Power in Development: Michel Foucault and the Relevance of his Work to the Third World', *Alternatives,* X (Winter 1984–5).
4. See S.M. Lélé, 'Sustainable Development: A Critical Review', *World Development,* vol. 19, no. 6 (1991).
5. C. Kay, *Latin American Theories of Development and Underdevelopment* (London, Routledge, 1989).
6. See respectively F.H. Cardoso & E. Faletto, *Dependency and Development in Latin America* (Berkeley, University of California Press, 1979) and G. O'Donnell, *Modernisation and Bureaucratic Authoritarianism: Studies in Southern American Politics* (Berkeley, Institute of International Studies, 1973).
7. I am reminded of the reaction by Nicos Poulantzas during the anti-Althusserian backlash, which he did not feel affected his work.
8. See for example, E. O'Malley, *Industry and Economic Development: The Challenge to the Latecomer* (Dublin, Gill & Macmillan, 1989); B. Girvin, *Between Two Worlds: Politics and Economy in Independent Ireland* (Dublin, Gill & Macmillan, 1989), and R. Munck, *The Irish Economy: Results and Prospects* (London, Pluto Press, forthcoming 1993).
9. N. Lechner, 'De la Revolución a la Democracia', *La Ciudad Futura,* no. 2 (1986), p. 33.
10. E. Laclau, *New Reflections on the Revolution of Our Time* (London, Verso, 1990), p. xv.
11. R. Mangabeira Unger, *A Alternativa Transformadora: Como Democratizar O Brasil* (Rio de Janeiro, Editora Guanabara Koogan, 1990), p. 11.
12. For some feel of the debate on socialist renewal in Latin America see EURAL, *Proyectos de Cambio: La Izquierda Democratica en América Latina* (Caracas, Editorial Nueva Sociedad, 1988). Also, A. Fernandez Jilberto & K. Biekart, 'Europa y la Socialdemocratización en América Latina: la Renovación Ideológica de la Izquierda en Chile', *Affers Internacionals* (Barcelona), no. 20, 1991, and H.C. Mansilla, 'Perspectivas Para el Movimiento Socialista en América Latina', *Nueva Sociedad* (Caracas), no. 108 (1991).
13. F.H. Cardoso, 'La Democracia en América Latina', *Punto de Vista,* no. 23 (1985), p. 8. For more detail on this topic see R. Munck, *Latin America: The Transition to Democracy* (London, Zed Books, 1989).

14. T.H. Marshall, *Class, Citizenship and Social Development* (Westport, Greenwood Press, 1973), p. 72.

15. R. Sklar, 'Developmental Democracy', *Comparative Studies in Society and History,* vol. 29, no. 4 (1987), p. 708.

16. J. A. Moises, 'Democracy Threatened: The Latin American Paradox', *Alternatives* 16 (1991), p. 150.

17. R. Sklar, *op. cit.*, p. 709.

18. F. Fukuyama, 'The End of History', *The National Interest* (Summer 1990), pp. 3–18.

19. B. Stauffer, 'After Socialism: Capitalism, Development, and the Search for Critical Alternatives', *Alternatives* 15 (1990), p. 425.

20. On which see the interesting book by S. Amin, *Maldevelopment: Anatomy of a Global Failure* (London, Zed Books, 1990).

6

Ethics in Development Studies:
The Example of Debt

by Stuart Corbridge

> Of course the Israelites needed the end of the world to come. Mr. Wroe does, above all. So much imperfection and contradiction, there is no putting it right. It must be demolished. And in the New World that follows, they themselves will be saved; which is to say they will become single in intent, contraries will be removed. Wroe's instincts will agree with his lusts which will agree with the desires of his rational mind and higher spirit, and will be sanctioned by his conscience. All will be made simple. The crooked path will be made straight. In another, new, world. Which is death. The removal of contraries is death.
>
> Jane Rogers: *Mr. Wroe's Virgins* (1991: 260–1).

Introduction

These are odd times to be thinking and writing about development studies. The old certainties no longer seem to hold true. In the 1950s, 1960s and 1970s one could confidently believe in certain grand theories about development. Advocates of modernisation could believe that growth and development were much the same thing and that development involved a process of catching up. Latecomer societies had to learn from those pioneer societies which had already moved to a state of modernity beyond the stage of Rostow-like 'take-off'. Meanwhile, dependency theorists and Marxists alike could look forward to the collapse of the capitalist world economy which held peripheral economies in a state of underdevelopment. A dose of autarky and/or socialism would cure such countries of the sins of maldevelopment and would free them from the chains of unequal exchange. A new world order would be built in the economies of Asia, Africa and Latin America, but not by dint of capitalism, or its associate, imperialism.

Today, these nostrums comfort us no longer (or comfort very few of us: for a different reading of the possibilities of a democratic socialist revolution, see Peet 1991). The 'facts' of development confirm neither the optimism of the early modernisers nor the pessimism/optimism of the (old) New Left. The gap between rich and poor countries continues to grow. In 1990 the richest 20 per cent of the world's countries had incomes

60 times greater than those of the poorest 20 per cent of the world's countries; in 1960 the ratio was 30:1. At the same time, some developing countries have developed and very few of these successes are to be found in the socialist world. Mao's China may have performed quite well in terms of the distribution of income, but its rate of growth of GDP was not impressive and neither was its record on human rights.

Amidst such complexity and contradictions, a new version of development pessimism can easily take hold. Theorists of the counter-revolution in development studies play on this sentiment when they maintain that development will come to a market-oriented Third World, but only over the course of several decades or even a century. The promise of a single Development Decade is no longer held out. Still others insist that it is the problematic of development itself which should be at issue. Development can so easily be imposed on other people, with the voices of these Others not being heeded or paid proper attention (Pieterse 1991). Development in the traditional senses of state-sponsored capitalism or socialism may then lead to the disempowerment of those on the margins of society – margins which might be so broad as to include women, natives, migrants and refugees (Trinh 1989). Development might also threaten the environment and the security of the global system. The technological fix may then turn out to be a technological nightmare (Shiva 1991).

It is right that these issues are faced up to and that the complexities of the modern world are recognised and not wished away. As Michael Mann so presciently observed: 'Societies are much *messier* than our theories of them' (Mann 1986: 4; emphasis in the original). At the same time, it seems clear to me that a sensitivity to complexity, contradiction and the voices of non-Western Others must not occlude a sensitivity to the needs and rights of distant strangers and to the responsibilities of richer countries, institutions and citizens towards them (Corbridge 1993). To this extent, I find myself in agreement with an editorial in the London *Guardian* newspaper, published on 25 April 1992. The leader maintains that: 'At a time when the original universalism of the UN is being invoked again to legitimate peacekeeping on a wide scale, the argument in favour of organised poverty prevention should have wider appeal. Whether it is civil war in Bosnia or child dehydration in Mali, we either commit ourselves to an internationalist approach or we give up ... The temptation to scoff at vision must be resisted' (p. 20; see also Friedmann 1992).

I also find myself in agreement with David Crocker when he makes a renewed call for the study of development ethics (Crocker 1991). Crocker points out that development is too easily taken for a positive discourse without normative content; either that, or its normative content is rendered unproblematic. What then disappears from view is a diverse set of questions which is bound up with the myriad practices of local and international development. Crocker spells out some of these questions at length and there is no need to repeat all of his arguments here (see also Goulet 1989; O'Neill 1986, 1991; Sen 1984, 1989).

Amongst the more pressing questions raised by Crocker are those which surround the employment consequences of mechanisation and the exploitation of cheap female labour by transnational corporations. Still broader questions relate to issues of different ethno-cultural conceptions of the 'good life' and inter-generational equity. The first of these issues was at the heart of the 1992 Rio summit on the environment: to what extent are growth and 'development' in some countries in the present and immediate future compatible with the ecological needs ('sustainability') of present and future generations in these same and other countries (see Adams 1990; Goodman and Redclift 1991)? The other issue is well illustrated by the Chipko movements in northern India; movements which involve women and men in defence of local trees and a wider moral economy of the peasantry (Guha 1989).

Crocker rightly concludes that these issues are not incidental to development theories or policies. There is an urgent need for 'moral reflection on a society's basic goals because such things as economic growth and modernisation may be morally problematic and in need of replacement, modification or supplementation with more adequate concepts of "fullness of being". We need critical and explicit reflection on the ends as well as the means of development, on the *what* as well as the *how*. Given that the non-normative sense of development can easily be confused with the normative senses, it is often best to speak of "authentic" or "good" development as the theoretical and practical goal of development ethics' (Crocker 1991: 467; emphasis in the original).

Crocker's review of the literature on development ethics is a valuable one. What is less easy to accept, however (as Crocker would himself acknowledge), is that questions relating to development ethics are answered easily or may be answered in the singular. John Toye is surely right to maintain that development is about trade-offs – that it is defined by a series of dilemmas that are resolved only be the creation of new (and perhaps less threatening) dilemmas (Toye 1987). These dilemmas need not function as development theory's equivalent of the Medusa's head, but they should caution us against a conception of development which is linked to claims about the perfectability of humankind. If the new development studies occupies any clear ground, it will be between the optimistic vision of a brave new world and the pessimism of original sin and/or continuing disempowerment.

So far, my remarks have been speculative and deliberately wide-ranging. In the remainder of this chapter I want to illustrate some of these initial concerns with reference to a particular example: the debt crisis of the developing world. The next section rehearses some well-known arguments about the origins, dynamics and dimensions of the debt crisis. It also examines how the debt crisis has been managed in accordance with an economic orthodoxy which stresses economic liberalisation and structural adjustment. I then consider the fairness and efficiency of this orthodoxy and briefly set out a series of competing policy measures which are informed by a more internationalist account of development ethics. The main part of the chapter concludes by reflecting critically on the arguments and policies set out in the previous section. Its point of focus is on the political and institutional arrangements which would be necessary to prosecute particular forms of debt crisis management. Finally, I try to offer a brief and perhaps necessarily inconclusive conclusion.

Policing the Debt Crisis
Most students of development are by now so familiar with the story of the debt crisis that one can talk of a 'standard narrative account' of indebted non-development (Corbridge 1992). The account begins in 1973 with the OPEC-inspired oil price shocks of that year and 1974. A rise in the price of oil created balance of payments problems in most non-oil exporting LDCs and pushed some OECD countries further into recession. Fortunately, the petrodollars which flowed to the Middle East were in turn recycled through London, New York and the Eurodollar markets to some middle-income countries, and particularly those in Latin America and Southeast Asia. In the late 1970s countries including Brazil and Mexico recorded high rates of growth of GDP and manufactured exports.

The good years came to an end, however, between 1979 and 1982. During this period oil prices were hiked again and some leading Western governments turned to monetarism as a way of dealing with the inflation which tormented their economies. Between 1978 and 1981 the six-month dollar London Inter-bank Offered Rate (LIBOR) increased from 9.2 per cent to 16.63 per cent in nominal terms. Meanwhile, real commodity prices were falling sharply for most non-oil products as the world economy moved into its deepest recession since the 1930s. With the debtor countries also facing a strong and ever-strengthening US dollar in the early-mid 1980s, it is perhaps not surprising that Brazil and Venezuela (in 1983) followed Mexico (August 1982) into default on their debt repayments. All of these countries were caught in a scissors crisis not apparently of their own making. A crisis loomed too in large parts of Africa, where debt had been contracted mainly to official creditors and not to the commercial banks.

The story thereafter may also be familiar. In an effort to secure the stability of the commercial banks (especially the big, US money-centre banks), the IMF was called upon to coordinate a series of rescue packages for countries caught in the debt crisis. The IMF agreed first to provide some refinancing for Mexico – and to a rescheduling of some of its loans due – on condition that the commercial banks agreed to abide by a similar package. The IMF also insisted that the indebted countries should begin to reform their economies by virtue of local processes of structural adjustment. In practice, this would mean efforts to reorient their economies towards the needs of the world market and the dictates of world market prices (often by currency devaluations), and efforts to wean domestic economies away from the largesse of public subsidies, public corruption and protectionism. Public expenditure would have to be brought under control to ensure that a trading surplus would not be threatened by domestic budget deficits.

The containment-austerity years of 1982–85 were softened by the introduction of the Baker and Brady plans in 1985 and 1989 respectively. The Baker initiative was announced in October 1985 at Seoul, at the annual joint meeting of the IMF and the World Bank. After first thanking his hosts and praising South Korea, whose 'market-oriented approach and emphasis on private initiative are a lesson for us all', Secretary Baker acknowledged that the industrial countries must take up some of the burden of adjustment in the developing countries' debt crisis. More exactly, Baker acknowledged the successes of the containment strategy, and he noted that the strategy had become more flexible with the introduction of Multi-year Rescheduling Arrangements (MYRAs) in 1984. He particularly endorsed the suggestion that MYRAs should be offered 'as rewards for countries that had made strong progress on policies to deal with their balance of payments problems' (World Bank 1989: xviii). At the same time, he proposed that: 'If the debt problem is to be solved, there must be a Program for Sustained Growth incorporating three essential and mutually reinforcing elements:

1. First and foremost, the adoption by principal debtor countries of comprehensive macroeconomic and structural policies, supported by the international financial institutions, to promote growth and balance of payments adjustment, and to reduce inflation.

2. Second, a continued central role for the IMF, in conjunction with increased and more effective structural adjustment lending from the multilateral development banks, both in support of the adoption by principal debtors of market-oriented policies for growth.

3. Third, increased lending by the private banks in support of comprehensive economic adjustment programs' (Baker 1985).

Thus was the 'Baker initiative' born and with it a new optimism on the debt crisis. The watchwords now were *adjustment with growth* and the promise seemed to be that new resources would be made available to some debtor countries (see also Selowsky and Van der Tak 1986). In part, these resources would be delivered by a 'serious effort to develop the programs of the World Bank and the Inter-American Development Bank ... (to) increase their disbursements to principal debtors by roughly 50 per cent from the current annual (1985) level of $6 billion' (Baker 1985). Other resources would flow in the form of foreign direct investment and as renewed and expanded private bank lending. At the end of his address, Secretary Baker suggested that the commitment 'by the banks to the entire group of heavily indebted, middle-income developing countries would be new net lending in the range of $20 billion for the next three years' (*ibid.*).

The Baker initiative was warmly received by the Western press. In February 1985 *Fortune Magazine* had run an article by Gary Hector entitled *Third World Debt – The Bomb Is Defused*. Hector claimed that: 'Evidence is building that the international debt crisis is over' (Hector 1985: 24). Although 'A feeling of hard times ... still pervades the major Latin American countries', on balance 'confidence is growing in the debt-restructuring process', and in the booming Latin American exports which were a complement to 'the US economic boom' (*ibid.*). Now the Baker initiative seemed to confirm such optimism (Morgan Guaranty Trust 1986). The context for Secretary Baker's address was a US economy at full capacity – a confident, Reaganite economy which seemed to have delivered a miracle to US citizens and which could now act as a locomotive for the rest of the world (and for the indebted countries in particular). The time was right to promise a less austere future for some indebted countries, to hold out the prospect of less protected markets in the industrial world, and to dangle the carrot of new bank loans as a reward for a continuing process of structural adjustment.

In March 1989 these carrots were defined anew when Secretary Brady spoke in support of a strategy of market-led revaluations and writedowns of debts outstanding. (By this time, the stock of commercial banks' claims on the Baker 17 countries had already fallen by more than $20 billion.) Following earlier speeches by President Mitterand of France, Chancellor Lawson of the UK, Japanese Finance Minister Miyazawa, and the Chairman of American Express, James Robinson, Secretary Brady was minded to build upon the officially sanctioned Bolivian buy-back scheme of 1988 and other well publicised developments in the secondary debt markets. Having made a ritual declaration that 'the fundamental principles of the current (Baker) strategy remain valid', Mr. Brady suggested that 'the path toward creditworthiness of severely indebted countries should involve debt and debt service reduction on a voluntary and case-by-case basis, in addition to rescheduling of principal and new money packages' (World Bank 1990: 21).

The main difference between the Brady initiative and 'the ad hoc debt reduction that had taken place until then through (a) market-based menu strategy was its inclusion of official support for debt and debt service reduction. The World Bank and the IMF were asked to provide funds for debt and debt service reduction operations for countries with high external debt burdens and strong adjustment programs' (*ibid.*). The expectation was that the IMF and the World Bank would commit resources to the Brady programme of the order of $20–25 billion over a three-year period from 1989. Japan was further expected to underwrite the Brady proposals – and further to socialise private bank debts – by committing up to $10 billion in cofinancing funds over a three- or four-year period. This was duly secured.

The Debt and Development Crisis of the 1980s

The socialisation of a good deal of private (especially US) bank debt is the first among many reasons for being sceptical of the standard narrative account of the debt crisis and of conventional procedures for dealing with that crisis. Notwithstanding a rhetoric of economic liberalisation and privatisation, it is clear that the debt crisis (so-called) has been policed mainly as a banking crisis and, secondarily, as an export crisis for some US companies used to doing business in Latin America. 'Development' has not been coupled to debt in quite the same way. Indeed, there is evidence that the debt crisis had been associated with *de facto* underdevelopment in many debtor countries. Such evidence is available in the form of official statistics (as with reference to GDP per capita, rates of public expenditure, the position of official reserves), and in the form of the telling prose style favoured by Susan George (amongst others: see also Altvater *et al.* 1991; Roddick 1988). In her book, *A Fate Worse Than Debt*, George recounts the plight of a Bolivian mother, Zona San José Carpinteros in La Paz, amidst the debt-induced evils of rising inflation and unemployment. Says the mother: 'Since everything is so expensive, I don't give my children breakfast any more. For lunch I give them a little rice soup. I don't buy sugar now that it has gone up. To eat, I have to make do any way I can, because the children can't get along without food. Us adults, we manage without when we have to. Sometimes I say to myself, "I'm going to give away my children to someone". But then I think of what my parents might do to me – that's what I'm afraid of' (George 1989: 147). This is what a 'lost decade of development' often means at the level of an individual household, and it is by no means a story confined to Bolivia or to Latin America. Many African countries were poorer in real terms (on a per capita basis) in 1990 than they were in

1960 (Onimode 1989). Their prospects for development have not been helped by an estimated net flow of resources from the indebted countries of more than $200 billion in the 1980s.

But what is to be done about this, and how and why? To begin to answer these questions we are compelled to offer a different narrative account of the debt-cum-development crises, and to establish that the economic, political and social costs associated with the debt management policies of the 1980s were needlessly high and unfairly so. This is not the place for a detailed exposition of such a narrative-argument (see Corbridge 1992). All I can offer here is a synopsis of the main areas of analysis which might be raised in such a discussion. They are three-fold:

Consider, first, the necessity of providing an alternative explanation of any sort. One strength of the prevailing orthodoxy on debt crisis management is that there is 'no alternative' to current policies. The IMF and the World Bank have both made it clear that: 'There is no viable alternative to adjustment' (World Bank 1987: 35). They have further argued that the debt crisis is (was?) likely to be of short duration. Throughout the 1980s the World Bank provided forecasts of world economic growth (and recovery) which ran consistently in excess of achieved rates of growth (Cole 1989). The Bank argued that precipitate actions were not required to cure the debt crisis; structural adjustment and world economic growth would provide the necessary and sufficient conditions for an end to localised and temporary crises of liquidity.

But there *are* alternatives to the prevailing orthodoxy (as changes and refinements within the orthodox view have themselves suggested). It might be that these alternatives are second-best or even unwieldy, but logically there are always alternative ways of running an economy and this needs to be clearly stated. One proposal which runs counter to the adjustment-containment package was put forward some years ago by Stephany Griffith-Jones and Osvaldo Sunkel. In their judgement, the debt crisis in Latin America stems from that continent's increasing, and increasingly dependent, integration into a world economy built around the expansion and privatisation of industrial and financial capitals. They argue that Latin America must reassert its own national and domestic economic agendas and should produce 'goods and services ... required by the majority sectors of the population, to improve their levels of living and their productivity' (Griffith-Jones and Sunkel 1986: 185). Still others have argued that indebted countries should default on their debts, using all available resources for local development initiatives (Payer 1991). Again, it matters less that such proposals are practicable (at this stage and for this first argument), than that they can be floated at all. One purpose of a focus on development ethics is to render problematic the proposition that there are no alternatives to a given form of social and economic organisation (and development).

Consider, next, the logic of structural adjustment and market-led economic recovery. The debt crisis of the 1980s was policed almost entirely on a country-by-country basis. Attempts to suggest that the debt crisis might signal a common crisis (Brandt 1983), or a crisis of global solvency, were strongly resisted by the creditor community. Individual countries, it was urged repeatedly, were suffering from temporary crises of liquidity brought on largely by local economic mismanagement and fiscal profligacy.

Now there is some truth to the argument, but consider also what is lost from view. Consider, for example, what might be called the macroeconomic and political implications of dealing with the debt-cum-banking crisis according to the principles of some on the New Right. Keynesian and Marxist critics have no difficulty in exposing the unhappy, if unintended, consequences of the conventional approach. In the case of the debtor countries such a formula is likely to lead to currency devaluations, local bank bailouts and a further socialisation of bank debt (ECLAC 1989) and rising rates of inflation and unemployment (Dornbusch and Edwards 1991). This cannot reasonably be considered an efficient economic outcome. (At any rate, the burden of proof should be on the proponents of structural adjustment *by austerity* to show that a given stream of potential future benefits, accruing to particular peoples in particular places over a given period of time, are greater than the present and future costs of such a process of adjustment. An attention to development ethics might suggest that real people in the present should not be condemned to further or more acute poverty and loss of power on the basis of abstract economic propositions about the future of an uncertain domestic and world economy.) It is not clear either how development is aided by selling abroad an excess of those products which ordinarily provide an individual family or country with a token or sign of its level of development. Nor is it clear that all debtor countries can run a trade surplus at the same time, especially when trade between the indebted countries has historically been very significant (Grimwade 1989).

In the case of creditor countries, there is reason to suppose that the imposition of strict financial disciplines in the indebted world works to promote unemployment and/or low growth in the manufacturing and (non-financial) services sectors of the developed world. Some estimates suggest that up to three million person-years of employment were lost in North America in the 1980s as a result of declining exports to the indebted countries. Great Britain, too, suffered a loss of exports to Latin America equivalent to 49 per cent in real terms between 1980 and 1983 (Marcel and Palma 1988: 389).

More serious still are the possible future trading implications of the debt crisis. In the 1980s Latin America's debtor countries were encouraged to run a collective trading surplus which in practice was absorbed mainly by the USA (and created largely by cutting back on imports). To continue to service a collective debt of almost one trillion US dollars, Latin America's debtors will have to generate a trading surplus equivalent to four or five percent of world trade. The problem is that, in the 1990s, the United States may itself be seeking to run a trade surplus of a not dissimilar magnitude (Corbridge and Agnew 1991; Lipietz 1989). The implications of such a scenario for Europe and Japan have not always been considered or understood.

In general terms, the implication is that individual initiatives for local debt management can portend wider instabilities at the level of international trade and capital flows. In Brandtian terms, the choice in an interdependent world economy may be between the recognition of shared problems and mutual interests or the prolongation of a common crisis. Orthodox 'accounting' procedures tend to underestimate the externalities associated with local containment and austerity programmes.

Thirdly, there is the matter of ethics and morality in a direct sense. Some on the New Right are opposed to a redistribution of resources either within or between countries if the income flows which presently exist have emerged by means of non-coercive market transactions (Nozick 1974). Some also maintain that a strategy of partial debt forgiveness is inconsistent with the requirement of international financial probity and the avoidance of moral hazard (Vaubel 1983). Bailing out indebted countries (and banks) is tantamount to throwing good money after bad; to rewarding the profligate while punishing those that have been prudent (like South Korea) or poor (like Bangladesh and Mali) (see Buiter and Srinivasan 1987). Peter Bauer maintains that debtor countries took out loans on a voluntary basis and in the knowledge that interest rates can go up as well as down. If the West has a moral duty to these countries, it is not to relieve them of any of the problems which they might now be facing. The West's duty is to encourage such countries to accept that individuals (and individual countries) are responsible for their own actions and resultant fates. Non-market writedowns of debt, or debt rollovers, are offensive morally, as well as being inflationary and economically counter-productive. Sadly, to date: 'Western governments have condoned Third World default and have even encouraged it by insisting on forbearance by both official and commercial creditors in the face of default, including default on very soft loans' (Bauer 1991: 63).

These arguments are not lightly made and nor should they be easily dismissed. (It should also be said that the IMF and the World Bank do not subscribe to such a stark moral prospectus; they are political actors bound to operate in the world as it now is.) Nevertheless, the effect of such arguments, and of policies enacted in part in accordance with them, is to hide from view two arguments of equal, if not greater moral force:

– is it reasonable, by virtue of structural adjustment, to condemn large numbers of people to a life devoid of some basic human needs?
– is it proper that the burdens of a market-led package of adjustment should fall most squarely upon the poor and the powerless of an indebted country when they were often not parties to, or major beneficiaries of, the 'profligacy' made possible by international credit money transfers?

In Rawlsian terms the answer to each question must be: 'no, it is neither fair nor reasonable'. John Rawls provides a theory of justice (Rawls 1971) which insists that 'freedom may never be sacrificed for an increase in material wellbeing' (Miller 1991: 422), but which also maintains that the interests of particular individuals should not be sacrificed to maximise an assumed aggregate welfare of a wider collectivity. His intervention in the field of American politics is thus of signal importance to the field of development ethics (albeit unintentionally), and, prospectively, to the case of the developing countries' debt crisis.

The Rawlsian theory of justice is a powerful exposition of the argument that 'there but for the grace of God go I'. Rawls forces us to put ourselves in the position of those who are less well off than ourselves for no good reason. Rawls does this by means of an appeal to the 'original position', or what he calls 'the veil of ignorance'. Imagine that the principles of a just society are to be drawn up by agents who are 'deprived of knowledge about their talents and abilities and about the place they occupy (and will occupy) in society' (Miller 1991: 422). Imagine, in other words, that the rich and the powerful are not already the rich and the powerful, and that the chances of becoming one of the rich and the powerful are far less than the chances of becoming one of the poor and the dispossessed. In such a situation – where on present odds one's chance of being born into a middle class family in the USA are much less than the chance of being born into destitution in the (indebted) developing world – the rational actor would want to re-arrange society so that at least minimal standards of freedom and livelihood are guaranteed for all. In this manner Rawls provides an account of a just society from first principles. Rawls presents an abstract model of justice which is based precisely upon a reasoned command to think that the needs and rights of distant strangers could easily – and but for the accident of birth – be the needs and rights of ourselves. In Rawlsian terms, the policing of the debt and development crisis of the 1980s and 1990s in terms of an overriding moral principle – in this case the principle of moral hazard – works to condemn fellow humans to forms of existence which few rational outsiders would be prepared to accept for themselves. It also fails to distinguish between the active and passive progenitors of the policies in which moral hazard is thought to reside. In practice, it ignores the actions of the private banks; it also ignores the decision of the US to force up interest rates from 1978.

A more reasonable policy of debt and development management would aim to ensure that repayments of debt are made only after present and future basic human needs have first been provided for in the indebted countries. Such a policy would also seek a balance in the burdens to be borne by the debtors and the creditors. As Carlos Diaz-Alejandro put it in 1984: 'Blaming victims is an appealing evasion of responsibility, especially when the victims are far from virtuous. But when sins are as heterogeneous as those of the Latin American regimes of the 1980s one wonders how well the exemplary mass punishment (structural adjustment) fits the alleged individual crime' (Diaz-Alejandro 1984: 335).

Development Ethics and Developmental Institutions

Diaz-Alejandro concludes his paper with some remarks on debt crisis management. Perhaps rather surprisingly, given the tenor of some of his remarks, he calls for a range of measures which are similar to those endorsed by his more conservative colleague, Jeffrey Sachs – a rather eclectic mix of 'better exchange rate management in the debtor countries, moderate IMF policies, faster OECD growth and modest systemic reform' as Sachs puts it (Sachs 1984: 394). That said, Diaz-Alejandro takes care to emphasise that the debt crisis is also a political crisis for most debtor countries. To the extent that private assets have been built up abroad by capital flight, these 'considerations indicate that the debt crisis is not just a North-South issue; for several Latin American countries it is also an issue of the distribution of domestic income and wealth' (Diaz-Alejandro 1984: 336).

I am sympathetic to the arguments set out by Diaz-Alejandro and to those related arguments and proposals set out by critics of a broadly Keynesian-Rawlsian persuasion (see Dornbusch 1985). I am even sympathetic in broad terms to Susan George's suggestion that the debt crisis must always be theorised in relation to questions of development and democracy. George still favours a strategy of debt repudiation, but she now recognises that this strategy is unlikely to work unless all countries agree on a total and collective repudiation of debts. Her Debt, Development and Democracy solution is thus a compromise. George writes that: 'The basis idea of a 3-D solution is that countries are allowed to pay back interest and principal over a long period of time in local currency, calculated so as not to create inflation. Their payments are credited to national development funds whose uses are determined by authentic representatives of the people working with those of the state. For the creditors, 3-D would come to be the same thing as cancellation, since the local currency would be used internally' (George 1989: 244). George insists that her proposals are not utopian. The international financial system can now bear the costs of cancellation, and in the North 'environmentalists, peace activists, women's movements, trade unions, farmers and export-oriented industries ... all have an interest in the changes that 3-D would encourage' (*ibid.*).

But is this the case, and what is hidden (if anything) in this formulation? What are the inherent problems in approaching the debt crisis in terms of development ethics and (for example) a Rawlsian theory of justice? Thus far, we have suggested: (i) that orthodox debt management policies in the 1980s were probably unfair in Rawlsian terms; (ii) that the orthodox policies of the 1980s might not have been sensible in their own terms – that is, in terms of promoting macro-economic efficiency and stability; and (iii) that there are alternatives to past and present policies for debt crisis management. Less easy to suggest, however, are the institutional forms in and through which these alternative policies might be put into operation (and argued for). In terms of justice, also, it is one thing to specify social and economic arrangements which are 'unjust' to some degree, and quite another to determine how a more just society should be constructed. There are two particular problems associated with using a Rawlsian framework for an account of development ethics. First, the work of John Rawls was written specifically for an American audience. Some might doubt that its logic can reasonably be extended to a global scale. Communitarians would take this line, as would others who are sceptical of the idea of a global moral community (Little 1982). (Proponents of 'global Rawlsianism' would counter that moral communities cannot be defined by national boundaries in an age of increased globalisation – see Beitz 1991. Second, Rawls's account of a just society is compatible with a wide range of social and economic institutions ranging from market socialism to a 'market economy in which material inequalities serve as incentives, increasing the stock of goods available for distribution' – see Miller 1991: 422–3. The latter specification of a just society is an important counter to those who argue that Rawlsian ethics are too sensitive to the fair carving up of a given-sized pie, and not sufficiently attentive to the need to increase the size of the pie at a time of mounting economic 'wants' – see Kirzner 1989.)

These issues need rather more thought than many on the centre-left are prepared to grant them and they strike at the heart of a new concern for development ethics (in the abstract). It is one thing to propose a cancellation or partial writedown of debts outstanding for reasons of equity and efficiency, and quite another to specify the wherewithals of such policies and their likely effects on particular places and target groups. Such policies would not be acceptable if they simply transferred further large sums of money to unaccountable elites in some indebted countries; nor would they always have the support of those countries and peoples who do not stand to benefit from such a transfer of resources. Such a policy might also be counter-productive if it could be shown (as perhaps it could be shown for the years 1982–3) that a generalised debt default would destabilise the international monetary system and thus plunge the world economy into a still deeper depression. Moreover, if democracy is not in place in a given indebted country (*pace* George), it might be that debt relief should only be offered in return for a relaxation of local control over a given space–economy. In this manner, the whole question of sovereignty – which itself is not incidental to development ethics – is thrown into sharp relief. Finally, debt relief leaves open the response that such actions betoken an unhelpful short-termism. Keynesians might believe that in the long run we are all dead, but, equally, most on the New Right profess to be thinking long-term (if not at a wide angle) and with regard to the attainment of a state of economic equilibrium which is not unstable in the short run. Put more simply, they would need to be assured that the eventual costs of behaving more 'fairly' now would not be increased and expanded economic costs and instabilities later on. 'Fairness' is not an easy concept to specify.

Conclusion

All the same, I am afraid of 'principle'. Ever since 1918 we (the UK), alone amongst the nations of the world, have been the slaves of 'sound' general principles regardless of particular circumstances. We have behaved as though the intermediate 'short periods' of the economist between one position of equilibrium and another really were short, whereas they can be long enough – and have been before now – to encompass the decline and downfall of nations ... Wasn't it Lord Melbourne who said that 'No statesman ever does anything really foolish except on principle'?

(Keynes in 1930; Keynes 1978: 379).

This chapter has attempted only to raise certain issues for debate and to illustrate some of the strengths and weaknesses of a development ethics perspective with regard to the specific case of the international debt crisis. It has not offered a consistent or a concerted discussion of the practical problems facing debt crisis managers, politicians and activists. If a conclusion can be drawn, it is only the simple one that a concern for 'development ethics' is bound to throw up as many questions as it is able to suggest answers. Ironically, perhaps, this returns us to Maynard Keynes and to his principled opposition to most 'timeless' principles.

Most proponents of development ethics would not be surprised by this. Once we give up a search for the millennium – for freely functioning markets or a socialist paradise – complexity and contradiction are seen to be the order of the day. All that development ethics can help us do is to accept this fact, while recognising that some contradictions and trade-offs may be more acceptable (for some peoples and some places over a given period of time) than some others.

The demise of grand theories in development studies need not shunt us towards either a state of despair or a committed local activism. As the example of the debt crisis makes clear, the empowerment of local peoples will usually depend on actions taken elsewhere by distant strangers and upon arguments and voices raised against those practices which *are* radically disempowering. A consideration of development ethics (per-haps in combination with 'grand theory') begins to allow us to combine the local with the global; to do what the old Oxfam poster so neatly prescribed – to think and act both globally and locally. In the case of the debt and development crisis, this means interrogating present policy arrangements to test their fairness or unfairness, and then, in the light of this, to begin to specify some combination of institutions and processes through which less unfair outcomes might be effected. Development ethics also puts a premium upon intellectual and policy honesty. Since there are always dilemmas associated with development, it is important that the costs of any given process of 'development' are specified as clearly as possible and are passed on to others to interrogate anew. Development ethics is not about certainty; at least not about certainty as Mr Wroe would have expected it, and wished for.

Relevant Literature

Adams, W. 1990. *Green Development: Environment and Sustainability in the Third World*. London, Routledge.

Altvater, E., K. Hubner, J. Lorentzen & R. Rojas (eds.). 1991. *The Poverty of Nations: a Guide to the Debt Crisis from Argentina to Zaire*. London, Zed Books.

Baker, J. 1985. Statement before the Joint Annual Meeting of the IMF and the World Bank, Seoul, South Korea, 8 Oct.

Bauer, P. 1991. *The Development Frontier: Essays in Applied Economics*. Hemel Hempstead, Harvester Wheatsheaf.

Beitz, C. 1991. 'Sovereignty and Morality in International Affairs', in D. Held (ed.) *Political Theory Today*, pp. 236–54. Cambridge, Polity Press.

Brandt, W. (Chairman of the Brandt Commission). 1983. *Common Crisis, North-South: Cooperation for World Recovery*. London, Pan Books.

Buiter, W. & T. Srinivasan. 1987. 'Rewarding the Profligate and Punishing the

Prudent and Poor: Some Recent Proposals for Debt Relief'. *World Development* 15, pp. 411–17.

Cole, S. 1989. 'World Bank Forecasts and Planning in the Third World'. *Environment and Planning A*, 21, pp. 175–96.

Corbridge, S. 1992. *Debt and Development*. Oxford, Blackwell.

— 1993. 'Marxisms, Modernities and Moralities: Development Praxis and the Claims of Distant Strangers'. In D. Booth (ed.), *New Directions in Social Development Research*, Cambridge, Cambridge University Press (forthcoming).

— & J. Agnew. 1991. 'The US Trade and Budget Deficits in Global Perspective: An Essay in Geopolitical-Economy'. *Society and Space* 9, pp. 71–90.

Crocker, D. 1991. 'Towards Development Ethics'. *World Development* 19, pp. 457–83.

Diaz-Alejandro, C. 1984. 'Latin American Debt: I Don't Think We Are in Kansas Any More'. *Brookings Papers on Economic Activity* 2, pp. 335–89.

Dornbusch, R. 1985. 'Policy and Performance Links between LDC Debtors and Industrial Countries'. *Brookings Papers on Economic Activity* 2, pp. 303–56.

— & S. Edwards (eds.). 1991. *The Macroeconomics of Populism in Latin America*. Chicago, University of Chicago Press/NBBR.

Economic Commission for Latin America and the Caribbean (ECLAC). 1989. *Economic Survey of Latin America and the Caribbean*. Santiago, United Nations.

Friedmann, J. 1992. *Empowerment: the Politics of Alternative Development*. Oxford, Blackwell.

George, S. 1989. *A Fate Worse than Debt*. Harmondsworth, Penguin Books.

Goodman, D. & M. Redclift. 1991. *Refashioning Nature: Food, Ecology and Culture*. London, Routledge.

Goulet, D. 1989. *Incentives for Development*. New York, New Horizons.

Griffith-Jones, S. & O. Sunkel. 1986. *Debt and Development Crises in Latin America: the End of an Illusion*. Oxford, Clarendon Press.

Grimwade, N. 1989. *International Trade: New Patterns of International Trade. Production and Investment*. London, Routledge.

Guha, R. 1989. *The Unquiet Woods: Ecological Change and Peasant Resistance in the Himalaya*. Delhi, Oxford University Press.

Hector, G. 1985. 'Third World Debt: the Bomb is Defused'. *Fortune* 18 February, pp. 24–9.

Keynes, J.M. 1978. *The Collected Writings of John Maynard Keynes*. Vol. XX, London, Macmillan.

Kirzner, I. 1989. *Discovery, Capitalism, and Distributive Justice*. Oxford, Blackwell.

Lipietz, A. 1989. 'The Debt Problem: European Integration and the Net Phase of World Crisis'. *New Left Review* 178, pp. 37–56.

Little, I. 1982. *Economic Development*. New York, Basic Books.

Mann, M. 1986. *The Sources of Social Power*. Vol. 1, Cambridge, Cambridge University Press.

Marcel, M. & G. Palma. 1988. 'Third World Debt and its Effects on the British Economy'. *Cambridge Journal of Economics* 12, pp. 361–400.

Miller, D. 1991. 'John Rawls'. In D. Miller (ed.), *The Blackwell Encyclopaedia of Political Thought*, pp. 422–3, Oxford, Blackwell.

Morgan Guaranty Trust. 1986. 'The Baker Initiative: the Perspective of the Banks'. *World Financial Markets* February.

Nozick, R. 1974. *Anarchy, State and Utopia*. Oxford, Blackwell.

O'Neill, O. 1986. *Faces of Hunger: an Essay on Poverty, Development and Justice*. London, Allen & Unwin.

— 1991. 'Transnational Justice'. In D. Held (ed.), *Political Theory Today*, pp. 276–304, Cambridge, Polity.

Onimode, B. (ed.). 1989. *The IMF, the World Bank and the African Debt*. Two vols., London, Zed Books.

Payer, C. 1991. *Lent and Lost: Foreign Credit and the Third World Debt Crisis*. London, Zed Books.

Peet, R. 1991. *Global Capitalism: Theories of Societal Evolution*. London, Routledge.

Pieterse, J. 1991. 'Dilemmas of Development Discourse and the Crisis of Developmentalism and the Comparative Method'. *Development and Change* 22, pp. 5–29.

Rawls, J. 1971. *A Theory of Justice*. Oxford, Oxford University Press.

Roddick, J. 1988. *The Dance of the Millions: Latin America and the Debt Crisis*. London, Latin America Bureau.

Rogers, J. 1991. *Mr. Wroe's Virgins*. London, Faber & Faber.

Sachs, J. 1984. 'External Debt and Macroeconomic Performance in Latin America and East Asia'. *Brookings Papers on Economic Activity* 2, pp. 523–74.

Selowsky, M. & H. van der Tak. 1986. 'The Debt Problem and Growth'. *World Development* 14, pp. 1107–24.

Sen, A.K. 1984. *Resources, Values and Development*. Oxford, Blackwell.

— 1989. 'Food and Freedom'. *World Development* 17, 769–81.

Shiva, V. 1991. *The Violence of the Green Revolution*. London, Zed Books.

Toye, J. 1987. *Dilemmas of Development: Reflections of the Counter-Revolution in Development Theory and Policy*. Oxford, Blackwell.

Trinh, T. Minh-ha. 1989. *Woman, Native, Other: Writing Postcoloniality and Feminism*. Bloomington, Indiana University Press.

Vaubel, R. 1983. 'The Moral Hazard of IMF Lending'. *The World Economy* 6, pp. 291–303.

World Bank. 1987. *World Development Report, 1987*. Washington, The World Bank.

— 1989, 1990. *World Debt Tables*. Washington, The World Bank.

7

Exploring Development Interfaces:
From the Transfer of Knowledge
to the Transformation of Meaning

by Norman Long and Magdalena Villarreal

Introduction

The Issue of Theory for Practice

A major preoccupation of those working in the sociology of development is how to resolve the relationship between theory and practice, often depicted in terms of the gulf that exists between theorists, who are locked into their 'ivory towers', and practitioners, who 'get their hands dirty'. This same general concern is expressed by Scott and Shore (1979) in their book *Why Sociology does not apply*, where they contrast two distinct kinds of knowledge: 'knowledge for understanding' as against 'knowledge for action'.

In responding to this preoccupation, it is not enough simply to argue for an 'enlightenment model' which sees theoretical work as influencing practitioners and policy-makers indirectly through the ways in which new concepts and interpretations of social process percolate into society at large, thus shaping the thinking of lay and professional persons alike.[1] We must take the implied critique of the gap between theory and practice and the issues this entails more seriously, especially if you work, as we do, at a university where 'intervention' is always placed high on the agenda.

We must struggle then to achieve a better integration of theoretical understanding and practical concerns, although we should not expect the divide between these to fall neatly into the field of 'theory and research' as against 'policy and intervention'. Obviously policy models and measures are themselves underpinned, either explicitly or implicitly, by certain theoretical interpretations and methodological strategies, just as theories are themselves laden with evaluative judgements and decisions. A first priority therefore is that of obtaining a better theoretical grasp of the problems of planned intervention and social change. But in order to do this, we must, as we have argued elsewhere (Long and Van der Ploeg

1989; Villarreal 1990), expose the limitations of certain sociological orthodoxies as well as existing 'interventionist' models. This is particularly urgent since we are presently confronted with, on the one hand, a resurgence of simplistic systems thinking and, on the other, a stress on 'ethnographic particularism' associated with the deconstructionist mood of the post-modern era.

One way forward, we suggest, is through the development of an actor-oriented approach which builds upon theoretical work aimed at reconciling structure and actor perspectives. This point of view was advanced in *An Introduction to the Sociology of Rural Development* (Long 1977; also Long 1984), but since then a number of relevant general theoretical studies dealing with issues of structure and 'agency', and the link between so-called 'micro' and 'macro' phenomena, have appeared (see, for example, Giddens 1979, 1984, 1987; Habermas 1987; Knorr-Cetina and Cicourel 1981; Alexander *et al.* 1987; Fielding 1988). These and similar contributions have stimulated the development of a more sophisticated treatment of social change which emphasises the interplay and mutual determination of 'internal' and 'external' factors and relationships, and which provides accounts of the life-worlds, strategies and rationalities of the different social actors involved.[2] Alongside these theoretical advances has emerged the growing need to identify a set of appropriate analytical concepts and a methodology for exploring intervention processes that would prove useful not only to the researcher but also to the field practitioner (Long and Long 1992). The present chapter is a modest attempt to respond to this challenge.

During the late 1970s and early 1980s, a number of social scientists turned towards neo-Marxist models for an explanation of the nature and consequences of uneven development. While this gave some new insights and a framework within which they could order their data and experiences, it did not in the end provide much practical help to those in the 'frontline' of planned development who were confronted with the day-to-day dilemmas of implementing policy and of interacting with so-called 'target' and 'non-target' groups. Many of the abstractions used were far removed from the detailed workings of everyday social practice and failed to explain the differential outcomes of structural change. Hence, while 'class struggle' and 'surplus extraction' might characterise some important features of capitalist intervention, they were seldom enough to explain the particular soical configurations and subjectivities that emerged. This approach in fact promoted a somewhat pessimistic view of the possibilities of initiating change 'from below', through the actions of local groups themselves or by means of outside planned interventions aimed at increasing the claim-making capacities of local people.

It is here that new types of theorisation and field methodologies based upon an actor-oriented approach can make an important contribution, though we must avoid setting ourselves up as the new 'gurus' of interventionism with yet another prefabricated solution to the problems of planned development. The neo-Marxist theoretical bubble may now have burst but we must guard against replacing it with the search for similar generic models of change. The essence of an actor-oriented approach is that its concepts are grounded in the everyday life experiences and consciousness of ordinary men and women.

In order to explore these issues more closely, we have chosen to focus upon one important field of application, namely that centring on the processes of knowledge acquisition, utilisation and transformation. Such processes are at the core of programmes of planned intervention and form the critical set of problems that define what is called 'extension science' (Röling 1988b).

The Systems Model in Agricultural Extension

While extension was for many years associated with Rogerian models of the adoption and diffusion of innovations (Rogers 1962, third edition 1983; Rogers and Shoemaker 1971) and with the Land Grant type of applied rural sociology (Lionberger 1960), over the last 10 years or so this has given way to a more thoroughgoing application of communication and systems theory (Beal *et al.* 1986). This is signalled by the mushrooming of research dealing with farmer knowledge and with the complex set of links between research establishments, extension services and the farming population. Simultaneously these developments have been accompanied by a growing interest in 'farming systems analysis', which is aimed at developing a multi-level, interdisciplinary approach to understanding farming practice, placed within the context of the wider ecological, technical, economic and social contraints and in relation to technological change in agriculture (Collinson 1982; Hildebrand 1981; Fresco 1986).

Most of these new-style extension, agronomy and rural sociological studies have been grounded in terms of systems thinking based on four central concepts: emergence, hierarchy, communication and control. It is argued that the interaction of elements within a system gives way to emergent properties which are irreducible, thus producing a 'whole' that 'is larger than the parts'. This whole is composed of different types of sub-systems which nest within each other and are functionally and hierarchically interrelated. Fresco and Westphal, for example, define a system as 'an arrangement of components or parts that interact according to some [specific] process and transform inputs into outputs'. They claim that 'agriculture can be described as a hierarchy of systems, ranging from the cell at the lowest level, through the plant or animal organs, the whole plant or animal, the crop or herd, the field or pasture, and the farm, to complex ecosystems such as the village and watershed culminating in the agricultural sector at the highest level' (1988: 401). Another element described as crucial is communication, which is necessary for purposes of regulation and control (Checkland 1981: 83). All systems are said to contain within them factors of control which can be manipulated to achieve desired change.

It is our view that such systems models are basically inadequate for developing a sound understanding of change processes and do not come to terms with important and complex issues involved in knowledge processes. We aim to show this through developing a critique of existing attempts to theorise and investigate the nature of agricultural knowledge processes and through elucidating the advantages of adopting an actor-oriented approach instead. This will take up the first part of the chapter.

The second part builds upon this argument by showing how one might extend the analysis of knowledge processes to cover the organisational and strategic elements involved in rural development interfaces. Interfaces are characterised by discontinuities in interests, values and power, and their dynamic entails negotiation, accommodation and the struggle over definitions and boundaries. A detailed study of them provides insights into the processes by which policy is transformed, how 'empowerment' and room for manoeuvre is created by both intervenors and 'clients', and how persons are enrolled in the 'projects' of others through the use of metaphors and images of development.

The Legacy of Havelock's Communication Model

Twenty years ago, Havelock (1969) suggested that the essence of knowledge utilisation is the linkage between two social systems, one of which is faced with a problem and the other with delineating options that facilitate its resolution. Since then this basic idea has been further elaborated and developed by himself and others in an attempt to conceptualise in more detail the nature of such linkage processes.

In 1986, Havelock provided a fuller explication of the critical elements involved, arguing that the descriptive term 'link' implies a continuous loop which forms part of 'a chain, a sequence of entities connected to one another in a series and serving a common purpose' and where each link has two sides that interpenetrate other links or elements of the same chain – in other words, what one might visualise as some kind of coupling device, such as that linking the individual carriages of a train. On top of this coupling image, Havelock adds a radio signalling metaphor when he describes knowledge utilisation links as actively engaged in the 'transfer of complex messages' between 'senders' and 'receivers'. He suggests that such dialogue or exchange is based essentially upon the movement of resources from a 'resourcer system' in an attempt to respond to certain needs emanating from a 'user system', although at the same time resource users 'stimulate the problem-solving processes of resource systems, at least at some level' (Havelock 1986: 228). Both images of course stress the discreteness and integrity of the elements or 'systems' that are articulated.

Havelock goes on to maintain that what 'is special about linkage theory is its explanation of how altogether new connections are formed, connections that extend perhaps to far-away resources and far-away users outside the normal environment. What we are looking at is the way in which one system can send messages that penetrate the self-protective layers and become planted in the on-going routines and problem-solving processes of the other' (Havelock 1986: 227).

Although some recognition of actor/interpretive processes is smuggled in, Havelock concludes by arguing that linkage is a natural process, but that it is 'generally slow, inefficient, error-prone, and costly. Furthermore, there are many links along potential knowledge-use chains that are either dangerously weak or missing altogether. That is why there is a great need to provide specialists in various linkage processes at strategic points along the knowledge chain' (Havelock 1986: 234).

This leads him to argue that machine and human interventions designed at improving the flow of messages are essential: hence the need for what have been variously called relay stations, transformers and synthesisers, as well as extension agents, animators (i.e., user system mobilisers), and what he characterises as 'linkage catalysts' or 'linkage process facilitators'.

Havelock's communication model remains a central orienting image for looking at knowledge dissemination and utilisation processes, forming the conceptual bedrock of much recent work on knowledge systems. For example, the model of agricultural knowledge and information systems promoted by Röling (1988b: 30) and Engel (Röling and Engel 1990) distinguishes between research, extension and farmer networks and institutions ('sub-systems') that are interlinked through a flow of information and other resources to form a synergic whole. Linkage mechanisms, which Röling describes, in his earlier work, as devices for bridging 'the gap between components of the system', stimulate communication between them, but because of certain resistances to the smooth flow of information, intervention by '*knowledge managers*' is also required 'to nudge [them] ... into compatible and complementary system roles'. Such intervention focuses upon 'institutional calibration' wherein the 'institutions can be compared to cogs in a gear box: each cog transforms knowledge up- or down-stream' (Röling

1988a: 54). In this way, Röling adds a further metaphor to the picture: this time a mechanical engineering one.

More recent contributions by Röling and Engel (1990) have softened up 'hard systems' thinking and imagery characteristic of earlier formulations. In harmony with Checkland (1985, 1981), they propose a 'soft systems methodology' which adopts a more inductive approach to systems modelling.

Checkland proposes a methodology based on 'the view that social reality is not a "given" but is a process in which an ever-changing social world is continuously recreated by its members' (Checkland 1981: 20). In an attempt to avoid the teleological trap of predefining 'system goals', the focus of systems research, he argues, should be 'problem situations in which there are felt to be unstructured problems, ones in which the designation of objectives is itself problematic' (Checkland 1981: 155). The first step then involves a detailed depiction of the social situation and circumstances, leading to the identification of the critical problems facing the actors and to the use of systems concepts to delineate and prioritise them. On the basis of this, one devises a series of procedures whereby the actors and researcher participate in the construction of a systems model and 'make joint decisions in order to enhance the emergent properties of their human activity system' (Röling and Engel 1990: 9). Accordingly, gaps in communication (missing links), latent conflicts, lack of access to critical resources (especially information), problems of coordination and task differentiation, and poor management practice can be exposed and plans laid to correct them. Once such 'pathologies' (Röling 1988: 39–41) are detected, it is a question of making the right choices, of identifying the control variables and designing a control strategy to correct them.

Knowledge as an Encounter of Horizons

Recently researchers have pinpointed certain critical limitations in this linkage approach, or what Dissanayake (1986: 280) has designated 'the transportational paradigm', to understanding knowledge processes. The model assumes that the process of knowledge dissemination/utilisation involves the transfer of a body of knowledge from one individual or social unit to another, rather than adopting a more dynamic view that acknowledges the joint creation of knowledge by both disseminators and users. This latter interpretation depicts knowledge as arising from an encounter of horizons, since the processing and absorption of new items of information and new discursive or cognitive frames can only take place on the basis of already existing stocks of knowledge and evaluative modes, which are themselves reshaped by the communicative experience. Moreover, although knowledge dissemination/creation is in essence an interpretative and cognitive process entailing the bridging of the gap between a familiar world and a less familiar (or even alien) set of meanings, knowledge is built upon the accumulated social experience, commitments and culturally-acquired dispositions of the actors involved.

Hence 'communicative action is not only a [cognitive] process of reaching understanding; in coming to an understanding about something in the world, actors are at the same time taking part in interactions through which they develop, confirm, and renew their memberships in social groups and their own identities. Communicative actions are not only processes of interpretation in which cultural knowledge is 'tested against the world'; they are at the same time processes of social integration and socialisation' (Habermas 1987: 39).

Processes of knowledge dissemination/creation simultaneously imply, therefore, several interconnected elements: actor strategies and capacities for drawing upon existing knowledge repertoires and absorbing new information, validation processes whereby newly introduced information and its sources are judged acceptable and useful or contested, and various transactions involving the exchange of specific material and symbolic benefits. Implicit in all this is the fact that the generation and utilisation of knowledge is not merely a matter of instrumentalities, technical efficiencies, or hermeneutics (i.e., the mediation of the understandings of others through the theoretical interpretation of our own), but involves aspects of control, authority and power that are embedded in social relationships. It is for this reason that there are likely to be striking dissonances between the different categories of actors involved in the production, dissemination and utilisation of knowledge, although, as several studies of 'experimenting' farmers (e.g., Richards 1985; Box 1987; Rhoades and Bebbington 1988) have convincingly shown, it is unlikely that the critical social divisions will coincide neatly with the distinctions between knowledge 'producers', 'disseminators' and 'users'. A recent study on the use of information technology (i.e., computerised production models) among Dutch farmers, for example, argues that the category of 'users' must be extended beyond farmers-as-clients to cover also government agencies and farmers' organisations wishing to use the technology to improve their competitiveness vis-à-vis other producer groups, to researchers and extension workers who deploy it to promote their own models of farming, and to agro-industrial enterprises that seek to tie customers to their business interests (Leeuwis 1991). Leeuwis's data suggest that conceptualisations of 'information needs' in terms of information technology are often problematic, as they are viewed as 'static', as if they could be 'predicted in advance and relate[d] to formal decision making models'. Dutch cucumber growers, he claims, choose a specific software programme considering all sorts of 'context' situations, such as solidarity between peripheral groups, personal ties, group composition and the need to avoid isolation (Leeuwis and Arkesteyn 1991).

This case lends support to the argument that so long as we conceptualise the issues of knowledge dissemination/utilisation simply in terms of 'linkage' concepts, without giving sufficient attention to human agency and the transformation of meaning at the point of intersection between different actors' life-worlds, and without analysing the social interactions involved, we will have missed the significance of knowledge itself. Our guiding notions, we suggest, should be, *discontinuity* not linkage, and *transformation* not transfer of meaning. Knowledge emerges as a product of the interaction and dialogue between specific actors. It is also multi-layered (there always exists a multiplicity of possible frames of meaning) and *fragmentary* and *diffuse* rather than unitary and systematised. Not only is it unlikely therefore that different parties (such as farmers, extensionists and researchers) would share the same priorities and parameters of knowledge, but one would also expect 'epistemic' communities (i.e., those that share roughly the same sources and modes of knowledge) to be differentiated internally in terms of knowledge repertoires and application. Therefore, engineering the creation of the conditions under which a *single* knowledge system (involving mutually beneficial exchanges and flows of information between the different actors) could emerge seems unattainable; and, if indeed one did succeed, this would be at the expense of innovativeness and adaptability to change, both of which depend upon the diversity and fluidity of knowledge rather than on integration and systematisation.

Discontinuities and Accommodations at Knowledge Interfaces
In order to explore these issues in more depth it is necessary to develop an analysis of '*interface situations*'. We define a social interface as a critical point of intersection between different social systems, fields or levels of social order where structural discontinuities, based upon differences of normative value and social interest, are most likely to be found (Long 1989).

Interface studies then are essentially concerned with the analysis of the *discontinuities* in social life. Such discontinuities are characterised by discrepancies in values, interests, knowledge and power. Interfaces typically occur at points where different, and often conflicting, life-worlds or social fields intersect. More concretely, they characterise social situations (what Giddens calls 'locales') wherein the interactions between actors become oriented around the problem of devising ways of 'bridging', accommodating to, or struggling against each other's different social and cognitive worlds. Interface analysis aims to elucidate the types of social discontinuities present in such situations and to characterise the different kinds of organisational and cultural forms that reproduce or transform them. Although the word 'interface' tends to convey the image of some kind of two-sided articulation or confrontation, interface situations are much more complex and multiple in nature.[3]

The interactions between government or outside agencies involved in implementing particular development programmes and the so-called recipients of the farming population cannot be adequately understood through the use of generalised conceptions such as 'state-peasant relations' or by resorting to normative concepts such as 'local partici-pation'. These interactions must be analysed as part of the ongoing processes of negotiation, adaptation and transfer of meaning that take place between the specific actors concerned. Interface analysis, which concentrates upon analysing critical junctures or arenas involving differences of normative value and social interest, entails not only understanding the struggles and power differentials taking place between the parties involved, but also an attempt to reveal the dynamics of cultural accommodation that makes it possible for the various 'world views' to interact.

This is a difficult research topic but one which, we believe, is central to understanding the intended and unintended results of planned inter-vention carried out 'from above' by public authorities or development agencies or initiated 'from below' by diverse local interests.

Some of the complexities involved in the interaction of governmental agencies with local groups are explored in the following three cases, which illustrate how the understanding of different (and possibly conflicting) forms of knowledge and ideology is central to the analysis of rural development.

The first concerns an extended Mexican case study (Arce and Long 1987) which focuses upon the dilemmas of Roberto, a *técnico* who tries to bridge the gap between the interests of peasant producers and the administrative structure and its priorities. As a *técnico*, Roberto was the 'frontline' implementor of SAM (Mexican Food System, a national programme which aimed at providing a degree of 'capitalisation' to rural producers of basic staples) in direct and regular interaction with his client population. He was expected to follow certain administrative procedures in the implementation of the programme. At the same time, however, he accumulated experience in dealing both with the demands of the admin-istrative system and its routines, and with those of his peasant clients.

The *técnico*'s involvement with these two contrasting, and often conflicting, social worlds produces a body of knowledge based upon individual experience which leads him to devise his own strategies of intervention in both the village and official administrative arenas.

Although it might appear that such strategies are highly idiosyncratic, being based upon the chronology of experience of particular individuals, in fact they are shaped by the possibilities for manoeuvre and discourse that already exist within the two arenas and by the dynamics of the structural contexts within which the different parties interact. The case shows how these different parties or social categories develop their own everyday shared understandings or models for action that originate from and acquire their potency and legitimation through social interaction and confrontation with opposing views and forms of organisation. The *técnico* described could not simply escape these influences and con- straints by attempting to ignore their existence, and if he did try to do so, he would lose legitimacy as a *técnico* in the eyes of both peasants and bureaucrats.

He launches a criticism of the shortcomings of the SAM and gives recognition to administrative malpractice. However, the end result is that he is labelled a 'troublemaker' (*un grilloso*) and sent to a special 'troublemakers unit' (i.e., to an isolated or 'problematic' zone) for remedial treatment. His lack of success in persuading his administrative boss to accept his solution for bridging the gap between peasant and government interests has the further repercussion that the peasants could use his case to confirm and reinforce their existing model of government practice and personnel. Hence their experience with this particular *técnico* refurbishes their beliefs in how the state works, although this same set of events may later also be used to justify further attempts to restructure the interface between them and intervening agencies and interests. The situation also becomes an important factor in the repro- duction of their particular livelihood strategies, which they effectively conceal from government, and in the reproduction of their own diverse configurations of knowledge. The combined effect of these various processes is to keep the social worlds of peasants and bureaucrats in opposition through the linking of contrasting everyday knowledge configurations and through the mutual generation of socially-constructed systems of ignorance.

The interaction and accommodation between world views entailing muffled and overt power processes as well as the interweaving of knowledge networks can be observed in a case study carried out in Mexico concerning a group of women beekeepers (see Long and Villarreal 1989; Villarreal 1990) organised as an Agro-Industrial Unit for Peasant Women. The group was formed upon state initiative, following a recently established law which stipulated the creation of peasant women's enterprises. Although each of the women attribute a different meaning to their participation in the beekeeping project and to the benefits they might procure from it, their interests are intertwined at certain points, addressing issues relating not only to the project itself, but to household strategies, to relations within their kin networks, etc. Thus, the enterprise comprises shared as well as conflicting definitions by the group members, involving matters such as the size of the enterprise (this was crucial as to whether it was a complementary or central activity for the women), the relations they assumed with groups and institutions outside the village, but also their self-definition as beekeepers, as women entrepreneurs or as housewives. The women struggled together against male villagers who labelled them lazy and irresponsible towards household chores, redoubling their efforts to care for their children and husbands. They contested the ideas of ministry officers who pressed them to enlarge their enterprise and to enter into the 'men's world of business'. However, during the process of interaction with each other, with their families and other people from the village, as well as with 'outside' intervenors from the ministry and even with us as researchers, the boundaries of the project and their roles as women in the face of it were constantly redefined. This redefinition involved not only their aims as beekeepers, but their prospects and projects as women in other fields of their everyday lives.

Our third case concerns a recent study of technological change (Hawkins 1991) which shows how issues of 'knowledge transfer' also necessitate a careful analysis of the interests and strategies pursued by those who produce, sell and/or promote technologies. The case suggests how we might integrate such political and economic dimensions into the analysis of agricultural knowledge processes.

Hawkins's study focuses on dairy and potato production in Cheshire, exploring the following issues: the sources of funding and direction of agricultural research in these fields over the past decade, the dissemination of new technologies from manufacturers to individual farmers, and the types of *interface networks* that emerge within these two contrasting commodity complexes, as well as the ways in which farmers integrate new technologies into farm production. Hawkins argues that new technologies have a dual nature: they are both a product or input into production and an information flow concerned with promoting a particular technological rationale. Technology development and dissemination is managed and shaped by specific public and private interests and is influenced by prevailing policy discourse and by market possibilities. As a result, the rate and direction of technological change varied, for example, between dairying (which tended to be production-oriented) and potato production (which was primarily market-oriented).

However, Hawkins maintains that it is crucial to 'disaggregate' these various sets of interests impinging upon the farm by identifying the particular social actors involved in the process. This leads her to isolate important differences in the commodity complexes and interface networks for milk and potatoes. The provision of technology to the farm and the networks and the channels through which this was achieved showed how the farm itself was enclosed within sets of interlinked agents (providing inputs and advice and organising outputs) that took somewhat different forms depending on the commodity complex. Whereas the potato complex was found to be highly integrated both vertically – with processors and prepackers also selling seed and providing advice – and horizontally – with agents selling combinations of inputs – the milk complex was rather segregated, with little evidence of vertical or horizontal integration for products. The study of interface networks highlighted three other interesting aspects: first, far from being in powerful market positions, agribusiness agents faced uncertain and constrained markets; second, locality was important, since farmers obtained many inputs from the nearby general merchant; and third, the offer of technical advice to farmers was a strategy for intensifying the link since as production became more technically complicated so farmers felt the need for more advice. Hence good technical advice was considered by agribusiness as a way of increasing farmers' loyalty: for example, many dairy farmers favoured ICI fertilisers which gave them access to a number of services from the company.

Technological change was not only important therefore at a product level but also through its advisory, or as Benvenuti (1975) terms it, its technico-administrative character, although as Hawkins shows later in her analysis of how farmers negotiate a degree of autonomy in managing technology, commodity networks and farm production, agribusiness is never able to completely undermine the independent decision-making capacity of farmers nor destroy the heterogeneity of farm enterprise, even within the same commodity complex. Even if farmers' decisions are influenced to a considerable extent by the ideas of their advisors, any such advice is, of course, filtered through the farmers' technological system and their own life-worlds. In this way there is what one might call 'an internalisation of externalities'. As Hawkins neatly puts it (1991: 279): 'The interface networks are sites for the dynamics of agribusiness extending markets and technical control to farmers, and [of] farmers reacting by adapting the offered technologies to suit themselves, shaping the networks and relating their actions perhaps to a slightly different logic to those of agribusiness.'

Knowledge Networks and Epistemic Communities
Consistent with this emphasis on viewing knowledge generation and acquisition in terms of encounters at multiple interfaces is Louk Box's (1989: 167) argument that agricultural knowledge systems should not be

conceptualised as overall structures made up of research, extension and farmer '*sub-systems*' (as suggested by Röling 1985, 1988). He proposes instead the notion of a multiplicity of *knowledge networks* through which certain types of information are communicated and legitimated, and between which there is often a critical lack of communication. Using the case of cassava production in the Dominican Republic, Box shows how the life-worlds of researchers, extensionists and farmers are partially sealed off from each other. He concludes that 'knowledge networks are highly segmented. They are, like the sierra landscape with its cleavages, holding communities apart. Instead of one knowledge system there are many complex networks, which lack articulation. The life-worlds of the participants, or their values, norms and interests, differ so greatly that they do not allow for communication and interaction between the parties' (Box 1989: 167).

These differences, often labelled pathological by system thinkers, are intrinsic to the everyday life of the actors, and constitute the social conditions for both change and continuity. A key problem for the analysis and management of so-called knowledge systems is, then, precisely the fragile, changeable or non-existent communication channels between the various parties involved, not the permanence and coherence of existing linkages. Moreover, as Box underlines, the knowledge repertoires of sierra migrants – who arrive with certain pre-existing social networks but also quickly create new ones – cannot therefore be detached from the social relationships and exchanges in which such knowledge exists.

In another study in the Dominican Republic, Box documents how small-scale traders (not extension officers) involved in the marketing of various types of agricultural produce played a central role in the diffusion of information concerning new varieties of sweet potato. Twenty per cent of farmer respondents indicated they preferred to receive advice from traders, as compared with only 5 per cent who showed a preference for official agricultural extensionists. In addition, there was widespread distrust among farmers about the quality of the planting materials distributed and the information given out by government agencies. Local producers bitterly recalled the last time government actively promoted a new variety: this tasted so bad that it was impossible to sell in the fresh food markets! (Box 1986: 104–5).

Another example of the way in which agricultural knowledge is embedded in particular social relations and cultural understandings comes from the Tonga of Mola Chiefdom in northern Zimbabwe (Schuthof 1989). Here we find three different and largely separate social networks relating to agricultural knowledge and practice: one centring upon the government agricultural extensionist whose job it is to promote a hybrid maize package, the second upon the religious specialist, 'the spirit medium' or rainmaker who deals primarily with matters pertaining to traditional staples and Tonga farming practice, and the third upon a group of 'innovative' farmers involved principally in market-oriented production. The community is also divided along religious lines between Christians and non-Christians. Schuthof records that while Christians usually consult the extensionist or knowledgeable local farmers when faced with agricultural problems, most non-Christians go directly to the local rainmaker who gives advice on the scheduling of agricultural practice, divines the causes and cures of plant diseases, blesses the seeds before planting, and intercedes on behalf of local people with aggrieved spirits for rain or to prevent wild animals from attacking them or from destroying their crops. For the bulk of the population, the rainmaker and his professed 'agricultural' knowledge and network of support and legitimation was more significant for shaping agricultural production decisions than the specialised agricultural knowledge and contacts provided by the extension staff. Indeed, Schuthof's brief study shows that only 1 per cent of the farmers of the area bothered to visit the extensionist and learn about the maize package he was supposed to promote, even though most farmers did in fact grow some improved maize variety. Understanding agricultural knowledge processes among the Tonga then required careful appreciation of the differentiated nature of local social networks, beliefs and power.

An early study of differences in the social networks of commercial and non-commercial farmers among the Plateau Tonga of Zambia (Jones 1966) showed how commercial producers developed closer, non-dependent friendship ties with nearby European farmers, from whom they obtained benefits such as advice on maize farming and certain farm inputs. Unlike the non-commercial farmers, however, who also sometimes visited European farmers (mostly ex-employers), usually 'to beg for something ... salt, a piglet, and in one case, a pile of old sacks', the commercial farmer avoided placing himself in a subordinate relationship and insisted on paying or reciprocating for any services rendered. One such farmer responded to the agricultural information he received by advising his European friend on the purchase of pigs from certain non-commercial farmers. Another case was that of a farmer borrowing money to pay off a debt on a tractor, in return for which he offered to place cattle on the European's land as collateral (Jones 1966: 280, 282).

These examples point to the existence of important differences in the nature and operation of knowledge networks within the same farming populations. Hence network analysis can help to identify the boundaries of *epistemic communities* (see above) and to characterise the structure and contents of particular communicator networks. As previous studies of communicator networks have shown (e.g., Allen and Cohen 1969; Long 1972; Long and Roberts 1984), certain individuals or groups often become the sociometric stars of a defined network of social ties, as well as the points of articulation with wider interactional fields. That is, they operate as 'gatekeepers' or 'brokers' to structurally more distant networks and social fields. Gatekeepers play a strategic role in both facilitating and blocking the flow of certain types of information and thus are of crucial importance in understanding the functioning of knowledge networks. Related to this issue is the proposition that effective dissemination of ideas and information within a network of individuals depends upon the existence of what Granovetter (1983) calls 'weak ties' which 'bridge divergent network segments that otherwise would be isolated from one another' (Milardo 1988: 17). Such weak ties have been shown to be particularly significant in obtaining access to diverse fields of information, such as, for example, those associated with seeking employment or housing, or information concerning prices in dispersed market locations. On the other hand, to act on information usually requires that individuals secure some support from others. This entails a minimum of normative consensus and, in some situations, the capacity for making rules and enforcing compliance from members (Moore 1973). The latter presupposes the existence of a relatively dense social network, which might also, paradoxically, hinder the absorption of new information and the quick adaptation to changed circumstances (Long 1984: 23, note14).

These and similar network findings provide a fertile source for ideas on how different types of social networks and exchange contents within networks affect the flow of information and processes of knowledge dissemination/creation. This is a fruitful but still neglected field of research.[4]

Knowledge Heterogeneity and Agency in Farm Practice

As the above examples indicate, farming populations are essentially heterogeneous in terms of the strategies that farmers adopt for solving the production and other problems they face. Varying ecological, demographic, market, politico-economic and socio-cultural conditions combine to generate differential patterns of farm enterprise, leading to differences in farm management styles, cropping patterns and levels of production. Implicit in this process, of course, is the differential use and transformation of knowledge: that is, farm knowledge varies and is accorded different social meanings depending upon how it is applied in the running of farms. This is readily seen in the use of different technologies (e.g., tractor, plough, hoe or axe) but is also evident in the specific meanings that a particular instrument or factor of production acquires as it is coordinated with other production and reproduction factors (Van der Ploeg 1986). Hence adopted technology is forever being reworked to fit with the production strategies, resource imperatives and social desires of the farmer or farm family.

Included in this, however, is not only the process by which 'new' technologies or packages are adopted, appropriated or transformed, but also the ongoing processes by which particular farmers combine different social domains based on, for example, the family, community, market, or state institutions. Since each domain (as the word suggests) implies some distinctive normative ordering, the farmer's task becomes that of selecting and coordinating the most appropriate normative and social commitments for organising the process of farm production and reproduction. The decisions the farmer makes of course are based upon value preferences and available stocks of knowledge, resources and relationships.

Viewed in this manner, the farmer is seen as an active strategiser who problematises situations, processes information and brings together the elements necessary for operating his farm. That is, a farmer is involved in constructing his/her own farming world, even if he/she internalises external modes of rationality (which may include the use of information technologies) and thus, as it were, appears simply to carry out the commands of outside agents. An interesting example of this is provided by Pile (1990) who analyses processes of cultural construction among dairy farmers in England. He shows how their forms of discourse and 'maps of meaning' conceptualise the power relations in which they are involved and how these frames of signification shape everyday social action and farming strategy. In this way, he brings out how dairy farmers perceive the character of the state and reason about the agricultural policies pursued by both the British Government and the European Community.

This line of argument leads once again to the importance of an actor-oriented approach to the understanding of knowledge processes. Central to the notion of social actor is the concept of human agency, which attributes to the actor (individual or social group) the capacity to process social experience and to devise ways of coping with life, even under the most extreme conditions of coercion. It is important, however, to stress that 'agency' is not simply an attribute of the individual actor. Agency is composed of social relations and can only become effective through them; it requires organising capacities. The ability to influence others or to pass on a command (e.g., to get them to accept a particular extension message) rests fundamentally on 'the actions of a chain of agents each of whom "translates" it in accordance with his/her own projects' ... and 'power is composed here and now by enrolling many actors in a given political and social scheme' (Latour 1986: 264). In other words, agency (and power) depend crucially upon the emergence of a network of actors who become partially, though hardly ever completely, enrolled in the 'project' of some other person or persons. Effective agency then requires the strategic generation/manipulation of a network of social relations and the channelling of specific items (such as claims, orders, goods, instruments and information) through certain 'nodal points' of interaction (Clegg 1989: 199). In order to accomplish this, it becomes essential for actors to win the struggles that take place over the attribution of specific social meanings to particular events, actions and ideas. Looked at from this point of view, particular development intervention models (or ideologies) become strategic weapons in the hands of the agencies charged with promoting them (Long and Van der Ploeg 1989).

This process is illustrated by Van der Ploeg's (1989) analysis of how small-scale producers in the Andes succumb to 'scientific' definitions of agricultural development. He shows that, although peasants have devised perfectly good solutions to their own production problems (here he is concerned with potato cultivation), their local knowledge gradually becomes marginalised by the type of scientific knowledge introduced by extensionists. The former, that is, becomes superfluous to the model of 'modern' production methods promoted by 'the experts', and development projects become a kind of commodity monopolised and sold by experts who exert 'authority' over their 'subjects'. In this way the rules, limits and procedures governing the negotiation between state agents and farmers and the resources made available are derived (in large part) from external interests and institutions. Hence, although it is possible to depict the relations between Andean peasants and outside experts or state officials in terms of a history of distrust and dependency, science and modern ideologies of development eventually come to command such a major influence on the outcomes of dealings with cultivators that they effectively prevent any exchange of knowledge and experience. This creates what Van der Ploeg calls 'a sphere of ignorance' whereby cultivators are labelled 'invisible men' in contrast to the 'experts' who are visible and authoritative.

Such processes, however, are by no means mechanical impositions from the outside. They necessarily entail negotiation over concepts, meanings and projects which are *internalised* to varying degrees by the different parties involved. Thus the ability of extensionists to transform the nature of agricultural practice is premised on two elements: their skills in handling interface encounters with peasants; and the ways in which the wider set of power relations (or 'chain of agents') feeds into the context, giving legitimacy to their actions and conceptions, and defining certain critical 'rules of the game'. Counter-balancing this is the fact that cultivators, too, assimilate information from each other, as well as from 'external' sources, in an attempt to create knowledge that is in tune with the situations they face.

This process of internalisation is further described in the study mentioned earlier concerning a Mexican women beekeepers' group. From the start, the implementors of the project saw these women as potential enterpreneurs and as *campesinas* (peasant women). But the women's self-images portrayed a different and varied picture. While some of them went along somewhat with the enterpreneurial, peasant image, most described themselves as housewives or as 'coarse and uncultivated' people (using the phrases '*patas rajadas*', which means 'with cracked soles', and '*rústicas*', 'rustic types', to label themselves), for whom beekeeping was an activity complementary to their main duties. Nevertheless, the project provided a series of encounters with the 'outside world' involving a confrontation between 'external' categorisations of themselves as women and their own diverse images and representations. As time passed the latter conceptions were reflected upon and partly modified, leading after a few years to the point where the notion of 'women entrepreneurs' was not entirely alien or incompatible with their other conceptions of self.

Power and the Social Construction of Knowledge

The foregoing discussion brings out the relationships between power and knowledge processes. Like power, knowledge is not simply something that is possessed, accumulated and unproblematically imposed upon others (Foucault in Gordon 1980: 78–108). Nor can it be measured precisely in terms of some notion of quantity or quality. It emerges out of processes of social interaction and, as suggested earlier, is essentially a joint product of the encounter of horizons. It must therefore, like power, be looked at relationally and not treated as if it could be depleted or used up. That someone has power or knowledge does not necessarily entail that others are without. A zero-sum model is thus misplaced. Nevertheless both power and knowledge may become reified in social life: that is, we often think of them as being real material things possessed by agents, and we tend to regard them as unquestioned 'givens'. This process of reification is, of course, an essential part of the ongoing struggles over meaning and the control of strategic relationships and resources that we discussed earlier. Knowledge encounters involve the struggle between agents whereby certain of them attempt to enroll others in their 'projects', getting them to accept particular frames of meaning and winning them over to their points of view. If they succeed then other parties 'delegate' power to them. These struggles focus around the 'fixing' of key points that have a controlling influence over the exchanges and attributions of meaning (including the acceptance of reified notions such as 'authority').

If, therefore, we recognise that we are dealing with 'multiple realities', potentially conflicting social and normative interests, and diverse and fragmented bodies of knowledge, then we must, as suggested above, look closely at the issue of whose interpretations or models (e.g., those of agricultural scientists, politicians, farmers, or extensionists) prevail over those of other actors and under what conditions. Knowledge processes are embedded in social processes that imply aspects of power, authority and legitimation; and they are just as likely to reflect and contribute to the conflict between social groups as they are to lead to the establishment of common perceptions and interests. And, if this is the normal state of affairs, then it becomes unreal to imagine that one can gently 'nudge' knowledge systems towards better modes of integration and coordination.

If we now look at knowledge dissemination/creation in this way we are forced to place it fully in its social context, not as a disembodied process made up of 'formal institutions', 'ideal-typical conceptions' or linkage mechanisms, but as involving specific actors and interacting individuals who become interrelated through networks of interest and through the sharing of certain knowledge frames. These networks, of course, are emergent and stretch beyond the immediate interactional context to encompass remoter regions. They also may, as Latour (1986) has remarked, involve more than simply social relationships: embedded in them are various material and 'extrasomatic' resources (such as telephone calls, farm records, genetic materials, and machines) that acquire social significance in the process of knowledge dissemination/creation.

The analysis of power processes should not therefore be restricted to an understanding of how social constraints and access to resources shape social action. Nor should it lead to the description of rigid hierarchical categories and hegemonic ideologies that 'oppress passive victims'. Standing back from the tendency to empathise ideologically with these hapless victims, one should, instead, explore the extent to which specific actors perceive themselves capable of manoeuvring within given contexts or networks and develop strategies for doing so. This is not to fail to recognise the often much restricted space for individual initiative but rather to examine, within the constraints encountered, how actors identify and create space for their own interests and for change (see Long 1984 for a fuller discussion of this notion of 'space for change').

For example, in a study of women day-labourers in Mexico, one particular worker had a clear perception of the fact that there was a shortage of labour and that the company needed skilled and fast workers.

Since she herself possessed the requisite qualities, this gave her a certain leverage over the company: she could pace her own work and banter with the foreman and farm manager, thus revealing what she called their 'softer sides'. Yet at the same time she was not prepared to give the company more physical labour than was absolutely necessary and was able, to a significant degree, to 'mould authority', thus enrolling the 'bosses' in her own 'circumstantial projects' (Torres 1992) – such as selecting the job she wished to do, allowing her more time to rest, or obtaining leave on grounds of health, or seeking a higher work position. It goes without saying that she did not of course achieve complete control over the organisation of her work, since the management staff were also intent upon enrolling her and the other workers in their projects, otherwise the company would have no *raison d'être*.

As we have argued elsewhere (Villarreal 1992), making room for manoeuvre implies a degree of consent, a degree of negotiation and a degree of power – not necessarily power stored in some economic or political position, but the possibility of control, of prerogative, of some degree of authority and capacity for action, be it front- or backstage, for flickering moments or for long periods. Power then is fluid and difficult or unnecessary to measure, but imperative to describe more precisely. It is not only the amount of power that makes a difference, but the possibility of gaining an edge over others and pressing it home situationally. Different people have different ways of enrolling others in their projects, of selling their own self-images and of trying to impose self-images on them,[5] all of which form part of a process of negotiation by which actors attempt to change certain components or conditions, while striving to maintain others. Hence power always implies struggle, negotiation and compromise. Even those categorised as 'oppressed' are not utterly passive victims and may become involved in active resistance. Likewise, the 'powerful' are not in complete control of the stage and the extent to which their power is forged by the so-called 'powerless' should not be underestimated.[6] Rather, as Scott points out, one must speak of resistance, accommodation and strategic compliance. Although resistance is rarely an overt, collective undertaking, individual acts of subtle defiance and the muffled voices of opposition and mobilisation nevertheless act to divert the possibly coercive or oppressive strategies of others. In this manner, accommodation and strategic compliance – sometimes shielding acts of defiance – become regular features of everyday social life (Scott 1985).

All this suggests that power differentials and struggles over social meaning are central to an understanding of knowledge processes. Knowledge is essentially a social construction that results from and is constantly being reshaped by the encounters and discontinuities that emerge at the points of intersection between actors' life-worlds. A systems perspective, we contend, fails to grasp the theoretical significance of these processes for analysing knowledge issues. It also evades making explicit the critical value decisions made by researchers or intervenors when applying systems models.

The Discourse and Dilemma of 'Empowerment'

This view sheds light on crucial dilemmas faced by development practitioners. For example, much recent work within development enterprises is oriented towards the aim of 'empowerment' of local groups (Chambers 1983; Kronenburg 1986). Although the concept of empowerment forms part of a neo-populist discourse supporting 'participatory' approaches that emphasise 'listening to the people', understanding the 'reasoning behind local knowledge', 'strengthening local organisational capacity' and developing 'alternative development strategies from below', it nevertheless seems to carry with it the connotation of power injected from outside aimed at shifting the balance of forces towards local interests. Hence it implies the idea of empowering people through strategic intervention by 'enlightened experts' who make use of 'people's science' (Richards 1985) and 'local intermediate organisations' (Esman and Uphoff 1984; Korten 1987) to promote development 'from below'. The need to take serious account of local people's solutions to the problems they face must be acknowledged, but the issues are often presented as involving the substitution of 'blueprint' by 'learning' approaches to the planning and management of projects (Korten 1987) or in terms of 'new' for 'old' style professionalism aimed at promoting participatory management and participatory research and evaluation methods (Chambers *et al.* 1989).[7]

Such formulations still do not escape the managerialist and interventionist undertones inherent in development work. That is, they tend to evoke the image of 'more knowledgeable and powerful outsiders' helping 'the powerless and less discerning local folk'. Of course, many field practitioners, who face the everyday problems of project implementation, show an acute awareness of this paradox of participatory strategies. For example, Kronenburg (1986) – himself a practitioner – provides an insightful description of some of the dilemmas of 'empowerment' experienced by implementors of a non-formal education programme in Kenya which was strongly committed to participatory and conscientising goals. Discussing the interplay between emancipatory and manipulative processes, he explains: 'There was contradiction looming in the thin line between the use of DEP [Development Education Programme] skills to enhance the capacity of communities and their members to decide on their own development priorities or to attain goals the facilitators themselves had set. Often, discussions on the topic of manipulation emerged at national ... workshops usually at a stage that trust between participants and facilitators had not fully developed. Yet, the possibility was always there that unwittingly participants would be following the path laid out by the facilitators.

'Closely related to the issue of emancipation versus manipulation is the power of the facilitator to either allow group dialogue to follow its course or to control the discussions by imposing various forms of discipline. By applying time limits on topics judged irrelevant or by emphasising topics familiar or foreseen for discussion, the facilitator could influence the direction of the discussion. This is a dilemma facilitators, applying a non-directive methodology ... are faced with continuously ... To forestall manipulation DEP workers attempted consciously to develop sensitivity to group needs and feelings. To do this optimally facilitators always operated in teams to provide counterweight to the undesired tendencies inherent to their work' (Kronenburg 1986: 163).

Kronenburg's account exposes the multi-faceted nature of power inherent in the relations between development practitioners and their local 'partners' in participatory projects. It also shows how external social commitments intrude into this arena and shape the outcomes of participatory activities. Hence his study adds weight to our earlier argument that social processes (and especially so-called 'planned' interventions) are highly complex and cannot easily be manipulated through the injection of external sources of power and authority. The issue he mentions of conflicting loyalties and ideologies, likewise, brings us back to the earlier discussion of negotiations over 'truth' claims, battles over images, and contesting interests which are implicit in the interlocking of life-worlds and actors' 'projects'.

The Kenyan project in fact illustrates the central importance of strategic agency[8] in the ways in which people (i.e., development practitioners as well as local participants) deal with and manipulate certain constraining and enabling elements in their endeavours to enrol each other in their individual or group 'projects'. The case also suggests the significance of social networks for gathering information, forming opinions, legitimising one's standpoint, and thus for generating differential power relations. The idea that designing participatory strategies based upon the effective use of local knowledge and organisation would enable one to avoid what Marglin (1990) calls 'the dominating knowledge' of science and Western 'scientific' management is clearly untenable.[9] The question of empowerment, then, brings us back to the central issue of the encounter between actors and their knowledge repertoires.

Conclusion

The foregoing discussion provides a brief profile of current empirical and theoretical interests essential for developing an actor-oriented analysis of knowledge processes and agrarian development. The agenda is extensive and the theoretical issues daunting. But it is our view that we have made important headway towards developing a revitalised socio-logical perspective that challenges systems models and interventionist thinking. Such an approach enables us, we believe, to build a better bridge between theoretical understanding and social practice. It does this by providing a set of sensitising analytical concepts based on an actor and interface perspective and a field methodology geared to developing theory 'from below'.[10] As suggested earlier, such a framework neces-sitates a thorough rethinking of issues of intervention, knowledge and power. Yet let us not be intimidated by the scale of the tasks before us. Though arduous, the path ahead is likely to be exhilarating and much more in tune with the needs and dilemmas of the frontline practitioner in search of a better understanding of intervention processes and of his or her role in them.

Notes

1. Janowitz (1972) argues that the sociologist must be fully regarded as part of the process he or she studies. Giddens (1987: 20) takes this further by arguing that 'the "findings" of the social sciences very often enter constitutively into the world they [the sociologists] describe', creating what he calls a 'double hermeneutic'.

2. For examples of an actor approach applied to agrarian change, see Arce 1986; Arce and Long 1987; Long 1988, 1989; Drinkwater 1988; Whatmore 1988; Long and Villarreal 1989; Van der Ploeg 1990; Marsden and Murdoch 1990; and Pile 1990.

3. The general notion of 'interface' conjures up the image of two surfaces coming into contact or of a modern computer system whose central proces-sing unit is linked to auxiliary equipment through a mechanism called the interface. It has also been used to characterise the situation where chemical substances interact but fail to combine to form a new composite solution. Our usage differs from these in that we wish to stress the dynamic and conflictive nature of social interface.

4. In order to advance such work, it is necessary to emphasise that 'network analysts are concerned with explanations of behaviour based upon the patterned interconnections of members, rather than the independent effects of personal dispositions or dyadic relationships. They avoid explanations of behaviour based on normative beliefs or categorical memberships like gender, race or class ...' (Milardo 1988: 15).

5. See Long and Van der Ploeg (1989) for a discussion of the 'trade of images' that takes place within intervention situations.

6. James Scott describes these issues beautifully in his book *Weapons of the Weak* (1985). His analysis falls somewhat short, however, in its reliance upon prefabricated class categories, which is his way of making the pieces (i.e., countervailing strategies) fit the puzzle (i.e., the persistence of hegemonic forms).

7. The furthering of participation goals is not, of course, new to models of planned development (Van Dusseldorp 1991) See also Frerks (1991) for a critical overview of concepts of participation in relation to planned intervention programmes.

8. De Vries (1992) suggests that, in respect of development situations, the various actors advance their own interpretations of agency: 'Thus for experts it entails the right to "represent" other people such as peasants and "recipients" of state services as "traditional", rationally risk-averse, marginalised or exploited. For front-line workers, it means the capacity to create room for manoeuvre by increasing discretion while negotiating the extent to which they are accountable to superiors or the beneficiaries. Agency means to farmers the capability to choose not to become recipients of state services, to confront the authorities or to adapt to them or if necessary to penetrate and manipulate state bureacracies.'

9. Marglin's analysis focuses upon the ideological dominance of Western systems of knowledge and their subordination and devaluation of other cultures and forms of knowledge. He distinguishes in ideal-typical terms between two kinds of knowledge, which he calls *techne* and *episteme*. The former represents a practical type of knowledge and is a product of a personalised social order (i.e., what modernisation theorists might designate as 'traditional' society), and the latter the kind associated with Western science and logical reasoning (i.e., 'modern' society). While making a number of powerful criticisms of existing development theories and policies, Marglin's argument founders, we believe, upon the rocks of dichotomisation since, like many previous writers, he posits a sharp distinction between a 'dominant Western' knowledge system and other 'traditional' knowledge systems.

10. See Long and Long (1992) for an exploration of the methodological implications of an actor-oriented theoretical approach to social research and development intervention.

Relevant Literature

Alexander, J.C., B. Giesen, R. Münch & N.J. Smelser (eds.). 1987. *The Micro-Macro Link*. Berkeley, University of California Press.

Allen, T.J. & S.I. Cohen. 1969. 'Information Flow in Research and Development Laboratories'. *Administrative Science Quarterly*, vol.14, pp. 12–19.

Arce, A. 1986. 'Agricultural Policy Administration in a Less Developed Country: The Case of SAM in Mexico'. Ph.D. Thesis, Manchester University.

— & N. Long. 1987. 'The Dynamics of Knowledge Interfaces between Mexican

Agricultural Bureaucrats and Peasants: a Case Study from Jalisco'. *Boletin de Estudios Latinoamericanos y del Caribe*, 43, pp. 5-30.

Beal, G.M., W. Dissanayake & S. Konoshima (eds.). 1986. *Knowledge Generation, Exchange, and Utilization*. Boulder, Colorado, Westview Press.

Benvenuti, B. 1975. 'General Systems Theory and Entrepreneurial Autonomy in Farming: Towards a New Feudalism or Towards Democratic Planning?' *Sociologia Ruralis*, XV, 1/2, pp. 47-62.

Box, L. 1986. 'Knowledge, Networks and Cultivators: Cassava in the Dominican Republic'. In N. Long, L. Box *et al.*

— 1987. 'Experimenting Cultivators: A Methodology for Adaptive Agricultural Research'. ODI Agricultural Administration (Research and Extension) Network *Discussion Paper 23*, Dec.

— 1989. 'Knowledge, Networks and Cultivators: Cassava in the Dominican Republic'. In N. Long (ed.), *Encounters at the Interface: A Perspective on Social Discontinuities in Rural Development*. Wageningen, The Agricultural University.

Chambers, R. 1983. *Rural Development: Putting the Last First*. London, Longman.

—, A. Pacey & L.A. Thrupp (eds.). 1989. *Farmer First: Farmer Innovation and Agricultural Research*. London, Intermediate Technology Publications.

Checkland, P. 1981, 2nd ed. 1988. *Systems Thinking, Systems Practice*. Chichester, Wiley.

— 1985. 'From Optimizing to Learning: a Development of Systems Thinking for the 1990s'. *Journal of the Operational Research Society*, 36(9), pp. 757–67.

Clegg, S.R. 1989. *Frameworks of Power*. London, Sage Publications.

Collinson, M. 1982. 'Farming System Research in Eastern Africa: The Experience of CIMMYT and Some National Agricultural Research Services, 1976–1981'. *MSU International Development Paper 3*, East Lansing, Michigan State University.

Dissanayake, W. 1986. 'Communication Models in Knowledge Generation, Dissemination and Utilization Activities'. In G.M. Beal *et al.* (eds.), *Knowledge Generation, Exchange, and Utilization*, Boulder, Colorado, Westview Press.

Drinkwater, J.M. 1988. 'The State and Agrarian Change in Zimbabwe's Communal Areas: An Application of Critical Theory'. Ph.D. Thesis, School of Development Studies, University of East Anglia.

Dusseldorp, D. van. 1991. 'Planned Development via Projects: its Necessity, Limitations and Possible Improvements'. *Sociologia Ruralis*, XXX, pp. 336–52.

Esman, M.J. & N.T. Uphoff. 1984. *Local Organizations: Intermediaries in Rural Development*. Ithaca and London, Cornell University Press.

Fielding, N.G. (ed.). 1988. *Actions and Structure*. London and Beverly Hills, Sage Publications.

Frerks, G.E. 1991. *Participation in Development Activities at the Local Level: Case Studies from a Sri Lankan Village*. Department of Sociology of Rural Development, Wageningen, The Agricultural University.

Fresco, L. 1986. *Cassava and Shifting Cultivation: A Systems Approach to Agricultural Technology Development*. Amsterdam, Royal Tropical Institute.

— & E. Westphal. 1988. 'A Hierarchical Classification of Farm Systems'. *Experimental Agriculture*, vol. 24, pp. 399–419.

Giddens, A. 1979. *Central Problems in Social Theory: Action, Structure and Contradiction in Social Analysis*. London, Macmillan Press.

— 1984. *The Constitution of Society: an Outline of the Theory of Structuration*. Cambridge, Polity Press.

— 1987. *Social Theory and Modern Sociology*. Cambridge, Polity Press; Stanford, Stanford University Press.

Gordon C. (ed.). 1980. *Power/Knowledge: Selected Interviews and Other Writings 1972–1977 by Michel Foucault*. United States, Pantheon Harvester Press.

Granovetter, M. 1983. 'The Strength of Weak Ties: A Network Theory Revisited'. In R. Collins (ed.), *Sociological Theory: 1983*, San Francisco, Jossey-Bass.

Habermas, J. 1987 (originally published in German 1981). *Theory of Communicative Action: Critique of Functionalist Reason*. Vol. II, Oxford, Polity Press.

Havelock, R.G. 1969. *Planning for Innovation through Dissemination and Utilisation of Knowledge*. Institute of Social Research/Centre for Research of Utilisation of Scientific Knowledge. Ann Arbor, University of Michigan.

— 1986. 'Modeling the Knowledge System'. In G.M. Beal *et al.* (eds.) *Knowledge Generation, Exchange and Utilization*, Boulder, Colorado, Westview Press.

Hawkins, E.A. 1991. 'Changing Technologies: Negotiating Autonomy on Cheshire Farms'. Ph.D. Thesis, London, South Bank Polytechnic.

Hildebrand, P.E. 1981. 'Combining Disciplines in Rapid Rural Appraisal'. *Agricultural Administration* 8, pp. 423–32.

Janowitz, M. 1972. *Sociological Models and Social Policy*. Morristown, New Jersey, General Learning Systems.

Jones, A.D. 1966. 'Social Networks of Farmers among the Plateau Tonga'. In D. Forde (ed.), *The New Elites of Tropical Africa*, Oxford, Oxford University Press for International African Institute.

Knorr-Cetina, K.D. & A.V. Cicourel (eds.). 1981. *Advances in Social Theory and Methodology: Toward an Integration of Micro- and Macro-Sociologies*. London and Henley, Routledge & Kegan Paul.

Korten, D.C. (ed.). 1987. *Community Management: Asian Experience and Perspectives*. West Hartford, Connecticut, Kumarian Press.

Kronenburg, J.B.M. 1986. *Empowerment of the Poor: A Comparative Analysis of Two Development Endeavours in Kenya*. Amsterdam, Royal Tropical Institute.

Latour, B. 1986. 'The Powers of Association'. In J. Law (ed.), *Power, Action and Belief: A New Sociology of Knowledge?* London, Boston and Henley, Routledge & Kegan Paul.

Leeuwis, C. 1991. 'From Electronic to Social Interfaces'. In D. Kuiper & N.

Röling (eds.), *Edited Proceedings of the European Seminar on Knowledge Management and Information Technology*, Wageningen, The Agricultural University.

— & M. Arkesteyn. 1991. 'Planned Technology Development and Local Initiative'. In *Sociologia Ruralis*, vol. XXXI, no. 2/3, pp. 140–61.

Lionberger, H. 1960. *Adoption of New Ideas and Practices*. Ames, Iowa State University Press.

Long, N. 1972. 'Kinship and Associational Networks among Transporters in Rural Peru: The Problem of the "Local" as against the "Cosmopolitan" Entrepreneur'. Paper presented to Seminar on Kinship and Social Networks, Institute of Latin American Studies, London University. See shortened version in N. Long and B. Roberts (1984: 181–95).

— 1977. *An Introduction to the Sociology of Rural Development*. London, Tavistock Publications.

— 1984. *Creating Space for Change: A Perspective on the Sociology of Development*. Inaugural Lecture, Wageningen, The Agricultural University. A shortened version appears in *Sociologia Ruralis*, XXIV, 3/4, pp. 168–84.

— 1988. 'Sociological Perspectives on Agrarian Development and State Intervention'. In A. Hall & J. Midgley (eds.), *Development Policies: Sociological Perspectives*, Manchester, Manchester University Press.

— 1989. 'Knowledge, Networks and Power: Discontinuities and Accommodations at the Interface'. Paper presented to the European Seminar on Knowledge Systems and Information Technology, International Agricultural Centre, Wageningen, 23–24 Nov.

— (ed.). 1989. *Encounters at the Interface: A Perspective on Social Discontinuities in Rural Development*. Wageningen, The Agricultural University.

— & A. Long (eds.). 1992. *Battlefields of Knowledge: The Interlocking of Theory and Practice in Social Research and Development*. London and New York, Routledge.

— & J.D. van der Ploeg. 1989. 'Demythologizing Planned Intervention: An Actor Perspective'. *Sociologia Ruralis*, XXIX, 3/4, pp. 226-49.

— & B. Roberts. 1984. *Miners, Peasants and Entrepreneurs*. Cambridge, Cambridge University Press.

— & M. Villarreal. 1989. 'The Changing Life-Worlds of Women in a Mexican Ejido: the Case of Beekeepers of Ayuquila and the Issues of Intervention'. In N. Long (ed.), 1989.

Marglin F.A. & S.A. Marglin (eds.). 1990. *Dominating Knowledge: Development Culture and Resistance*. Oxford, Clarendon, WIDER Studies in Development Economics.

Marsden, T. & J. Murdoch. 1990. 'Restructuring Rurality: Key Areas for Development in Assessing Rural Change'. Working Paper, Department of Planning, Housing and Development, South Bank Polytechnic, London.

Milardo, R.M. (ed.) 1988. *Families and Social Networks*. London, Sage Publications.

Moore, S.F. 1973. 'Law and Social Change: the Semi-autonomous Social Field as an Appropriate Subject of Study'. In *Law Society Review*, Summer, pp. 719–46.

Pile, S. 1990. *The Private Farmer: Transformation and Legitimation in Advanced Capitalist Agriculture*. Aldershot, Dartmouth Publishing Company.

Ploeg, J. van der. 1986. 'The Agricultural Labour Process and Commoditization'. In N. Long *et al.*, *The Commoditization Debate: Labour Process, Strategy and Social Network*, Wageningen, The Agricultural University.

— 1989. 'Knowledge Systems, Metaphor and Interface: The Case of Potatoes in the Peruvian Highlands'. In N. Long (ed.), *Encounters at the Interface: A Perspective on Social Discontinuities in Rural Development*, Wageningen, The Agricultural University.

— 1990. *Labour, Markets, and Agricultural Production*. Boulder, San Fransisco, Oxford, Westview Special Studies in Agriculture and Policy, Westview Press.

Richards, P. 1985. *Indigenous Agricultural Revolution*. London and Boulder, Colorado, Hutchinson and Westview Press.

Rhoades, R.E. & A. Bebbington. 1988. 'Farmers Who Experiment: An Untapped Resource for Agricultural Research and Development'. Paper presented at the International Congress on Plant Physiology, New Delhi, 15–20 Feb.

Rogers, E.M. 1962, 3rd ed. 1983. *The Diffusion of Innovations*. New York, The Free Press of Glencoe.

— & F.F. Shoemaker. 1971. *Communication of Innovations: A Cross-Cultural Approach*. New York, Free Press.

Röling, N. 1988a. 'Extension, Knowledge Systems and the Research-Technology Transfer Interface', Unpublished paper, Department of Extension, Wageningen, The Agricultural University.

— 1988b. *Extension Science, Information Systems in Agricultural Development*. Cambridge, Cambridge University Press.

— & Engel, P. 1990. 'Information Technology from a Knowledge Systems Perspective: Concepts and Issues'. In *Knowledge in Society: The International Journal of Knowledge Transfer*, 3, 3.

Schuthof, P. 1989. 'Common Wisdom and Shared Knowledge: Knowledge Networks among the Tonga of Mola Chiefdom in Zimbabwe'. Unpublished Report, Centre of Applied Social Studies, University of Zimbabwe, and Department of Rural Extension and Adult Education, Wageningen Agricultural University.

Scott, J.C. 1985. *Weapons of the Weak: Everyday Forms of Peasant Resistance*. New Haven and London, Yale University Press.

Scott, R.A. & A.R. Shore. 1979. *Why Sociology Does Not Apply: A Study of the Use of Sociology in Public Policy*. New York, Elsevier.

Sutherland, A. 1987. 'Sociology in Farming Systems Research'. *Occasional Paper 6*, Agricultural Administration Unit, London, Overseas Development Institute.

Torres, G. 1992. 'The Force of Irony: A Study of the Everyday Life-Worlds of Agricultural Labourers in Western Mexico'. Forthcoming in N. Long (ed.)

Social Constructions of Agrarian Life: Meanings, Purposes and Powers in Western Mexico.

Villarreal, M. 1990. 'A Struggle over Images: Issues on Power, Gender and Intervention in a Mexican Village'. M.Sc. Thesis, Wageningen, The Agricultural University.

— 1992. 'The Poverty of Practice: Power, Gender and Intervention from an Actor-oriented Perspective'. In N. Long & A. Long (eds.), *Battlefields of Knowledge: The Interlocking of Theory and Practice in Social Research and Development*, London and New York, Routledge.

Vries, P. de. 1992. 'A Research Journey: On Actors, Concepts and the Text'. In N. Long & A. Long (eds.).

Whatmore, S. 1988. 'The "Other Half" of the Family Farm: An Analysis of the Position of Farm Wives in the Familial Gender Division of Labour on the Farm'. Ph.D. Thesis, University of London.

8

Gender Studies: Whose Agenda?

by Janet Townsend

Gender Studies in the 1990s

An eminent development theorist once adjured a conference audience to 'avoid the concrete peasant!' (This was someone whose work on the peasantry and on land reform I much respect, emphasising the need to look beyond the individual to the deep structures of reality.) In the 1990s we are closer to saying, 'Seek out the concrete peasant and enquire into her private life!'

Gender studies take us straight into people's most private lives, and this immediately brings the role of the researcher into question. Empowerment becomes the first and most essential requirement of both planning and development (Sen and Grown 1987; Moser 1989). The researcher must examine the specific articulation of patriarchy in private as well as public space (Walby 1990). In old-fashioned feminist terms, the personal becomes political. In gender studies seeking to lead us out of the impasse, development is defined in terms of the personal: personal empowerment in private and public space. This is highly antipathetic to traditional development studies, which have overwhelmingly concerned themselves with generalisation, with representative samples, with prediction and with the public domain (Townsend 1988; Radcliffe with Townsend 1988).

'There are six main structures which make up a system of patriarchy: paid work, housework, sexuality, culture, violence and the state' (Walby 1990). Clearly, in development studies we need to change the phrasing from 'paid work: housework' to 'production: reproduction', despite the analytical difficulties (Redclift 1985). We then see that of these six categories, development studies have concerned themselves with only two: paid work, or production, and the state. Culture and reproduction are left to anthropologists, while sexuality and domestic forms of violence are rarely studied even by them.

Gender studies are also subject to the post-modern critique. The single most important advance in feminist theory is that the existence of gender relations has been shown to be a problem (Flax 1987). Gender can no longer be treated as a simple, natural fact. 'Sex' refers to the anatomical differences between male and female, which are much the same across space and over time; gender, the socially constructed differences and relations between males and females, varies greatly from place to place and from time to time. The post-modern critique goes beyond this and sees the categories 'women', 'men' and 'gender' as themselves essentialist and reductionist; in post-modern language, there are a number of overlapping, cross-cutting discourses of femininities and masculinities which are historically and culturally variable and could potentially take an infinite number of forms. Gender is then a reductionist, essentialist term. Development studies have been criticised by gender studies as having falsely universalised on the basis of limited perspectives; now gender studies face the same critique. In practice there are enough common features and routinised interconnections to make it sensible to compare gender relations in the West over the last 150 years or so (Walby 1990). I contend that these Western gender relations now impinge on almost all the people studied in 'development' to such a degree that they too now have comparable experiences.

This chapter will follow Caroline Moser's history of gender planning in the Third World (1989) and draw on my own experience of research to emphasise the need for empowerment and the practical, theoretical and ethical difficulties of gender studies which seek to promote empowerment. I shall also make reference to extensive and intensive forms of research, since this is an issue which often confuses discussion. We need both kinds of research (Sayer 1984): extensive research, which looks at the common properties and general patterns of a population as a whole; and intensive research, which examines some causal process in a limited number of cases.

From Welfare to Empowerment

Moser has distinguished five historical approaches to 'women in development' outside the socialist bloc (Moser 1989). She identifies the approaches which have been tried, and which are so critical to gender studies, as welfare, equity, anti-poverty, efficiency and empowerment.

The Welfare Approach
First, under the welfare approach, in the 1950s and 1960s, women were included in programmes for vulnerable groups. Women were part of 'relief aid'; 'economic aid' went to men. Women were passive recipients, mothers who had to be reached for the sake of their children; women received handouts, food aid, programmes against malnutrition, programmes for family planning. Women were a delivery channel for welfare, and their work in producing wealth was ignored. Many development schemes failed because people forgot about women's farm work,

for instance (Palmer 1985). The welfare approach perceived women as passive. Women were socially regarded as victims (Moser 1989).

The welfare approach is not dead in development practice, nor is it dead in the development literature. It should be. Women as passive receivers of 'development' are simply a false model of reality. The only field in which the welfare approach may be applicable is refugee studies. Refugees, whether Kurds in Turkey or Afghans in Pakistan, may actually be denied the right to produce. Refugees are a highly exceptional case, and even for them women's reproductive and managerial roles are critical, as among the Saharawis (Lawless and Monahans 1987).

Equity

In 1970, Esther Boserup described women's role in economic development: although her work lacks theory (Beneria and Sen 1981), it was a courageous attempt to deploy deficient data, and it did render women visible. We shall see that the invisibility of women is still a problem in the 1990s. Boserup presented development as negative for women; the idea was carried forward strongly in the United States. Equity became the name of the game. The themes of the UN Decade for Women, 1975–85, were development, peace and equality. Equality was the preoccupation of First World feminism, peace of the socialist bloc, development of the Third World. All three groups wanted recognition that women are active, not passive. It was felt that, far from promoting sexual equality, development had marginalised and excluded women; the answer was to integrate women into development. Top-down legislation was to make women visible and give them equal rights.

There was an array of difficulties with the equity approach (Moser 1989).

– Ironically, integrating women into development proved superfluous: often the problem was that they had been only too well integrated already, often into more work in worse conditions. It was often increased exploitation of women that was making economic growth possible, as in the Four Little Tigers so beloved of the World Bank (Taiwan, South Korea, Hong Kong and Singapore).

– Under the Decade for Women, programmes were created to increase equity, but there were no indicators, and no baseline, so monitoring was impossible. How was equity to be measured?

– Above all, no-one was willing to redistribute power to women. Whether we start at the top or start at the bottom: the United Nations is male dominated, so are governments, bureaucracies, aid agencies and poor people. Equity programmes were characteristically top-down, and even at the top there was no will to redistribute power to women. Under the equity approach, there were legal gains, but they were often curtailed in practice; this was classic, ineffective, 'top-down' development. It remains a clear priority to secure legal rights to women, whether in the ownership of their own bodies, in access to title for dwelling or land, or in access to livelihood, but the equity approach delivered little.

The equity approach was all doublethink and contradictions: i) the idea of 'integrating women' was ludicrous; ii) no-one knew what success would look like; iii) much legislation changed nothing in practice; iv) equity without a gain in power for women was self-contradictory.

Anti-Poverty Approaches

Moser points out that anti-poverty approaches seemed an escape. We may say that because, frankly, we were unwilling to interfere in the relations between men and women, whether in England or Nigeria, we shifted to meeting women's practical needs. Anti-poverty schemes tended to remain small projects, run by aid agencies, trying to meet the needs articulated by women themselves without threatening social change. The problem is that these needs are what is called for to make society work as it is, not to change it. Moser has also argued (1987), following Maxine Molyneux (1985), that these are *practical gender needs*. Women want water because society has made it women's problem. Everybody needs water, and food, and health, and income; women are just a delivery mechanism, expressing a need they feel on behalf of other people. To suffer less male violence, to gain more control over their own lives, to achieve some autonomy – these would be strategic changes, meeting *strategic gender needs*; but anti-poverty approaches preferred to avoid these sensitive areas.

Women in Development

Women in Development (WID) incorporates equity, anti-poverty and *efficiency*, now the dominant approach. Deniz Kandiyoti (1988) has shown how, in the 1980s, in sections of the World Bank and various United Nations agencies, women become the answer to everything. There is supposed to be no conflict between helping women and promoting development; on the contrary, assisting women will always pay dividends in straight economic terms. Greater equity for women can go with increased productivity, and an increase in women's participation in production for the market will give them both equity and efficiency. It is forgotten that it did not do so in China (Molyneux 1981; Croll 1987). And women are seen as a cheap option, for both production and welfare. Where extra income goes to women rather than men, there is a greater gain in family welfare. The World Bank is very enthusiastic about this.

It all sounds very 'efficient'. Once again, the problems are presented as technical, not political, and theory and practice are riddled with contradiction. Moser describes women as having a triple role in developing countries: in production (or income generation), in reproduction (biological and social) and in community management. It is supposed to be possible to take advantage of women's triple role, and simultaneously to use women to increase production, to use them in their reproductive roles to buffer the shocks of brutal structural adjustment policies, and to make them more efficient managers of poverty. And this will all be cheap. As Kandiyoti has shown (1988), the criteria for success in women's projects from, say, the Food and Agriculture Organisation of the United Nations or the World Bank are much less stringent than for men's projects. Kandiyoti and Moser argue convincingly that the actual programmes under the efficiency approach are not about real growth, or change, or even treating women on equal terms. Conflicts of interest are ignored, whether between women and men or between groups of women; so are conflicting demands on women. Under the efficiency approach, women are still just a cheap delivery system for current objectives.

Empowerment

The empowerment approach arises from the writings and grassroots experience of Third World women (Sen and Grown 1987). Third World feminists have a vision of economic and social development geared to human needs through wider control over and access to political power: empowerment. Development theory should take this very seriously. Third World women talk about 'empowering ourselves through organisations' (Sen and Grown 1987). Third World feminists identify the same needs, but they have quite different means of achieving them. Gita Sen and Caren Grown (1987), Irene Dankelman and Joan Davidson (1987), Caroline Moser and Linda Peake (eds., 1987) all see the limitations of top-down government legislation, top-down 'basic needs' programmes. Third World feminists recognise the triple role of women, but they seek to use it politically, to build change through the struggle for practical needs. Women's daily struggles around issues of primary relevance to their lives become politicised: food prices, the cost of living, drains, the lack of social services, the disappearance of their children at the hands of repressive regimes (Moser 1989; Sen and Grown 1987). Women's daily struggles become the means to empowerment. Struggles for empowerment take place in the home, the state and the workplace.

Empowerment is the approach which allows for diversity and difference rather than simply universalising falsely from Western perspectives.

Not even empowerment is a panacea. Already, in many countries, grassroots organisations of all kinds are being asked to take on tasks for which they just have neither the scale nor the expertise. In Latin America, there is a real fear that the recent channelling of resources into them, particularly by USAID, will simply lead to failure and the discrediting of grassroots development (Lehmann 1988). Small organisations are being asked to take over almost overnight from the state, without time, resources or experience. Sen and Grown note the same problem with women's organisations (1987).

Land Settlement and Sustainable Livelihoods

Empowerment should nevertheless command the attention of every development researcher in the 1990s, not only in work with women or in gender studies but across the board. My own research experience will illustrate this, and will demonstrate many of the difficulties. Theory in development, like all other forms of theory, is dependent upon and reflects a certain set of social experiences; individual experience is merely an extreme case. We do not have an Archimedes point outside the world, outside human life and our embeddedness within it, from which to construct theory. We construct it and accept or reject it from our own experience.

Since 1965, I have been involved in research with people trying to make farms out of the rainforest in Latin America – the pioneers on the frontier of colonisation, or the people blamed for deforestation, according to your point of view. For all this time, it has been a very depressing field. One is working with people who are striving to make a sustainable livelihood for themselves and their children, often at the cost of great suffering and risk. In South America, most of them fail, and lose their farms, sometimes their lives; much land goes from forest to non-sustainable crops, and then to non-sustainable cattle ranching. Environmental degradation is normal. Human impoverishment and failure are also normal. My doctoral research was in the middle Magdalena valley, Colombia, which has been transformed while I have known it from rainforest to farms to ranches of low productivity, low wages and low employment; the profits are in land speculation and urban banks. The profitable land uses in the valley now are for the cocaine trade: airstrips and processing laboratories. In the 1960s the army terrorised the countryside, but now the great fear is of the paramilitary death squads, followed by the cocaine dealers and lastly the army and the guerrillas. Living standards are higher, but life is more insecure than ever.

Hulme (1987) has shown that state-sponsored land settlement schemes have been a persistent and popular 'development strategy' in poor countries, despite overwhelming evidence that they usually fail to meet their objectives. (They have also generated a huge literature which reveals only a constant failure to learn from experience – see Hulme, 1988.) Essentially, the administrative and infrastructural requirements of successful land settlement are too great to be practicable; other options are normally more cost-effective. I have continued to work on colonisation not because I see it as a good source of sustainable livelihoods, but because I find myself in sympathy with the settlers, who are so much at the mercy of the national and international political economy which is destroying physical and human resources. Most of my field research has been in Colombia and Mexico. My perspectives on the problems have shifted radically at least three times.

A Pathway to Understanding: Personal Experiences

First Conversion: Farmers as Scientists

I began my doctoral research with a longstanding conviction that my own culture had produced rather a poor design for living. We had an unsatisfactory and unenviable society, but had made certain technical advances which could, I thought, be of benefit to other societies, which might profit from them to make a better job of living than we did. I belonged to the long-lived 'transfer of technology' school of which writers like Robert Chambers (Chambers *et al.* 1989) are so critical. This is prehistory – I had not heard of social change, of dependency or of political economy, and my supervisor regarded postgraduate training as an undesirable waste of time. I was also under the illusion that intensive research was not really geography, and my work was both gender-blind and male-biased. As a doctoral research student, I was sent to Colombia from 1966 to 1968, to study the ignorant peasants who had been displaced from the highlands by rural violence and were destroying the forest resources of the middle Magdalena (Townsend 1976). Unfortunately, it took me much of this time to realise how completely I had been misdirected and to undergo my first conversion.

I found, of course, capable people making remarkable adaptations to their new environment, but at the mercy of the political economy of Colombia. It took me a long time to realise that there was no technical solution known for their problems and that the agronomists, hydrologists and forestry experts who pontificated on the ignorance of the settlers had themselves no alternative, viable, farming or forestry system. The area was under the control of the Regional Corporation of the Magdalena and Cauca valleys, which sought to achieve top-down solutions on a basis of no effective expertise. New researchers today should bear in mind that there are very few areas in developing countries where the experts actually know how to make a profit under prevailing conditions on a given farm, let alone how to achieve sustainable development. And that is in long-settled areas; for 'new' areas of land settlement they have even less idea.

In the middle Magdalena, settlers talked to me. They lived in fear under terrifying social conflict, but they had great faith in the power of the written word, the power of experts. They set a great value on my level of education; they saw knowledge as power; they believed in the value of truth; none of us had heard of the post-modern discourse. Like me, the settlers believed that if they could get their story told, it would make a difference to their problems. In fact, no-one in the Colombian establishment would believe me: I had used informal interviews, not a questionnaire, and they regarded this as subjective and unscientific. I had imposed my perceptions on my respondents. The respondents were stupid, traditional, ignorant and destructive; the skills and eagerness to learn that I described were figments of my imagination.

In 1974, I used psychological tests and computers (with repertory grids) to demonstrate that the settlers' ideas about good land use were much the same as those of their agricultural advisers, but that the settlers did not have the resources to put them into practice (Townsend 1977). To my surprise, this also convinced no-one. I had failed to realise, in all this time, how convenient these beliefs were to the Ministry of Land Reform, to academics and to experts; 'proof', with or without computers, was irrelevant. The settlers, like so many of the poor and powerless, were very effectively denied a voice. They were silenced, disqualified and excluded; legitimate knowledge was the prerogative of the elite.

I continued work on these problems, seeing more and more how far settlers were restricted by market conditions and by institutional reality. The settlers seemed puppets at the mercy of the world system, or at least of the laws of motion of capital. We all saw how limited was the power of 'truth' as excellent analyses came to be shown on peak-time television and pop stars adopted the cause of the Indians of Amazonia, apparently not to their benefit.

Second Conversion: Women's Voices

In 1984, I began to study the plight of the women among the pioneers, and met my second conversion. My first conversion had shown me how poor settlers were silenced, devalued and disqualified; now I learned how women's work was rendered invisible. I had of course talked with women pioneers a great deal before: I had stayed in their houses, camped near their houses, talked all night by the cooking fire. I had used very loosely structured interviews, open conversation and, once, repertory grid techniques. My primary informant had usually been the man of the house, although some interviews were conducted with the family. Indeed, in order to allow the man to concentrate on the repertory grid, my research assistant had entertained the women and children! I had always had an androcentric agenda, a male-centred agenda. I had been interested in the experiences and prospects of the farming household. Even chatting with the women, I had never enquired about their personal lives as they did about mine; it seemed intrusive.

When, in 1984, there was an amnesty and I was able to return to the Magdalena valley, I discovered that many of my assumptions about the women pioneers were quite wrong. I had thought of the women and children as a reserve army of labour on the farm; in fact, in the middle Magdalena, females are almost excluded from farm work. (This is true in many other areas of ex-rainforest in Latin America.) We used household questionnaires, and discovered for the first time that women in the Magdalena valley are in a minority; many girls leave for the cities.

We discovered that women in the Magdalena valley were housewives, engaged in reproductive tasks and often painfully isolated (Townsend and Wilson de Acosta 1987).

Ben White (1984) quotes a student as saying: 'When I use quantitative data, everyone else believes them but I don't; when I use qualitative data, no-one else believes them but I do.' White argues that the remedy is to improve both kinds of data, not to set them in opposition; I would agree very strongly. Quick and dirty surveys, yielding crude but quantifiable extensive data, have an invaluable role in cross-cultural research and in rapid appraisal. In this case, Sally Wilson de Acosta and I had taken questionnaires and informal interviews to a sample of one in 10 households in one settler village, and to every household along a particular trail through the forest. Only when the paper came out of the computer did we realise that the ratio between adult males and adult females in that area was 2:1 (Townsend and Wilson de Acosta 1987). Our notes recorded the preponderance of men in certain households, but failed to record the absence of complementary households with a preponderance of women.

Again, the settlers asked us to send reports to the Ministries of Health, of Transport and of Agriculture; they knew that this was unlikely to help them, but wanted to take even the outside chance of having their stories heard. They talked freely to us and allowed us to weigh their small children; we sent the reports to the ministries and to the people surveyed, but the Ministry of Health did not redistribute resources; it merely used the evidence to appeal to the World Health Organisation for help, unsuccessfully.

So what were we doing this for? In academic terms, we could demonstrate that in the Serrania de San Lucas females are almost excluded from work in the forest or the fields, and that girls leave the area from a very early age, even pre-teens. Women's work is almost confined to reproduction; girls, who are defined out of production, are seen as a potential cost, and many of them are sent to kin or contacts in the cities, to work as domestic servants and – in theory – to be educated

(I was able to confirm this pattern in two other areas of the Magdalena valley in 1987). We could demonstrate the appalling living conditions of these settlers, and the evidence of malnutrition and disease in the children. One family had 20 hectares of land titled, yet the four children under five in the household achieved only 50, 55, 75 and 94 per cent of the expected weight for their age (94 per cent for the baby, still breast-fed).

This study, then, was an exercise in seeking to render invisible women visible – an exercise properly belonging to the 1970s when the invisibility of women in development was the great problem and was to be rectified by studying them. By the 1980s, we recognised that the important issue is not women's invisibility – that it is not some strange historical accident. The issue is the causes of that invisibility, women's subordination, and the discourse which denigrates women and women's work. But this is much more difficult to confront. In exactly the same way, the male settlers with whom I had worked earlier were denied a voice and any voices raised on their behalf were skilfully disqualified. The project of development studies in the 1990s must be to change the discourse, to empower the powerless.

The demands of lecturing limited what I could do next, but I then conducted a literature survey of women in colonisation in Latin America, and to a lesser extent in Africa, Asia and even a little in North America. I found that women around the world tended to have some quite similar experiences in colonisation or land settlement. If the colonisation was planned, they were often left out of the plans; planners thought of moving 'men without lands to lands without men', of moving 'a man with a family'.

Commonly, colonisation meant: i) that women lost economic rights, such as title to land; ii) that they lost access to income; iii) that their workload was increased; and iv) above all that they lost their social networks and suffered severely from isolation.

Quite often, this was a move from an extended to a nuclear family, with a wholly new dynamic and new tensions. This pattern was identified by Chambers (1969) in his classic *Settlement Schemes in Tropical Africa*, and has been documented for India, Sri Lanka, Malaysia, Thailand, Kenya, Nigeria, Brazil, Bolivia ... There are meaningful and useful comparisons to be made across these areas, for all their diversity, but study must be comparative rather than universalising, attuned to changes and contrasts rather than developing laws (Fraser and Nicholson 1988).

But what is the point of documenting more and more negative experiences which people have in common? Donny Meertens (now at Amsterdam) and I wanted to conduct some more positive research in Colombia, Peru and Bolivia, finding out how women evaluated their problems, and what solutions they proposed. Not many people ask the male settlers what solutions they see (although I had tried to); no-one asks the women. We thought it might shed some new light. The cocaine wars in Colombia and Peru frustrated our project to deploy teams of action researchers to find out.

My third shift of perspective came last year. My Colombian friends advised against a return to the field there, and I went to Mexico. In Mexico, I used the same questionnaire – and I began to learn to use life histories. And I found that I still had a male agenda; I had still been blind to women's central concerns; I had still left the personal out of account.

Third Conversion: The Personal is Political

The aim of the Mexico project, 1990 and 1991, is to develop with pioneer women some guidelines for women's grassroots organisations in areas of land settlement in Mexico, and perhaps some guidelines for the planners. Six of us (five Mexican women and I) have now worked in five areas of Mexico where there is land settlement of tropical forest.

We have used questionnaires for background, extensive data on gender divisions of labour, demography and farm characteristics; unstructured interviews and workshops for attitudes and opinions; and tape-recorded life histories for more intensive research. The team comprises a geographer (myself), a biologist, two sociologists and two agronomists. We confined ourselves to Spanish-speaking communities to avoid working with translators. We worked in Los Tuxtlas (Veracruz), Tehuantepec (Oaxaca), Palenque (Chiapas), Balancan (Tabasco) and Champoton (Campeche). Analysis is still underway; the research is supported by ESRC, Durham University and the Colegio de Michoacan.

In these places, the creation of the settlement had been a painful process with many years of great hardship; the pioneers have made a community out of the forest. Benita, at 58, can say, 'My children don't suffer as we suffered' in building these settlements. But all the communities are now facing an agrarian crisis, exacerbated by current national policies.

In the wet tropical areas of Mexico, as in Colombia, 'the cattle are eating up the people'; there are now twice as many cattle as there are people in rural Mexico. When they first felled the forest, the pioneers began by living from their crops; they cleared and burned the forest and sowed maize, beans, gourds and chillies in the ashes. Usually, 'The men felled, the women sowed', but in some communities women were rigorously excluded from work in the fields. Women were there to sustain the male labour force, to provide sexual services and above all to create the future labour force. (I find it interesting that the sex ratio in these communities is balanced, not dramatically masculine, as in Colombia. There is not the same expulsion of girls.) Now, the forest is running out, and crop production is not sustainable without heavy expenditure, so they are moving from crops to cattle. This is the 'grass revolution of the American tropics' (Parsons 1976) or 'hamburger and frankfurter imperialism' (Feder 1982), to taste.

Cattle are costly, and offer little employment for unskilled labour. There is a tremendous contraction in labour needs. Even in the *ejidos* (Mexican peasants' collective lands), this is a time of intense differentiation – essentially the have-cows and the have-no-cows. Many people leave. We met one youth in a community on the Caribbean coast when we interviewed his family, and met him again a few days later in the middle of the Isthmus of Tehuantepec where his brother was opening up the forest ... These communities are suffering intense differentiation and out-migration. Where there is forest, it is still felled to grow maize for family consumption; when the forest runs out, food must be bought and family strategies must change.

This brings a family crisis. With the shift from crops to cattle, far less labour is needed, paid work becomes scarce and many adults become superfluous. Children have always been an asset; labour has always been an asset; women have been reproducers. Suddenly the need is for labour with non-traditional skills. Women do not know how to produce such labour. Women are not educated; most left school 'because my mother was ill'. Now, money must be earned. Food must be bought. The traditional solution is to move on and clear more forest, but there is little forest left in Mexico, and some effective attempts are being made to protect it.

Marital conflict over fertility is widespread. So recently, these families needed all the children they could breed; now, they are in labour surplus with little prospect for the unskilled. Many young couples say they only want two children and are acting on this. Usually this is the man's decision. Alicia is 15; she has one baby, and her husband plans that she will be sterilised after the next. She is illiterate and has no skills outside the house; no woman in her village earns a living. Conversely, many women in their 30s already have eight or 10 children and do not want any more, but have husbands who see their masculinity threatened by contraception. Domestic violence is common, and often associated with drunkenness.

I said that I came to the women in these localities with a male agenda. My concern was with sustainable livelihoods, differentiation, sources of income, education, services ... I habitually talked at the household level, having a socialist feminist preoccupation with production. I was fascinated by the possibilities of home gardens for sustainable agriculture, for instance. When we asked women to talk about their lives so that we could better understand what it was to be a woman in their community, the focus shifted. I expected them to dwell on events such as their courtship and marriage, bereavements and shifts of wealth and poverty. These things did figure, but the central themes of life histories were:

1. The way they and their families had suffered from the impact of alcoholism or of long-term illness. This figured very largely in their accounts of differentiation within the community.

2. Domestic violence, marital rape and marital conflicts over fertility.

These themes also emerged in workshops. Earlier, I quoted Walby's view (1990) that there are six main structures which make up a system of patriarchy: production, reproduction, culture, sexuality, violence and the state. In workshops and life histories, women questioned all these structures. They challenged their virtual exclusion from production, the devaluation of their reproductive work, the local construction of femininity, their lack of control over their own sexuality, their vulnerability to domestic violence and the patriarchal nature of the local state.

These women have a low opinion of Western technical achievements, because we do not have a technical fix for alcoholism. Many women questioned us at length about contraception and sterilisation. Then they thought, logically enough, that if there is a technical fix which protects you from having babies, there should be one which protects you from wanting alcohol. Not one that you take yourself to help resist the need, but one that someone can slip in your coffee, like a love philtre ...

One interview wove together the themes we had heard from many women; I'd like to quote from it. Lucia is 39 and has 10 children; she was very ill with the last pregnancy, and was advised to have no more. Vicente drinks; he has been repeatedly violent to her since they were married, and to the eldest daughter. He has drunk away nearly all they made pioneering together. The forest is running out.

Magnolia, Lucia's second daughter, had won two school contests in distant towns. 'The teachers told me: "She must keep on studying. She's got a head for learning." But we didn't have enough to send her out there, out of here. If I had had – she would have studied. She might have been able to help us eventually ...

'Men who don't have education work in the fields. That's the only thing they are good for.'

I asked: 'Do they go and work with cattle?'

Lucia: 'No, not with cattle ... There isn't work any more in the fields. They're full of stones ... the more you sow them, the more you use them up; they're only good to plant grass to feed cattle ... When I got married, we went to work in the fields. The soil was good, we planted rice, corn. We both worked equally ... Afterwards only the men would go to tend to the cattle, milk them, inject them, everything … Our job (the women's job) had finished. The fields weren't planted any more … They say we'll have to start working like before. But I don't think so, because the soil isn't good any more.'

'It made me very sad to see that I wasn't feeling well and there wasn't anybody to be with my children, at least to see that they were all right. So I cried and I thought to myself: I'll never go with him again, but, as he drinks, he raped me and this is why I'm pregnant now … If I could have chosen, I would have stopped with my third or fourth child … '

'I don't have anything, not a cent. That's the way he wants it. He has been told that his way is not the right way, but he insists women shouldn't have money, and who is going to convince him otherwise? … Men go not only to drink but also to brothels … They spend a lot of money. I just cry and tell him about the money the children need so much.'

'I tried to get the (contraceptive) injections through a sister of mine because she too suffers because of her husband who also beats her and forces her … But at least she's got money … because she works. She sells some fruit, lemons, she's got a lot of lemons and something else I can't remember, oh, yes, coconuts. She sells coconuts. So she's got an income and she can afford the injections … There's a clinic where you can go to discuss these matters, but you need your husband's signature … the husband must sign or else they won't see you. That's why I'm so sad, there isn't any hope. The doctor told me that he would operate on me because I still had some good years left to bear children, at least five more, but I needed my husband's signature.'

'I tell you, nobody knows it better than the one who is living through it, the one who is living this whole thing. Anyone can say, "This woman is very stupid".'

So what are the recommendations? How do these women define their strategic and practical gender needs? How would we as outsiders define them? Would it help them to have the *ejido* or the farm held jointly, not just by the man, as it is usually? It would help them to have the right to contraception in their own right, but that is known anyway; it is said, truly or falsely, that the availability of contraceptives from clinics is only acceptable and practicable at all so long as the man has right of refusal … In a sense, these women were not looking for guidelines for women in colonisation or guidelines for planners or for the state. They were not providing take-away answers; they were looking for the overthrow of patriarchy, which is rather more difficult.

We nevertheless concluded that there is a very positive role for women 'promoters' in these areas. Women are well aware that they share certain needs, that these needs are not being met and that action they may be able to take as women may help them. One community had experienced 'promoters' and reported very positively. In the short term, public services are painfully lacking. Latrines are rare, and in one community all water must be carried a kilometre from a polluted source; teachers are usually absent; there is a desperate need for income generation. The women are avid for training programmes. Basic needs are very much in the foreground as practical gender needs. Alcoholism and domestic violence will be much more intractable and women's proposed solutions are much more tentative, but the need to seek these strategic gender needs is as deeply felt as hunger and thirst. In the long term, changes are needed at the level of the state. New policies on colonisation are needed; rural areas need a return of economic support and a reduction of support to ranching; women need rights in the family farm. Deep transformations will be required in society; England does a little better for women than Mexico over alcoholism and domestic violence, but is no more willing to grant rights in land to farmers' wives.

Conclusions

So who sets the agenda? Aihwa Ong (1988) has warned us, 'When feminists look overseas, they frequently seek to establish *their* authority on the backs of non-Western women, determining for them the meanings and goals of their lives'. If we simply present the text to present the women, the operation may be merely voyeuristic (Hawkesworth 1989) and reduce the women once again to Others. As researchers, we arrived in these Mexican communities with a socialist-feminist agenda, to be presented with a mix of practical requirements and feminist rebellion. We can try to 'resist the tendency to write our subjectively defined world on to an Other that lies outside it', but I doubt whether we can 'jettison our conceptual baggage' as Ong requires (1988). Only one of our team of five was born a Mexican peasant, and she has experienced higher education since then. We believe that we built a real coalition of interest with many women in these communities (Goetz 1991), but they had no control over our activities once we left.

Working with indigenous women pioneers in Mexico, a team from the Centre for Indigenous Studies are producing a publication, available in Tzeltal, Tzotzil or Spanish, in print or on cassette, in which the women describe the experience of colonisation (Calvo *et al.*, 1991). The team recorded group meetings with the women and some life histories; they then compiled a connected narrative from the recordings, recorded this, took it back to the women, played it to them and corrected it as they required before finally publishing it. Most of the women are illiterate, but there are cassette recorders in their communities on which they can hear the text. So, these pioneer women are now close to owning their representation of their history. This research qualifies as supporting the capacity of women to increase their own self-reliance and internal strength. Our research budget did not allow us to return to our respondents, but I have just given you my selection and translation of Lucia's words, my representation of her life. How far does this have value or validity?

What of the work we have yet to complete and publish (Ursula Arrevillaga, Jennie Bain, Socorro Cancino, Silvana Pacheco, Elia Perez, Janet Townsend)? (We have returned preliminary typed reports to each community.) We plan two main publications. First, a report to be published by the Colegio de Michoacan on the lives of pioneer women; this will consist of selected life histories, each set in the context of its locality, and a summary of our recommendations, drawn from life histories and workshops – since we cannot check back with respondents, names will be fictional. This report will be directed at Non-Government Organisations active in rural Mexico, and at government departments. Second, a book in English (also to be published in Spanish in Mexico if we can arrange it) setting selected life histories in context for a more academic readership, and examining the lessons of life histories and workshops in the light of my work in Colombia and the literature on women pioneers. This last sounds like a classic colonial discourse: can that be avoided?

In academic terms, this research can only yield a very partial narrative of gender in pioneer Mexico, since there are no male voices. Pioneer men talked to us, but there was no attempt to represent men's lives – perhaps through life histories and workshops – or to understand the experiences and feelings which lead them to beat and rape their wives and to have recourse to alcohol.

This research was planned to facilitate empowerment. Can any short-term research achieve this? A single workshop is only a moment in the life of an individual or community, however deeply felt its conclusions. We believe that real progress will be achieved by building coalitions (Goetz 1991), which is by definition a long-term operation. I note that our recommendations, when stated briefly and baldly above, sound very much as if they are being imposed by academics, although we believe that we derived them from the women, and that they can help. We can only hope that our findings will have a resonance in these and other communities, and will aid understanding of the lives of pioneer women.

'One of the *raisons d'être* of the human sciences is surely to comprehend the "otherness" of other cultures. There are few tasks more urgent in a multi-cultural society and an interdependent world, and yet one of modern geography's greatest betrayals was its devaluaton of the specificities of places and people' (Gregory, 1989).

Certainly academics can do nothing to promote empowerment without a recognition of diversity and difference. Can we hope also not to colonise our subjects?

Relevant Literature

Beneria, L. & G. Sen. 1981. 'Accumulation, Reproduction and Women's Work in Economic Development: Boserup Revisited'. *Signs* 7(2), pp. 279–98.

Boserup, E. 1970. *Women's Role in Economic Development*. London and Baltimore, Allen & Unwin.

Calvo, A., A.M. Garza, M.F. Paz & J.M. Ruiz. 1991. *Sk'op Antzetik: Una Historia de Mujeres en la Selva de Chiapas*. San Cristobal de las Casas, Centro de Estudios Indigenas.

Chambers, R. 1969. *Settlement Schemes in Tropical Africa*. London, Routledge & Kegan Paul.

— 1983. *Rural Development: Putting the Last First*. London, Longman.

—, A. Pacey & L.A. Thrupp (eds.). 1989. *Farmer First: Farmer Innovation and Agricultural Research*. London, Intermediate Technology Publications.

Croll, E.J. 1987. 'New Peasant Family Forms in Rural China'. *Journal of Peasant Studies* 24, pp. 469–99.

Dankelman, I. & J. Davidson. 1987. *Women and Environment in the Third World: Alliance for the Future*. London, Earthscan.

Feder, E. 1982. *Lean Cows, Fat Ranchers*. Mimeo.

Flax, J. 1987. 'Postmodernism and Gender Relations in Feminist Theory'. *Signs* 12 (4), pp. 621–43.

Fraser, N. & L.J. Nicholson. 1988. 'Social Criticism without Philosophy: an Encounter between Feminism and Postmodernism'. *Communication*, 10 (3–4), pp. 345–66.

Goetz, A.M. 1991. 'Feminism and the Claim to Know'. In R. Grant & K. Newland (eds.), *Gender in International Relations*, pp. 133–57, Milton Keynes, Open University Press.

Gregory, D. 1989. 'The Crisis of Modernity: Human Geography and Critical Social Theory'. In R. Peet and N.W. Thrift (eds.) *New Models in Geography*, London, Unwin Hyman.

Hawkesworth, M. 1989. 'Knowers, Knowing, Known: Feminist Theory and the Claims of Truth'. *Signs* 14 (13), pp. 533–57.

Hulme, D. 1987. 'State-sponsored Land Settlement Policies: Theory and Practice'. *Development and Change*, 18, pp. 413–36.

— 1988. 'Land Settlement Schemes and Rural Development: a Review Article'. *Sociologia Ruralis* XXVIII (1), pp. 42–61.

Kandiyoti, D. 1988. *Women and Rural Development Policies: the Changing Agenda*. Brighton, Institute of Development Studies Discussion Paper 244.

Lawless, R.I. & L. Monahan (eds.). 1987. *War and Refugees: The Western Sahara Conflict*. London and New York, Pinter.

Lehmann, D. 1988. 'Basismo as if Reality Really Mattered'. Paper presented at Development Studies Association Annual Conference, Birmingham.

Molyneux, M. 1981. 'Women's Emancipation Under Socialism: a Model for the Third World?' *World Development* 9, pp. 1019–38.

— 1985. 'Mobilization without Emancipation? Women's Interests, the State and Revolution in Nicaragua'. *Feminist Studies* 11 (2), pp. 227–54.

Momsen, J.H. & J.G. Townsend (eds.). 1987. *Geography of Gender in the Third World*. London, Hutchinson Education; New York, State University of New York Press.

Moser, C.O.N. 1987. 'Conceptual Framework for Analysis and Policy-making'. In Moser & Peake (eds.), pp. 12–32.

— 1989. 'Gender Planning in the Third World: Meeting Strategic and Practical Gender Needs'. *World Development* 17 (11), pp. 1799–825.

— & L. Peake. 1987. *Women, Human Settlements and Housing*. London, Tavistock Publications.

Ong, A. 1988. 'Colonialism and Modernity: Feminist Re-presentations of Women in Non-western Societies'. *Inscriptions*, 3–4, pp. 79–93.

Palmer, I. (ed.). 1985. *Women's Roles and Gender Differences in Development: Cases for Planners*. West Hartford, Kumarian Press.

Parsons, J.J. 1976. 'Forest to Pasture: Development or Destruction?' *Revista de Biologia Tropical* 24 (Suppl. 1), pp. 121–38.

Radcliffe, S. with J.G. Townsend. 1988. *Gender in the Third World: a Geographical Bibliography*. Brighton, Institute of Development Studies, Development Bibliography 2.

Redclift, N. 1985. 'The Contested Domain: Gender, Accumulation and the Labour Process'. In N. Redclift & M. Mingione (eds.) *Beyond Employment: Household, Gender and Subsistence*, Oxford, Blackwell.

Sayer, A. 1984, *Method in Social Science: a Realist Approach*. London, Hutchinson Education.

Sen, G. & C. Grown. 1987. *Development, Crises and Alternative Visions: Third World Women's Perspectives*. New York, Monthly Review Press.

Townsend, J.G. 1976. *Land and Society in the Middle Magdalena Valley, Colombia*. Oxford, unpublished Ph.D. thesis.

— 1977. 'Perceived Worlds of the Colonists of Tropical Rainforest, Colombia'. *Transactions, Institute of British Geographers* New Series 2(4), pp. 430–57.

— 1988. *Women in Developing Countries: a Select, Annotated Bibliography for Development Organizations*. Brighton, Institute of Development Studies, Development Bibliography 1.

— & S. Wilson de Acosta. 1987. 'Gender Roles in Colonization of Rainforest: a Colombian Case Study'. In J.H. Momsen and J.G. Townsend (eds.), pp. 240–58.

Walby, S. 1990. *Theorizing Patriarchy*. Oxford, Blackwell.

White, B. 1984. 'Measuring Time Allocation, Decision-making and Agrarian Changes Affecting Rural Women: Examples from Recent Research in Indonesia'. *Bulletin of the Institute of Development Studies*, 15 (3), pp. 18–33.

9

Modernity, Post-modernity and the New Social Movements

by Frans J. Schuurman

Introduction

It was in the dark European Middle Ages that the expression 'the pen is mightier than the sword' was coined. It was a period in which the Catholic Church was the prime bearer of an unswaying hegemonic ideology. In the name of the Word, wars were fought and the Word created new realities on the smouldering remains left by the Sword. However, after the Renaissance, but especially after the onset of the Enlightenment, the Word increasingly acquired secular connotations. The Word became translated into Theory. The Enlightenment gave birth to modernity, a belief in rational politico-economic projects leading to universal human emancipation. Socialism and capitalism became the foremost projects of modernity.

The emerging idea within social sciences about the 'makeability' of society led, however, to an increasing dialectical relation with reality. Theory and reality began to develop their own internal dynamics. As a result theory had the tendency to move faster than reality. Among social scientists the notion grew that if theory did not match reality then reality was wrong.

Nowadays, the once-hegemonic emancipation projects of modernity are under heavy post-modern fire. The artillery is not only aimed at the universality of the modernity project (i.e., the universal significance and applicability of the emancipation project) but also at its realisability. According to Lyotard, modernity lost its credibility with Auschwitz and Stalin.

Development theories, whether Marxist, neo-Marxist or of the modernisation brand, have had their fair share of post-modern critique in the 1980s.

The attack on the modernisation theories, led in the second half of the 1960s by the radical Left, resulted for some time in an upsurge of dependency, modes of production and world system theories. The enthusiastic debates, however, increasingly showed an academic involution as well as a negation of the divergent reality in underdeveloped countries. This enabled the neo-conservative counter-revolutionaries (see Toye 1987) to gain strength from the mid-1970s onwards. Currently, with the demise of international socialism, this latter trend in development theory has gained a near-hegemonic position, at least in the most important international development institutions.

It was not only the post-modern critique which the radical development theories had to endure. A sometimes devastating critique was coined from within its own circles. The teleological and economic determinist nature of (neo)Marxist development theories has especially been criticised (Bernstein 1979; Booth 1985; Mouzelis 1988; Corbridge 1989). Post-modernism, however, added another more general dimension to the critiques.

It was not only the awareness that reality in the developing countries took on such a pluralist character that no metanarrative adequately could explain it. It was specifically the disenchantment with metanarratives as such that constituted the main core of the post-modernist point of view. As mentioned above, modernity was considered to have gone down the drain with Stalin and Auschwitz. The metanarrative of human emancipation, in terms of the Enlightenment ideals of liberty, equality and fraternity through a trust in truth, reason and morality, was supposed to have become unattainable along the lines stipulated within the socialist or modernisation projects.

There is, however, no homogeneity within post-modernism in the reaction concerning this grand disillusion. Some, like Baudrillard, have shifted to an extreme nihilistic position where every collective emancipatory project, whether inside or outside the old discredited metanarratives, is doomed to failure (Norris 1990). The attempt to construct collective identities is illusionary because of the non-existence of a final truth as the object of collective action and the impossibility of a discourse construction as a true representation of reality.

Not all post-modernists share this point of view, however. Writers like Foucault and Deleuze, also disillusioned with the modernity project, occupied less extreme positions and pointed out the existence of multiple discourses within society which act as counterpoints to the hegemonic power ideology which tries to colonise the inner life-world.

Disillusionment with the progressive role of the labour proletariat and the virtual disappearance of socialism as a political project led to a scramble by radical social scientists for a post-modern and post-Marxist position. Increasingly, attention fell upon the so-called new social movements in the North as well as in the South as collective attempts within civil society to create new identities and to thwart the hegemonic attempts of the mainstream ideology to colonise the inner life-spaces.

Initially the bulk of the literature concentrated on new social movements in the industrialised countries: the peace and ecology movements and the women's movements. Initially also, the theoretical interpretations of these movements underlined the possible discovery of a new revolutionary subject, a new agent which could play a central role in a fundamental reform of society. Movements as such were divided into 'real' social movements (defined as true historic agents) and mere protesting collectivities. Later on in the 1980s the interpretations turned out to be more diffuse, for two apparent reasons.

First, the movements themselves developed a growing heterogeneity in ideology and strategy. The schism between the *Fundis* and the *Realos* in the German ecological movement could provide an example in this respect (Scott 1990). Second, the increasing influence of post-modern critique led the social movement 'watchers' to place less confidence in the former transformative metanarratives (à la Touraine 1989 and Castells 1983) concerning new social movements. The new line adopted was that new social movements were associations within the subaltern classes where (embryonic) processes took place concerning the creation of new, non-commoditive values, new lines of horizontal communication – in short the creation of a new identity (Evers 1985), an identity, contrary to the universality of the modernity projects, with its own localised goals of emancipation, which did not lead to a bid for political power, but was based in local movements with multiple identities located in civil society, stressing new ways of social communication (solidarity and mutual understanding) and a new harmonic relationship with nature.

Increasingly, studies of new social movements in underdeveloped countries took aboard this post-modern inspired interpretation of new social movements (e.g., Razeto 1986 and Friedmann 1989b). This post-modern account of social movements at least does not carry with it the nihilistic notions of an extreme post-modern position where collective identities are non-existent and where there is 'indifference towards difference'. Furthermore, a pragmatic and realistic post-modernism offers a powerful analytical tool: the deconstruction not only of metanarratives but also of lower-order discourses. Deconstructing identities and discourses within the gamut of social movements could warn us against an unrealistic interpretation of these movements.

Still, in spite of the value of a post-modern deconstruction of modernist narratives, I would like to launch a general caution against post-modern inspired interpretations of new social movements in the South as well as in the North. I think that in this respect we could very well be facing another example of theory moving faster than reality, another example of teleological theorising. I will limit my arguments to social movements in the South, specifically in Latin America. But the drift of the arguments to be presented (i.e., social movements still form part of the modernity project) I consider also valid for social movements in the Western industrialised countries.

Beyond the Paradox of Epimenides

Putting forward a critique of post-modern approaches results in an uneasy feeling of getting entangled in the paradox of Epimenides about the Cretan who stated that all people from Crete were liars. If 'the crisis of representation' is the central message of post-modernity then criticising post-modern interpretations of the nature of social movements is exactly what post-modernity is all about. The only way to solve this sort of paradox is to question its assumptions. So, the question could be raised whether the Cretan really is from Crete or whether the post-modern critique really is post-modern.

Boyne and Rattansi (1990) make a distinction between modernity and modernism. With a reference to Berman they characterise modernity as 'a maelstrom that promises adventure, joy and growth, transformation of ourselves and the world, but also threatens to destroy cherished traditions and securities; it unites by cutting across class, region and ideology and yet disintegrates through incessant change, contradiction and ambiguity' (p. 2). Also they mention the 'two sides of modernity', being 'progressive union of scientific objectivity and politico-economic rationality ...' (p. 5).

Modernism, on the other hand, is '[preoccupied] with highlighting the means of representation, the disruption of narrative, and the contradiction and fragmentation in subjectivity and identity ...' According to Boyne's and Rattansi's account of modernism, it always constituted a critique of modernity by refusing to endorse 'any simplistic beliefs in the progressive capacity of science and technology ... nor did it hold with positivism and the idea of the integrated individual subject ...' (p. 8). What Boyne and Rattansi subsequently claim, and I agree with them in this respect, is that this distinction between modernism and post-modernism (as a 'self-proclaimed commitment to heterogeneity, fragmentation and difference') tends to become blurred. This means that the post-modern critique of the representation crisis in modernity actually is based itself on a critical tradition within modernism. If this proposition has any validity, it allows us to criticise the post-modern interpretation of social movements from a modernist point of view.

The arguments I would like to bring forward are cast in terms of a number of disjunctive discourses: firstly, the disjuncture or disarticulation between the above-mentioned post-modern inspired scientific interpretations of new social movements on the one hand and the discourses of the movements themselves on the other hand; secondly, the disjuncture between the discourses of Latin American political parties and those of the social movements; and lastly, I would like to stress the heterogeneity of discourses within the conglomerate of new social movements themselves.

My major point is that new social movements in the South are not by any means post-modern. Categorising the creation of new values, new life-styles, new ways of communication and new ways of collective action as post-modern denies the history of the movements and misinterprets what they are all about. Whatever the relevance of characterising Northern societies as post-industrial and post-modern, Southern societies for sure are not. It would be against common sense to interpret under-developed countries as post-industrial.

On the contrary, what characterises these countries is an aborted modernity project where the Enlightenment ideals of liberty, equality and fraternity are much farther out of sight than they ever were in the North. It would be counterproductive and politically conservative to interpret the failure of the modernity project in the South as a post-modern condition. I agree with Jürgen Habermas (1990) when he says that the modernity project in the North is still unfinished, which leads him to oppose the post-modernists. I certainly would apply the notion of an unfinished modernity project to the underdeveloped countries. It would be politically naive and demobilising to view social movements in the South solely as breeding grounds of a new post-modern identity.

The history of many of these movements started in the 1970s when many countries in Latin America suffered from the political and economic consequences of military rule. The political, economic and cultural exclusion of the subaltern classes in that period was such that all sorts of popular organisations came into existence to defend their sheer physical existence and other basic human rights. In various countries (in some more than others) these movements played an important role in finally bringing down the military (Munck 1989). The influence of social movements on the political system, however, tended to diminish after the fall of the military dictatorships.

Redemocratisation?

The 1980s are known in Latin America as *la década perdida* (the lost decade) with the ending of military rule as about the only bright element. The return to power of civilian regimes has been labelled as redemocratisation. The latter term however is not as unproblematic as it seems. In the first place, it suggests that before the instalment of the authoritarian military regimes in the 1970s Latin America had a democratic tradition. But history shows that, with a few periodic exceptions in some countries, the Latin American political system can be better described in terms of oligarchic rule, populism and corporatism than in terms of democracy (Touraine 1989 and Huber Stephens 1989). In the second place, the concept of redemocratisation suggests that democracy is now reigning in Latin America. But let us look at some economic and political facts.

Present 'democratic' regimes in Latin America tend to continue the neo-liberal economic model initiated by the military: a policy of the free market and an open door for foreign investment. The large-scale privatisation of government-owned enterprises has recently been added. The social polarisation and the falling living standards for the millions of Latin American poor which took on such marked characteristics during military rule are being continued by the present economic model. According to ECLA reports, no less than 44 per cent of Latin Americans live below the poverty line. Average per capita income in Latin America decreased in the 1980s by 8 per cent; in Argentina, Peru and Bolivia it fell by 25 per cent. Minimum urban wages have declined by 74 per cent in Peru, 50 per cent in Mexico, 30 per cent in Brazil and 21 per cent in Chile. There has been an overall decline of 50 per cent in state expenditure on health care and education (Petras and Morley 1991). Mortality rates (especially for children) and large-scale undernourishment increased. The cholera epidemic, starting in Peru, was not an accidental occurrence.

Yet, in spite of increasing poverty, Latin America was a net exporter of capital ($200 billion between 1982 and 1989). Corruption in government circles is widespread. Ex-presidents Alan García of Peru and Lusinchi of Venezuela are facing serious charges in this respect, as are various Brazilian ex-ministers.

In short, democracy has not until now brought any important benefits for the Latin American poor.

Maybe then there is democracy in a political sense? The answer depends of course on how one defines democracy. Of the standard denotation of democracy probably only the element of free elections applies in Latin America. There is still no representative political system, para-military death squads harassing and killing progressives are active in an increasing number of countries, and the military still has the (now unspoken) power to veto political decisions.

For these reasons it is factually incorrect to speak of a redemocratisation in Latin America. In the case of Chile, the term redemocratisation has been wisely avoided by the new powerholders. The Concertación, the alliance between socialists and Christian democrats, prefers to use the concept of 'transition to democracy'.

The present significance of social movements in Latin America cannot be interpreted without looking at origins and trajectories. In the next paragraphs I will try to do that for the Chilean case.

The Heritage of Authoritarian Rule in Chile

After Pinochet's *coup d'état* of 11 September 1973, the regime immediately began to rearrange the political-administrative system. The National Congress was disbanded, political parties were declared illegal, local and regional civil servants were fired, and leaders of popular organisations (originating in the Frei and Allende period) were replaced.

In 1975 the neo-liberal economic package was introduced at a fast pace. The public budget was reduced by 27 per cent, interest tariffs were liberated and import duties reduced. This resulted in a negative economic growth of 12.9 per cent in 1975. In the next year real wages were down to 62 per cent of the 1970 level. The inflow of transnational capital dismantled the national industrial sector. The percentage of wage labourers decreased dramatically from 22.3 per cent in 1974 to 7.5 per cent in 1984. The percentage of people 'employed' within the informal economy increased from 18 per cent in 1970 to 30 per cent in 1989. Recent figures show that from 1979–89 the top 40 per cent of the income categories increased their share of the GNP from 71.8 per cent to 77 per cent. The share of the poorest 40 per cent went down from 14 per cent to 11.8 per cent.

From 1976 to 1980 foreign investments and the growth of the export sector led to a macro-economic growth. Yet, in 1982, this neo-liberal 'Chicago' model led to a sudden sharpening of the unemployment rate, leading to large-scale protests the following year, known as *Protesta Nacional*. All in all, the low-income groups increasingly paid the price for this policy of structural adjustment. They experienced a severe decline in health services, educational standards and income.

Obviously, this economic model needed a large degree of political repression, executed by the DINA secret police (renamed CNI in 1977). The number of political assassinations (especially during the first months after the coup) during the Pinochet regime is not exactly known; estimates vary between 9,000 and 30,000.

The concept of marginality cannot adequately describe the situation of the low-income groups in this period. *Exclusion* would be a better-suited concept. The poor did not participate in whatever economic growth there was, and there was a total lack of political participation. The relations between state and society were severed.

Nevertheless, the political repression and the dramatic decline in living standards of the poorer part of the population led to the constitution of new social actors. Already in October 1973 the first human rights organisation was created: the *Comité de Cooperación para la Paz en Chile* (transformed in 1976 to *Vicaria de la Solidaridad*), a joint initiative of Catholic and Protestant churches. In later years other human rights organisations were created, such as CODEPU (*Comité de Defensa de los Derechos del Pueblo*) and SERPAJ (*Servicio de Paz y Justicia*).

In 1975 the first *pobladores* organisations were founded, basically of two types. The first of these functioned at the grassroots level and are commonly known as *Organizaciones Económicas Populares* (OEPs). The activities engaged in were subsistence-oriented, like joint cooking (*ollas comunes*), joint buying of food at the local market, basic health care (*grupos de salud*), etc.

The second type of *pobladores* organisations functioned at a higher level and were aimed at representing low-income neighbourhoods. In 1976 the first of these was created, the *Coordinadora Metropolitana de Pobladores* (METRO), followed shortly by organisations like *Solidaridad, Dignidad, Comité Unitario de Pobladores* (CUP) and *Pobladores Unidos*. These organisations were closely linked to the underground political parties and this led to much mutual distrust; coalitions came and went.

Women played an important role in the human rights organisations and in the grassroots OEPs. The first specifically feminist organisation was formed in 1977, *El Círculo de Estudios de la Mujer*, a small group of middle-class women. In the period of the National Protest (1983–4) an explosive development of women's organisations took place, e.g., *La Morada, Movimiento por Emancipación de la Mujer Chilena* (MEMCH '83) and *Centro de Servicios y Promoción de la Mujer* (DOMOS).

Giving in to external as well as internal political pressures, the Pinochet regime felt confident enough to allow a plebiscite in 1988 and let the Chilean people decide on continuation of Pinochet's presidential term. The victorious 'No' of October 1988 was a bitter pill to swallow for the Pinochetistas.

With the political parties (except for the communists) legalised by then, the stage was set for the beginning of the election campaigns. Looking at the three major actors (the state, the political parties and the conglomerate of social movements), the situation in the pre-election period can briefly be characterised as follows. The state (i.e., the military) was busily engaged in making life as difficult as possible for the opposition in case they should win the elections of December 1989. For example, legislation was changed in such a way that top civil servants could not be fired by a new government; the copper reserve fund was nearly emptied by a premature payment of external debts; and potentially incriminating files were destroyed. The political parties tried to re-establish links with their voters, a troublesome process ridden with problems as we will see. Finally, the social movements were engaged in forming new coalitions and formulating political demands.

The Transition to Democracy
and the Quest for a Progressive Political Project

Although the opposition won the December 1989 elections and subsequently took over the presidency in March 1990, there are still a number of factors which justify the use of the concept of transition to democracy rather than redemocratisation.

As in Argentina, the Chilean military gave up their direct and visible involvement in politics. However, indirectly they still have considerable political influence. Unlike Argentina, the Chilean military leaders left the political scene unscathed, although as an institution the army lost a lot of prestige. General Pinochet remained in his position as commander-in-chief of the army and still acts as a Nemesis for the government of President Patricio Aylwin. In Argentina, the junta members of the dirty war (Generals Videla, Viola, Galtieri, etc.) were put on trial in 1985 and sentenced to long-term imprisonment, but released in December 1990 by President Menem. During the period 1983–90 Argentina had four military rebellions, headed by the so-called *carapintadas*. According to ex-president Raúl Alfonsín, 'one cannot rule in Argentina without the military'. As in neighbouring Argentina, in Chile the army is still present in the background and acts as a constraint on civilian governments.

Although the ban on political parties was lifted and free elections announced, pre-election activities in Chile still took place within an authoritarian context. The opposition parties were allowed much less propaganda time (e.g., on television) than other (self-defined) democratic parties which were more or less sympathetic to the existing military regime. Also, the military junta changed the spatial boundaries of the constituencies, expecting a major electoral benefit from this gerrymandering. Finally, although the opposition parties (united in the Concertación) won the parliamentary and presidential elections, there were still many 'Pinochetistas' present in the government apparatus at the national and local level.

Although these arguments already indicate the limitations of the new democracy, there is another, perhaps more fundamental, reason for using the term 'transition to democracy'. Democracy as a concept refers to the way in which the following three actors interrelate: the state, political parties and civil society (consisting of a conglomerate of social actors). Political parties should be the platform on which the demands of a plurality of social actors are translated into political projects. The state and parliament constitute the scene where these political projects are translated, via a process of consensus and/or compromise, into policy measures.

This descriptive definition of democracy points to three potential bottlenecks which are totally ignored by a Fukuyama-like euphoria concerning the victory of liberal democracy. The first bottleneck concerns the relation between political parties and social actors. If political parties wield a discourse that does not articulate with the daily-life experiences of social actors then these parties can hardly be described as political representations of those social actors.

The second bottleneck is the process of consensus and/or compromise leading to the concrete policy measures. This process is for most social actors rather nebulous and subsequently political parties get accused of engaging in wheeling and dealing. The third bottleneck is the final consequence of this, i.e., that categories of social actors do not feel that their demands are being met by policy measures. This being the case, social actors can respond in two ways: either they organise themselves into social movements and engage in extra-parliamentary action, or they retreat into private life and refrain from any action whatsoever (including voting).

This disjuncture between political and social discourses and practices within a so-called democratic system also arises in developed countries but it is more pronounced in the underdeveloped world. Approached in this way, the North can also be characterised as being in a transition to democracy, but that need not concern us here.

It is important to point out that problems in the emerged democracies in Latin America are not only of a much more poignant nature than in the Northern countries but also are a result of a different historical trajectory of the political system.

In the case of Chile, the disjuncture between political and social discourses (between *lo político* and *lo social*) was deepened during the Pinochet regime. Nearly 17 years of dictatorship led to a destruction of civil society through systematic repression of 'dangerous' forms of collective identity. Political repression thus tends to lead to an atomisation, an individualisation within civil society. Still, the negative effects on the low-income groups of the Chilean economic model and the outrage of the violation of human rights increasingly led to the emergence of social movements as new social actors.

For the socialists, the fall of the Berlin Wall in 1989 came at a very inopportune moment. Together with the Christian democrats they had formed the major opposition party, the Concertación. The problem, then, which the socialists faced was how to define a progressive socialist project in the pre-election period. Besides the obvious problems of being in one party with the conservative Christian democrats and the threatening presence of Pinochet, the socialists found themselves in an ideological crisis which saw them lose ground to the more conservative elements within the Concertación. Reverting to the notion of *poder popular* (popular power, the slogan during the Allende regime) during the pre-election campaign was out of the question.

As we know, the Concertación won the elections in December 1989 and, since March 1990, has governed with a Christian democrat for president: Patricio Aylwin. In the meantime, there is an ongoing discussion in socialist circles on where to look for the elements to construct a progressive political ideology. Municipal elections were to be held in June 1992 and the socialist parties thought it opportune to sharpen their political profile within the coalition. Still confronted with the constraints mentioned earlier, there are some calls on the political Left to look more closely at the dynamics of civil society to see whether it is possible to construct, primarily at a basic and pragmatic political level, the foundation of a new progressive ideology. The actors in civil society towards which the political Left is looking are constituted by the social movements in Chile. It seems that the responsibility for constructing an alternative socialist-like or social-democratic paradigm is being laid at the doorstep of the *sociedad civil* instead of the *sociedad política*. The problem, however, is that with the absence of a political ideology as an articulating mechanism it will be very difficult if not impossible for the social movements (a heterogeneous conglomerate) to join forces and form a political project. This would lead to a stalemate, where both actors are waiting for the other to make a move.

For the time being, the relation between political parties and social movements can best be described as one of disjunctive discourses.

The Disjuncture between Political and Social Discourses

The potential role of the Chilean social movements in the transition process has two interrelated aspects. In the first place there is the necessity to strengthen the organisation, to deepen the identity, in short to constitute the social movement as a social actor. As mentioned above, nearly 17 years of political repression of 'dangerous' forms of collective identity led to an atomisation, an individualisation within civil society.

The second aspect of the role of social movements in the transition process concerns the political translation of the potential reinforced status as a social actor. This aspect has been hotly debated in the international literature on social movements (e.g., Evers 1985; Fuentes and Frank 1989; Dhanagare and John 1988). There are those authors who see in the strengthening of social movements/actors a new way of doing politics. This identity-forming process is considered to be hindered by looking for attachments to the political arena. Alienating tendencies are supposed to exert a negative influence on the identity of social movements (e.g., Evers 1985). Others, however, stress the importance of linking up with social-democratic parties as the only way of effectively improving the fate of the poor (e.g., Dhanagare and John 1988). In general, the two notions are considered mutually exclusive, but, as I will indicate in the conclusion to this chapter, this should not necessarily be the case.

Considering the two above-mentioned aspects (identity formation and the link to the political platform) of the role of social movements in the current transition process in Chile, the following remarks are of importance.

1. The strengthening of the movements as a social actor has not been facilitated by the political parties. Political fragmentation within the social movements is an old phenomenon in Chile, and was again manifest from 1985 onwards when the political parties increasingly regained legality. For example, when the trade union CUT (*Central Unitaria de Trabajadores*) was officially reconstituted in 1988, the functions in the directive were divided according to membership of political parties instead of reflecting representation from the bottom upwards. In addition, there has been a massive move, starting around 1985, by leaders of social movements to functions within political parties. Many social movements were virtually beheaded in their leadership. The feminist movement especially lost many people. Because of the strong ties between many social movements and political parties, it is difficult for these social actors to construct their identities in an autonomous manner.

2. Something potentially positive can nonetheless be discerned in this. If many social movements have strong ties with political parties, one could suppose that these movements have a direct line to the political arena. But this is not as simple as it seems. Leaders of social movements could be more closely affiliated to their party than to the movement itself. In addition, the social movements phenomenon has for a long time taken a very marginal position in political parties. The latter are much more concerned with gaining state power than with constructing a representative political identity for themselves.

In the pre-election period in Chile, social movements were not seen as a social actor with whom political parties should enter into discussion, with the exception of the trade union CUT. The point is not only that political parties have a strong étatist attitude, but also that in spite of the links with social movements two different languages are spoken.

3. At the time of Allende the concept of *poder popular* (popular power) acted as an articulating mechanism between grassroots organisations, political parties of the Left and the state. As mentioned in the introduction to this chapter, the current situation is entirely different. Not only has the socialist paradigm apparently lost its attraction, but Pinochet's role as Nemesis to the newly-won democracy is inhibiting socialist parties in developing a too-radical political programme even if they could and wanted to.

The character of social movements has also changed. During the Allende period the existence of grassroots organisations was a result of initiatives taken by Allende's political party, the Unidad Popular. By contrast, the social movements which emerged during the Pinochet regime have a much more autonomous background. In spite of the penetration of political parties into the social movements mentioned earlier, the parties do not know how to relate to many of these movements. When, during the pre-election period, a representative of the Concertación visited an *olla común* he stated that if the Concertación won the elections there would be no longer be any need for *ollas comunes*. The reaction of the women in question was rather negative: 'It is for us to decide what to do with our organisation.' The intention of this political representative was well-meant but at the same time it was a total negation of what these women had brought about during years of repression. This lack of a suitable political discourse, understandable and acceptable for the subaltern classes, hinders the political articulation of the social movements.

In addition to a strong identity as a social actor, the existence of a suitable political project is certainly a necessary precondition to articulating the heterogeneity of social movements to the political platform.

The Heterogeneity of Social Movements' Discourses
It is useful to stress that there exists no homogeneous discourse in the wide field of Latin American social movements. One attempt to systematise this heterogeneity of discourses within the world of social movements was made by Eugenio Tironi (1987). Based on an analysis of discourses in several social movements in Santiago, Tironi constructed the following matrix:

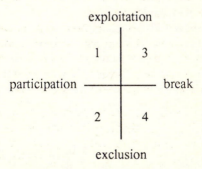

The variable on the vertical axis is 'social identity' (based upon a continuum between feeling exploited and feeling excluded). The horizontal axis is 'relation with the system' (varying between participation within the wider political, economic and cultural context, and a breaking away from that context).

The cells in the matrix were characterised by Tironi as follows:

ad 1. This quadrant includes actors who feel exploited by the system, yet look for increased participation. The prototype of this social actor is the trade union. Trade unionists have an *obrero* (worker) identity and direct themselves towards the state, the employers and the political parties in order to participate in the system on a more equal footing.

ad 2. This is the world of the *pobladores* movements. *Pobladores* feel excluded, neglected by the state, and as such want recognition as citizens, as *ciudadanos*. Their demands concern issues such as access to decent housing and health services. Sometimes the actors in this quadrant are supposed to be prone to populist regimes.

ad 3. This is the revolutionary quadrant, consisting of actors who feel exploited on all fronts (politically, economically and culturally) by the (capitalist) system and do not adhere to the rules of the game like the trade union militant. They place themselves outside of the system and engage in armed battle.

ad 4. The actors in this quadrant not only feel excluded, but deeply mistrust the state and political parties which have always let them down. As such these actors have increasingly engaged in defensive, subsistence-oriented collective activities like the soup kitchens. Writing about these collectives, the Chilean author Luis Razeto (1986) emphasises the existence of affective values instead of an instrumental-political orient-ation. As such he detects an autonomous discourse not directed towards participation but towards the construction of an alternative life-style, based upon an economy of solidarity.

Tironi's matrix is a useful heuristic device for differentiating between discourses of social movements. But it does not overcome the drawback that it suggests that individuals finding themselves in one quadrant, because of an analysis of the discourse of their social movement, can still have multiple subject positions with the accompanying array of discour-ses. Membership of quadrant 4 does not guarantee that you invariably want a break with the system. There is a difference between, on the one hand, the discourse at the level of the movement itself and, on the other hand, the discourse at the individual level. The fact that people belong to a certain social movement does not mean that they have the same outlook on life (social identity).

In an interview with the board of a small trade union in Santiago, I asked each individual to divide the Chilean society into two or three segments and to situate himself in one of the segments. The answers showed a wide variety and included a differentiation into poor and rich, into *pobladores* and the rest, into *obreros* (blue-collar workers) and white-collar workers. Some post-modernists would point out that there is not necessarily a contradiction between the answers: all three positions could be combined into one and the same person. The resulting discourse can as such not be determined by using a classification scheme which tries to objectify the place of the individual in the wider context. Someone who can be 'objectively' classified as a blue-collar worker might very well have a discourse based upon being a *poblador* as well.

I agree with this post-modernist interpretation. But what is then ignored is the fact that one can be discriminated against in all three positions mentioned earlier: for being poor, for being a *poblador* and for being a labourer. This commonly experienced discrimination can drive people together into social movements which try to handle a discourse in which the several domains of discrimination are covered.

Yet the proof of the pudding comes at the moment that discourse is translated into action. Action undertaken based on an individual discourse of being a *poblador* differs from a discourse in which you grant yourself an *obrero* identity. These are crucial points in the life-cycle of social movements: first, to construct a common discourse in spite of the different individual interpretations of how society functions and along what lines one feels discriminated against, and after that, to move from discourse to action, where care must be taken that the proposed action covers all the various points of possible discrimination on the individual level. This can, however, only be done if the initial discourse used as a rallying point for potential members is broadened in order not to lose membership; a difficult task for every social movement. The ecological movement in Germany provides an example of the internal conflict to which this can lead (Scott 1990). To be able to grasp this dimension fully calls for an actor-oriented approach which is beyond the purpose of this chapter.

The point to grasp is that discourses within and between social movements differ, and it is as such difficult for these movements to construct an articulating discourse to unify themselves and to express themselves in a coherent way in a political project.

Also to be taken into account is that a discourse position is not static: movements and individuals go from one discourse to another depending upon the way their own identity construction takes place and depending upon the reactions of other social and political actors.

Membership of a subaltern class does not (contrary to the structuralist vision) predetermine the discourse. Multiple subject positions taken up by one individual might lead to the handling of different discourses, dependent upon the context. To give another example: women in popular neighbourhoods potentially have a number of discourses at their disposal to define their relation with the wider political, economic and cultural context. They can choose between the discourses of the feminist movement, of the 'barrio' movement, of the subsistence-oriented organisations, etc. Granted, it is due to the deconstructionist critique of post-modernity that this anti-structuralist interpretation of the relation between individual subject positions and discourses finds increasing acceptance. Yet, what fails is the recognition that the various subject positions in the examples given have a common denominator, i.e., the feeling of being exploited, excluded or discriminated against.

Social Movements and the New Modernity Project

In the past decade Latin America witnessed the demise of authoritarian regimes and a return to civilian rule. Social movements found themselves increasingly confronted with a political context in which the old political parties took up their usual place and role in society. Economically, the context was defined by either a structural adjustment policy or (in the case of Chile) a continuation of the economic model created by the military. Formally, the Latin American governments are democratic, but in many instances this democracy does not work for the poor.

What does this mean for the position and the discourses of social movements? On the one hand, there are those social movements which uphold a basically defensive discourse based upon a distrust of policy-makers. It would, however, be a tragic mistake to take the survival strategy of these movements as embryonic signs of a new way of life. On the other hand, there are social movements with a more pro-active attitude, trying to influence political parties or putting pressure on the government to incorporate them into the socio-economic and political system, commonly referred to as democracy. In both cases, my feeling is that this latter option constitutes the final target of Latin American social movements: to be incorporated into the modernity project however piecemeal that may be. I do not refer here to Fukuyama's interpretation of democracy in the sense of a neo-liberal economic system ruled by a free market ideology. I mean incorporation into a 'new' modernity project where the state assumes responsibility for its citizens, where Citizenship and Participation (in short Emancipation) fly high in the banner of state policy.

It would be counterproductive for social movements to take seriously the advice of certain social movement scientists above all to keep an autonomous discourse all the way, or your inner life-world will be incorporated within the hegemonic ideology, be it democracy or otherwise. What I would like to stress is the absolute necessity for progressive political parties and so-called democratic government to recognise their responsibility and indeed incorporate the poor finally into the democratic project, because without that democracy cannot be.

Should one give up emancipation because of post-modern criticism, should one abstain from trying to construct a feasible progressive political project because it incorporates you into a non-existent reality? Not even for the industrialised Northern countries would I prescribe such advice, let alone for the excluded masses in the South which are and always have been outside modernity and finally want in.

The foregoing gives the impression of a rather instrumental analysis of what a social movement is about. I realise very well that membership of a social movement includes much more than just an instrumentalist choice. Affective values play a very important role, the feeling of belonging to a greater receptive collectivity in a situation where individuals are constantly discriminated against. This however should not sidetrack us from valuing these movements as trying to attain the goal of citizenship and political participation.

The field of social movements research is riddled with many disjunctive discourses, between the researchers themselves, between researchers and the social movements, between political parties and the social movements and within the social movements themselves. Denying these disjunctive discourses and romanticising these social movements seems to me counterproductive. Leftist political parties are in search of a tenable progressive political project where democracy is really given a material content, and these social movements could play a very important role in the construction of such a project. To overcome disjunctive discourses it is vital to view these movements in terms of an emancipatory force trying to enter into the aborted modernity project in underdeveloped countries.

Discourse Imperialism?
Many forms of social movements in the Third World have been and still are supported by international Non-Governmental Organisations (NGOs). Especially in Latin America, this support dates back to the exclusionary economic policy instigated by the military regimes in the 1970s and 1980s. The subsequent creation of defensive, subsistence-oriented organisations within civil society was in many cases actively supported by international NGOs. The (perforce) autonomous discourses of these social movements found a willing ear in the NGO world, which at that time was influenced by notions such as self-reliance, coming from dependency theories.

The continued and spreading relations between Northern NGOs and social movements in the South – with the latter in a position of financial dependency – begs the question about a possible discourse imperialism imposed by the Northern NGOs. In spite of their praxis-oriented image, the developmental NGOs in the North are tireless discourse-producers. The past two decades have witnessed the coming and going of several developmental fads and related discourses as solutions for the poor in the Third World: cooperatives, integrated rural development, attention to the environment, women, and the urban poor in general. New discourses were developed according to an interplay of widely varying factors: disappointment with certain development projects, changing societal and political conditions in the North (related to late-Fordism, the oil crisis, the demise of socialism, etc.), and the growing impasse in development theories. Grassroots organisations in the South were practically forced to develop similar discourses if they wanted to keep the financial resources flowing. Consequently, many of these organisations have become very apt in applying 'trigger-words' in their project proposals.

I do not want to imply that grassroots organisations and NGOs in the Third World which receive foreign aid develop discourses which are totally alien to their situation. Of course, the emphasis on items such as emancipation of women or sustainable development, presently favoured by the Northern NGOs, also has relevance in the Third World. The point is that the dependent relation with foreign donors could lead to an internalisation of the donor's discourse without either party realising it.

While the discourses of many Northern NGOs still favour concepts such as autonomy and self-reliance, the people in many Third World countries (especially in Latin America) are trying to give substance to the redemocratisation process in their societies. Grassroots organisations and local NGOs tend to think less and less in terms of autonomous, defensive strategies.

At present, political empowerment of the poor is the name of the game. Grassroots organisations and local NGOs in the South could play an important role in bridging the gap between civil society and the political system. These organisations would benefit from a discourse revision in the developmental agencies in the North and a much greater subsequent emphasis on political empowerment (see, e.g., Clark 1991).

Relevant Literature

Albertsen, N. 1988. 'Postmodernism, Post-Fordism, and Critical Social Theory'. *Environment and Planning* D 6, pp. 339–65.

Barros, R. 1986. 'The Left and Democracy: Recent Debates in Latin America'. *Telos* 68, pp. 49–70.

Belden Fields, A. 1988. 'In Defense of Political Economy and Systemic Analysis: a Critique of Prevailing Theoretical Approaches to the New Social Movements'. In Nelson and Grossberg (eds.), *Marxism and the Interpretation of Culture*, Urbana, University of Illinois Press, pp. 141–56.

Berman, M. 1982. *The Experience of Modernity: All that is Solid Melts into Air*. New York, Simon and Schuster.

Bernstein, H. 1979. 'Sociology of Underdevelopment vs. Sociology of Development?' In D. Lehmann (ed.), *Development Theory*, London, Cass, pp. 77–106.

Booth, D. 1985. 'Marxism and Development Sociology: Interpreting the Impasse'. *World Development* 13 (7), pp. 761–87.

Boulding, E. 1989. 'Cultural Perspectives on Development: the Relevance of Sociology and Anthropology'. *Alternatives* XIV, pp. 107–22.

Boyne, R. & A. Rattansi. 1990. *Postmodernism and Society*. London, Macmillan.

Calderon, F. & A. Piscitelli. 1990. 'Paradigm Crisis and Social Movements: a Latin American Perspective'. In Oyen (ed.), *Comparative Methodology*. London, Sage Publications, pp. 81–96.

Castells, M. 1983. *The City and the Grassroots*. London, Edward Arnolds.

Clark, J. 1991. *Democratizing Development: The Role of Voluntary Organizations*. London, Earthscan.

Corbridge, S. 1989. 'Marxism, Post-Marxism and the Geography of Development'. In R. Peet and N. Thrift (eds.), *New Models in Geography* (vol. 1). London, Unwin Hyman, pp. 224–54.

Crocker, D. 1991. 'Towards Development Ethics'. *World Development* 19 (5), pp. 457–83.

Dear, M. 1986. 'Postmodernism and Planning'. *Environment and Planning* D 4, pp. 367–84.

Dhanagare, D. & J. John. 1988. 'Cyclical Movements towards the "Eternal"'. *Economic and Political Weekly*, 21 May, 1988, pp. 1089–92.

Dubois, M. 1991. 'The Governance of the Third World: a Foucauldian Perspective on Power Relations in Development'. *Alternatives* 16, pp. 1–30.

Evers, T. 1985. 'Identity: the Hidden Side of New Social Movements in Latin America'. In D. Slater (ed.), *New Social Movements and the State in Latin America*, Amsterdam, CEDLA.

Falabella, G. 1983. 'Social Movements under Economic Restructuring and Authoritarian Political Conditions: Some Recent Latin American Experiences'. Paper for the annual meeting of the American Sociological Association, Detroit.

Fincher, R. 1987. 'Defining and Explaining Urban Social Movements'. *Urban Geography* 8 (2), pp. 152–60.

Friedmann, J. 1988. 'From Social to Political Power: Collective Self-empowerment and Social Change'. *Journal für Entwicklungspolitik* 2, 63–74.

— 1989a. 'The Latin American Barrio Movement as a Social Movement: Contribution to a Debate'. *International Journal of Urban and Regional Research* 13 (3), pp. 501–10.

— 1989b. 'La Dialéctica de la Razón'. *Revista EURE* 15 (46), pp. 29–46.

Fuentes, M. and A.G. Frank. 1989. 'Ten Theses on Social Movements'. *World Development* 17 (2), pp. 179–91.

Habermas, J. 1990. 'What does Socialism Mean Today? the Rectifying Revolution and the Need for New Thinking on the Left'. *New Left Review* 183, pp. 3–21.

Huber Stephens, E. 1989. 'Capitalist Development and Democracy in South America'. *Politics and Society* 17 (3), pp. 281–352.

Long, N. 1990. 'From Paradigm Lost to Paradigm Regained? the Case for an

Actor-Oriented Sociology of Development'. *European Review of Latin American and Caribbean Studies* 49, pp. 3–24.

Lyotard, J.-F. 1984. *The Postmodern Condition*. Manchester, Manchester University Press.

Mainwaring, S. 1987. 'Urban Popular Movements, Identity, and Democratization in Brazil'. *Comparative Political Studies* 20 (2), pp. 131–59.

Manzo, K. 1991. 'Modernist Discourse and the Crisis of Development Theory'. *Studies in Comparative International Development* 26 (2), pp. 3–36.

Mathur, G. 1989. 'The Current Impasse in Development Thinking: the Metaphysic of Power'. *Alternatives* XIV, pp. 463–79.

Mouzelis, N. 1988. 'Sociology of Development: Reflections on the Present Crisis'. *Sociology* 22 (1), pp. 23–44.

Munck, R. 1989. *Latin America: the Transition to Democracy*. London, Zed Books.

Nederveen Pieterse, J. 1991. 'Dilemmas of Development Discourse: the Crisis of Developmentalism and the Comparative Method'. *Development and Change* 22, pp. 5–29.

Norris, C. 1990. 'Lost in the Funhouse: Baudrillard and the Politics of Postmodernism'. In R. Boyne and A. Rattansi, pp. 119–54.

Parajuli, P. 1991. 'Power and Knowledge in Development Discourse: New Social Movements and the State in India'. *International Social Science Journal* 127, pp. 173–90.

Petras, J. & M. Morley. 1991. 'Latin America: Poverty of Democracy and Democracy of Poverty'. *Economic and Political Weekly* 25 (30), pp. 103–11.

Razeto, L. 1986. *Economia Popular de Solidaridad*. Santiago de Chile, Area Pastoral de la Conferencia Episcopal de Chile.

Scott, A. 1990. *Ideology and the New Social Movements*. London.

Sklair, L. 1988. 'Transcending the Impasse: Metatheory, Theory, and Empirical Research in the Sociology of Development and Underdevelopment'. *World Development* 16 (6), pp. 697–709.

Tironi, E. 1987. 'Pobladores e Integracion Social'. *Proposiciones* 14, Santiago, pp. 64–85.

Touraine, A. 1989. *América Latina: Política y Sociedad*. Madrid, Espasa-Calpe.

Toye, J. 1987. *Dilemmas of Development*. Oxford, Blackwell.

Trainer, F. 1989. 'Reconstructing Radical Development Theory'. *Alternatives* XIV, pp. 481–515.

Vandergeest, P. & F. Buttel. 1988. 'Marx, Weber, and Development Sociology: Beyond the Impasse'. *World Development* 16 (6), pp. 683–95.

10

Sustainable Development and the Greening of Development Theory

by Bill Adams

What is Sustainable Development?

Retrospective discussions of sustainable development theory in the 1980s will inevitably fasten upon the phrase 'sustainable development', and the emphasis placed upon environmental issues in development planning. In the very few years between the publication of *The World Conservation Strategy* (IUCN 1980) and *Caring for the Earth* (IUCN 1991), sustainable development became the dominant *leitmotif* of the discourse of development planners, commentators and bureaucrats. By the end of the 1980s the phrase was widespread in the reports of international consultancies and the agencies that employed them (Rich 1991); it had become an accepted part of the rhetoric of Third World and First World politicians, and had provided a potent new slogan and campaigning theme of First World environmental Non-Governmental Organisations. Lélé suggests that sustainable development is 'poised to become the development paradigm of the 1990s' (1991: 607).

The 1980s, then, were the decade of 'sustainable development'. But what is it that has apparently come to dominate discourse about the poor, and the degraded environments they endure and create? The phrase is undoubtedly popular, it seems to command widespread support, to release considerable emotional appeal, and to provide a way for sometimes very different interests to express something of their attitude to nature and the development process.

However, in terms of development theory, is it useful? It is far from clear whether sustainable development offers a new paradigm, or simply a green wash over business-as-usual. In practice most commentators use it loosely and in an untheorised way. The most-quoted definition, that of the World Commission on Environment and Development, is a classic of

NOTE: I would like to thank the participants at the NICCOS Seminar on 'Development Theories in the Nineties' held at Nijmegen, the Netherlands, in November 1991 for their comments on an earlier version of this paper. I am particularly grateful to Bas Arts for his detailed written comments. – Bill Adams

its kind: 'development that meets the needs of the present without compromising the ability of future generations to meet their own needs' (Brundtland 1987: 43). This is neat, but far from a clear base upon which to build new theoretical ideas about development.

In many ways, sustainable development is more of a slogan than a tight theoretical concept (Conroy 1988). Lélé speaks of disenchantment with 'a fashionable phrase that everyone pays homage to but nobody can define' (1991: 607). Michael Redclift calls sustainable development a 'development truism' (Redclift 1987: 3), and argues that 'its very strength is its vagueness' (1987: 4). Lélé provides a clear analysis of the weaknesses that follow from 'the absence of a clear theoretical and analytical framework' (1991: 607).

However, the real significance of this lack of clear definition is, surely, that the very success of sustainable development lies in its flexibility. It embraces diverse and highly complex ideas, yet manages to seem both unifying and simple (Adams 1990). O'Riordan sees the related concept of sustainability as a 'mediating term designed to bridge the gulf between "developers" and "environmentalists" ' (1988: 29). Through the 1980s, sustainable development indeed gained a remarkable currency, not because of its analytical power, but because of its tradeability, and the facility with which it could be used to package diverse and sometimes radically opposing concepts.

Although thinking about sustainable development is diverse, there is a clearly discernible mainstream within it (Lélé 1991). This is formed from three documents that between them span the years between the United Nations Conference on the Human Environment in Stockholm in 1972 and that on Environment and Development in Rio de Janeiro in 1992. The landmarks in the sustainable development debate are without doubt the *World Conservation Strategy* (IUCN 1980), *Our Common Future* (Brundtland 1987) and *Caring for the Earth* (IUCN 1991). These comprise the mainstream of sustainable development thinking, and I describe elements within that mainstream below. They are not by any means, however, the only elements in the debate. The mainstream draws upon just one end of the spectrum of ideas about sustainable development. Other streams provide a very different, and far less reformist, agenda for development action.

The World Conservation Strategy
The World Conservation Strategy (WCS) was prepared through the 1970s by the International Union for the Conservation of Nature and Natural Resources (IUCN), the World Wildlife Fund (WWF) and the United Nations Environment Programme (UNEP), and published in 1980 (IUCN 1980). The WCS represented a significant watershed in thinking

about conservation, because it marked a move away from prevention towards attempting a cure for the loss of wildlife species and habitats, and because it 'confirmed a growing belief that the assimilation of aims of both conservation and development was the key to a sustainable society' (McCormick 1986: 177). The WCS embodied ideas that had been developed, particularly in IUCN, for more than a decade. Conservation and development were the themes of the IUCN General Assembly in Banff in Canada in 1972, and IUCN and UNEP began to develop the notion of a strategic approach to conservation in 1975 (McCormick 1986). By 1977 a draft was being prepared. There was extensive consultation with UNESCO and FAO and the amendments these agencies requested were included.

Like its successors, the WCS was a consensus document. IUCN's member organisations and the other international agencies had different agendas, and the WCS also had to embrace a range of different concepts and ideas about conservation. O'Riordan describes it as 'a transitional document' (1988: 36), one that sought 'to be a mediating bridge between the conservationists of the developed world and the suspicious leaderships of the developing world' (1988: 37). The first draft was 'essentially a wildlife conservation textbook', but it is claimed that the final version had become 'a consensus between the practitioners of conservation and development' (Talbot 1984: 14).

The World Conservation Strategy identified three objectives for conservation. The first two were 'maintenance of essential ecological processes' and 'preservation of genetic diversity'. 'Essential ecological processes' are those 'governed, supported or strongly moderated by ecosystems and are essential for food production, health, and other aspects of human survival and sustainable development'. 'Preservation of genetic diversity' involves the variety of genetic material in both indigenous crop plants and animals. Such genetic diversity has a potential contribution to future production. Wild species are also important because they might serve a useful economic purpose: 'we cannot predict what species may become useful to us' (IUCN 1980: paragraph 3.2). Genetic diversity is both an 'insurance' (e.g., against crop diseases), and an investment for the future (e.g., crop breeding or pharmaceuticals) (paragraph 3.2). From these principles flows the third, the sustainable utilisation of resources.

These proposals for conservation in the WCS are anthropocentric and pragmatic. Conservation is defined as 'the management of human use of the biosphere so that it may yield the greatest sustainable benefit to present generations while maintaining its potential to meet the needs and aspirations of future generations'. The WCS emphasised the usefulness of species and ecosystems for human subsistence and economic development. O'Riordan (1988) points out that the WCS leans heavily on the ecologically-based concept of sustainable utilisation. Traditional wildlife conservation policies are also presented in this light. Thus arguments are advanced for the establishment of parks and reserves because of their indirect ecological benefits (such as control of run-off from forested watersheds) or direct economic returns from paying visitors.

Environmental modification is a natural and necessary part of development, but not all such modification will achieve 'the social and economic objectives of development' (IUCN 1980: paragraph 1.12). The solution is to give conservation a high priority in the development process, and 'to integrate every stage of the conservation and development processes, from their initial setting of policies to their eventual implementation and operation' (paragraph 9.1). Thus every sector (health, energy, industry) involves conservation, 'that aspect of management which ensures that utilisation is sustainable' (paragraph 1.6). This integration will end the apparent conflict between conservation and development which previously obtained.

Our Common Future

The report of the World Commission on Environment and Development is the second major element within the mainstream of sustainable development. The Commission's report, *Our Common Future* (Brundtland 1987), was presented to the UN General Assembly in 1987. The Commission followed the multilateralist and interdependent route charted by its predecessors, the Brandt Reports (Brandt 1980, 1983). The Brandt Reports set out much of the ground on which Brundtland builds, both in terms of general principles and in the approach to (if not the priority given to) environmental problems. *North-South* (Brandt 1980) discusses measures 'which together would offer new horizons for international relations, the world economy, and for developing countries' (Brandt 1980: 64). Those 'new horizons' include the environment, both globally ('the biosphere is our common heritage and must be preserved by cooperation' – 1980: 73), and in the countries of the South themselves. The Brandt Reports are themselves part of a longer evolution of thinking about economic interdependence and the Keynesian vision of the Bretton Woods system of international financial management to create a stable, growing and interdependent world economy. However, Corbridge argues that *North-South* was 'a text explicitly written for Northern politicians and appealing (apparently) to their instincts for enlightened self-interest' (Corbridge 1986: 222). The first Brandt initiative, of course, ran into the sand in the early 1980s amid growing protectionism. Corbridge suggests that Brandt's concept of mutuality is 'too imprecise and too impotent to serve as a useful guide to political action on behalf of the world's poor' (Corbridge 1982: 253).

The Brundtland Report, *Our Common Future*, attempts to recapture the 'spirit of Stockholm 1972'; it places elements of the sustainable development debate within the economic and political context of international development, and it puts environmental issues firmly on the political agenda. It also made the UN General Assembly discuss environment and development as one single issue. The Brundtland Report starts from the premise that development and environment issues cannot be separated: 'It is therefore futile to attempt to deal with environmental problems without a broader perspective that encompasses the factors underlying world poverty and international inequality' (Brundtland 1987: 3). The reciprocal links between poverty and environment are recognised, poverty being seen 'as a major cause and effect of global environmental problems' (Brundtland 1987: 3).

In *Our Common Future*, sustainable development is based on two concepts. The first is the concept of basic needs and the corollary of the primacy of development action for the poor. The second involves the idea of environmental limits. These limits are not, however, those set by the environment itself, but by technology and social organisation. Physical sustainability cannot be secured without policies which actively consider access to resources and the distribution of costs and benefits. Whereas the WCS started from the premise of the need to conserve ecosystems and sought to demonstrate why this made good economic sense (and – although the point was underplayed – could promote equity), *Our Common Future* starts with people, and goes on to discuss what kind of environmental policies are required to achieve certain socio-economic goals.

Mainstream Thinking in Sustainable Development
'Mainstream' thinking sees sustainable development as something that takes place without threatening economic growth. *Our Common Future* calls for a new form of growth, sustainable, environmentally aware, egalitarian, integrating economic and social development: 'material- and energy-intensive and more equitable in its impact' (Brundtland 1987: 52). *Our Common Future* lies centrally within the existing economic paradigms of the industrialised North. Growth is the most prominent feature of its policy objectives (see Table 1).

Economic growth is seen as the only way to tackle poverty, and hence to achieve environment-development objectives. The Brundtland Report's vision of sustainable development is predicated on the need to maintain and revitalise the world economy. This means 'more rapid economic growth in both industrial and developing countries, freer market access for the products of developing countries, lower interest rates, greater technology transfer, and significantly larger capital flows, both concessional and commercial' (Brundtland 1987: 89).

Table 1

Critical objectives for environment and development policies proposed in the Brundtland Report

1. Reviving growth
2. Changing the quality of growth
3. Meeting essential needs for jobs, food, energy, water and sanitation
4. Ensuring a sustainable level of population
5. Conserving and enhancing the resource base
6. Reorientating technology and managing risk
7. Merging environment and economics in decision making

Source: Brundtland 1987: 49

In the classification of Cotgrove (1982) it is firmly cornucopian rather than catastrophist. It is poverty which puts pressure on the Third World environment, and it is economic growth which will remove that pressure. Furthermore it is only the ending of dependence which will enable these countries to 'outpace' their environmental problems. But what of the pressures of that growth itself? What about demands for energy and raw materials, about pollution? *Our Common Future* hopes to have its cake and eat it: 'The Commission's overall assessment is that the international economy must speed up world growth while respecting environmental constraints' (Brundtland 1987: 89). It does not say how this balancing trick is to be achieved.

Abandonment of fixed exchange rates in 1971, volatility in currency markets, and eventually the destabilisation of oil prices and the oil crisis of 1973 (Strange 1986) coincided with the sudden flowering of concern about 'limits to growth' as part of environmentalism. This too stressed global interdependence, but with an altogether different message about the desirability and possibility of continued growth. The reconciliation of these difficulties created formal statements of sustainable development. It is not surprising that those ideas should be based on the resurgence of Keynesian thinking represented by the Brandt Reports, a return to principles of an organised, managed and growing world economy. It is less clear whether the skilful consensus-writing of the Brundtland Report tackles the fundamental issues. For example, Stewart argues that the Brundtland Report 'runs a grave risk of overstating the possibilities and nurturing frustration and disillusion' (Stewart 1988: 119).

These ideas about the importance of continued economic growth for sustainable development contrast strongly with those of the 'zero growth' school of environmentalism in the 1970s (the 'physicalists' – Corbridge 1986: 194). 'Limits to growth' ideas have occasioned considerable hostility from economists and radical commentators. The 'neo-Malthusian' arguments about overpopulation, in books such as *Population, Resources and Environment* (Ehrlich and Ehrlich 1970) and *The Population Bomb* (Ehrlich 1972), and the global computer models of Forrester (1971) and Meadows *et al.* (1972) were fiercely criticised. Beckerman, for example, suggests that 'a failure to maintain economic growth means continued poverty, deprivation, disease, squalor, degradation and slavery to soul-destroying toil for countless millions of the world's population' (Beckerman 1974: 9). The sharpness of the debate in the 1970s perhaps hides the continuing logical appeal of those economists tackling the issue of steady-state economics (notably Daly 1973, 1977).

Furthermore, although debates within and about environmental economics have been central to the growing debate about sustainable development (e.g., Goodland and Ledec 1984; Turner 1988), these have have once again bypassed issues of zero growth. Ironically, of course, the success of the Brundtland Report is in part at least the result of its realism in avoiding such radical ideas.

Mainstream thinking about sustainable development not only fails to challenge the capitalist growth paradigm, it is also remarkably resistant to ecocentrist or biocentrist elements within environmentalism. Environmentalism embraces both ecocentrism and technocentrism (O'Riordan 1981; O'Riordan and Turner 1983). Ecocentrism is transcendentalist in tradition, and includes notions of bioethics and biorights. The rise in interest in 'deep ecology' (Devall and Sessions 1985) falls clearly within this tradition. Technocentrism is rationalist, technocratic and managerial.

The World Conservation Strategy puts certain moral arguments for conservation. Humankind has become a 'major evolutionary force', with the capacity to effect radical changes in the biosphere but not fully able to control those changes. As a result, the WCS argues, 'we are morally obliged – to our descendants and to other creatures – to act prudently' (paragraph 3.3). However, the proposals of the WCS do not build on this moral position, but instead focus on pragmatic, utilitarian and technocentrist ideas.

The technocentrist elements within sustainable development involve ideas of ecosystem management, rational utilisation of resources and land, and normative 'rational' planning. In terms of their effect on developmentalism, technocentrist approaches are therefore inherently reformist (Adams 1990). The WCS, of course, builds on several decades of previous thinking, particularly within UNESCO and IUCN. Thus

UNESCO sponsored the 1961 symposium conference on 'Man's Place in the Island Ecosystem' at the 10th Pacific Science Congress in Honolulu (Fosberg 1963) and IUCN promoted ecological guidelines for economic development that took account of environmental issues, for example the book *Ecological Principles for Economic Development* (Dasmann *et al.* 1973).

Mainstream thinking about sustainable development also lacks a clear framework for analysing political economy. The WCS was intended 'to stimulate a more focused approach to the management of living resources and to provide policy guidance on how this can be carried out' (IUCN 1980: vi). It had little to say about the structures of wealth and power that constrain implementation. Redclift suggests that the WCS did not 'even begin to examine the social and political changes that would be necessary to meet conservation goals' (Redclift 1984: 50).

The WCS stops short of a political economic analysis of the world economy, or of poverty. It draws on neo-populist ideas, and in particular on critiques of the failures of large-scale centrally-planned development projects and programmes. In its place, there is a celebration of indigenous knowledge and a call for local participation in development. It argues that traditional wildlife conservation interests are entirely compatible with the growing demand for a 'people-centred' development. Such development should aim to achieve a wider distribution of basic needs in terms of nutrition, health, education, family welfare, fuller employment, greater income security, protection from environmental degradation. The WCS thus aligns itself with the various poor-first, farmer-first and 'development from below' schools of thought in development (e.g., Chambers 1983). Like them, it has more to say about rural development than about strategies of industrialisation and urbanisation, and thus is more readily applicable to the least industrialised countries of the Third World such as sub-Saharan Africa than to those countries that are more industrialised and urbanised, such as Brazil or the NICs of East Asia.

Mainstream thinking about sustainable development, as represented in the *World Conservation Strategy* (IUCN, 1980) and *Our Common Future* (Brundtland, 1987) and *Caring for the Earth* (IUCN, 1991), is technocentrist and not ecocentrist, reformist and not radical and is situated firmly within a paradigm of continued capitalist economic growth. It offers little theoretical critique of that paradigm.

Counterpoints in the Sustainable Development Debate

What I have described here as the 'mainstream' is not the only element in the sustainable development debate. There are also a range of more radical ideas. I will mention three. The first is the attempt to distinguish theoretically a 'green alternative' in world development. Friberg and

Hettne (1985) argue that there is a 'green counterpoint' to both 'blue' (market, liberal, capitalist) and 'red' (state, socialist) development strategies. They see this as opposing the institutionalisation of the 'modern complex' of bureaucracy, industrialism, urbanism, the market economy, the technical/scientific system and militarism (Friberg and Hettne 1985: 207). Friberg and Hettne argue that Marxism contains 'its own mainstream-counterpoint contradiction' (1985: 207). 'Green counterpoint' ideas differ from neo-populism in containing elements of 'an ecological consciousness (encompassing the total global ecological system)', and a 'strong commitment to a just world order' (1985: 208).

Friberg and Hettne argue that development is social transformation, and is 'anti-systemic' in the sense that it must be directed at the damaging and crisis-creating features which are an integral part of the world system. The 'Green Counterpoint' is 'opposed and dialectically related' to the dominant development paradigm (1985: 207) and the philosophy of the modern world system (c.f. Aseniero 1985: 51). Developmentalism ('a common corporate industrial culture based on the values of competitive individualism, rationality, growth, efficiency, specialisation, centralisation and big scale' – Friberg and Hettne 1985: 231), underpins both capitalist and socialist approaches to development.

The 'road of continued modernisation' would allow the world economy to expand to a ceiling, to be replaced by a socialist world government. The green strategy of 'demodernisation' would involve gradual withdrawal from the modern capitalist world economy and the launch of a 'new, non-modern, non-capitalist development project' (Friberg and Hettne 1985: 235). This new project would be based on 'the "progressive" (i.e., not exploitative and dehumanising) elements of pre-capitalist social orders and later innovations' (1985: 235). 'Green' principles of 'endogenous development' (1985: 220) suggest that the social unit of development should be a culturally defined community (whose development is rooted in its values and institutions), that each community should be self-reliant and that development should be characterised by social justice and 'ecological balance'.

The green project draws its strength from an alliance of three groups. The first consists of 'traditionalists' who wish to resist capitalist penetration in the form of state-building, commercialisation and industrialisation. These will be mostly in the global periphery and will include 'non-Western civilisations and religions, old nations and tribes, local communities, kinship groups, peasants and independent producers, informal economies, feminist culture, etc.' (Friberg and Hettne 1985: 235). The second group is 'marginalised people', including the unemployed, the mentally ill, handicapped people and people in de-humanising jobs who have lost 'a meaningful function in the mega-machine' (1985:

264) through pressures for increased productivity, rationalisation and automation. The third group consists of the 'post-materialists' who dominate Western environmentalism (Cotgrove 1982), 'young, well-educated and committed to post-materialist values' (Friberg and Hettne 1985: 236).

The second radical thrust relevant to the sustainable development debate is essentially an extension of radical socialist thinking. Amin argues that 'green' ideas are not new, but have roots in peasant communism and utopian socialism: 'the revolt of the oppressed and exploited has always produced the ideology of a just, equal and mutual counter-system' (Amin 1985: 273). He argues that 'the Greens – mistakenly – do not acknowledge that their counter-society is in fact nothing more than the communism espoused by Marx' (1985: 273).

Radical development theory, indeed radical theory in general, has had something of a blind spot with regard to nature and environmental degradation. The 'environmental crisis' of the 1970s passed most radical thinkers by, simply enriching anti-capitalist rhetoric (Enzensberger 1974: 9). By contrast, Enzensberger argued that real scientific problems lay behind the bourgeois packaging of the environmental movement, and that the capitalist mode of production 'has catastrophic consequences' (1974: 10). Subsequent work has substantially confirmed this interest in the environment, particularly in the context of the Third World (e.g., Blaikie 1985; Blaikie and Brookfield 1987; Adams 1990).

Redclift called for 'a fundamental revision of Marxist political economy, to reflect the urgency of the South's environmental crisis' (1984: 18). Pepper outlined an 'ecosocialism' involving the redefinition of needs, the redistribution of resources and the reassessment of the industrial mode of production. More radical ecosocialism would go further, and focus on new forms of production which replace private ownership in favour of social justice, and seek new forms of social order which 'eliminate alienation, state control, and centralisation' (Pepper 1984: 197). Brown comments: 'We will have to retrace our steps along the road of capitalist development to find a new social mix of goods and services that use up less scarce resources and do less harm to the environment' (Brown 1976: 9).

The traditions of social anarchism and utopian socialism offer a perhaps stronger platform for the development of a radical theory relevant to sustainable development. There is a strong resemblance between certain 'green' ideas about community, scale, control and technology (among deep ecologists and bioregionalists for example) and the social anarchism or anarcho-communism of Kropotkin (Kropotkin 1972, 1974; Galois 1976). Kropotkin believed 'that true individualism can only be cultivated by the conscious and reflective interaction of people with a social environment which supports their personal freedom and growth' (Breitbart 1981: 136). By contrast, environmentalist thinking such as *Blueprint for Survival* (Goldsmith *et al.* 1972) suggests an ecological imperative for action to achieve utopia, the human dimensions of which are secondary (Pepper 1984).

Murray Bookchin argues that 'in the final analysis, it is impossible to achieve a harmonisation of people and nature without creating a human community that lives in a lasting balance with its natural environment' (Bookchin 1979: 23). He proposes anarchist concepts of 'a balanced community, a face-to-face democracy, a humanistic technology and a decentralised society'. To Bookchin the 'ecological crisis' is just part of a larger problem, with imbalances in relations between people and nature reflecting (and resulting from) imbalances in and ruptures in the relations between people and hence within society. He suggests that there is a 'crisis in social ecology'. Western society is 'being organised round immense urban belts, a highly industrialised agriculture and, capping both, a swollen, bureaucratised, anonymous state apparatus' (1979: 25). By extension, Third World societies are being modelled in the same way, by the same forces. Bookchin's 'ecological anarchism' is essentially anti-industrial, anti-bureaucracy and anti-state. It demands 'revolutionary opposition' to the norms of society. If extended to the Third World, such thinking engages centrally with a number of the core themes of sustainable development.

The third area of radical thought relevant to sustainable development is ecofeminism. This develops the argument that both women and nature are subjugated by patriarchal industrialism and capitalism (Mies 1986, Shiva 1988). Modern science is a 'masculine and patriarchal project which necessarily entailed the subjugation of both nature and women' (Shiva 1988: 15). Shiva's analysis builds on an account of the struggles of Indian women over environment and property rights, particularly the place of common property resources.

Shiva argues that the destruction of forest in India and the displacement of women are both structurally linked to the reductionist (and capitalist) paradigm of science. Any attempt to deal with deforestation that comes from the same patriarchal scientific and capitalist source will fail. It will only compound the crisis of human survival and that of environmental degradation. She argues that a gender-based ideology of patriarchy underlies ecological destruction, and she calls for a 'non gender-based ideology of liberation' (Shiva 1988: xvii). Rediscovery of 'the feminist principle in nature', and of the view of the earth as sustainer and provider, depends on a successful ideological challenge to established male-dominated modes of thinking about knowledge, wealth and value.

Conclusions

Sustainable development is a flag of convenience under which diverse ships sail, and it is this catholic scope that goes a long way to explain its power and popularity as a term in debates about development. One drawback of this, however, is that within the rhetoric there is no agreed and clear theoretical core. Theoretical clarification is necessary both for debate to continue, and for sustainable development to have any long-term credibility. Lélé suggests that clarification of terms, concepts and analytical methods in sustainable development is necessary to broaden social acceptance and political support. To this end, Lélé argues that proponents and analysts of sustainable development need to focus on five issues: first, to reject the temptation to focus on economic growth; second, to recognise the 'internal inconsistences and inadequacies of neo-classical economics' (Lélé 1991: 618) and to redirect economic analyses; third, to accept the structural, technological and cultural causes of poverty and environmental degradation; fourth, to understand that sustainable development has multiple dimensions; fifth, to 'explore what patterns and levels of resource demand would be compatible with different forms or levels of ecological or social sustainability, and different notions of equity and justice' (1991: 618).

Within this agenda lies a significant tension for sustainable development advocates between reformist and radical approaches (Adams 1990). As Lélé has commented, proponents suffer from the 'difference between the urge to take strong stands on fundamental concerns and the need to gain wide political acceptance and support (1991: 618). The strength, and yet the long-term risk, in sustainable development is precisely this blend of radical and reformist agendas. Only theoretical debate can chart a synthesis or a credible path through this particular minefield.

Table 2

Priority Requirements of Caring for the Earth

1) Respect and care for the community of life
2) Improve the quality of human life
3) Conserve the Earth's vitality and diversity
4) Minimise the depletion of non-renewable resources
5) Keep within the Earth's carrying capacity
6) Change personal attitudes and practices
7) Enable communities to care for their own environments
8) Provide a national framework for integrating development and conservation
9) Forge a global alliance

Lélé's belief that a consensus on these lines is starting to emerge is confirmed by the revised conservation strategy, *Caring for the Earth,* published in 1991 by the same agencies that produced the WCS. *Caring for the Earth* (IUCN 1991) identifies a series of nine principles for sustainable development (Table 2). These include familiar concerns from the original WCS (for example the continued emphasis on the Earth's 'carrying capacity'), but there is also explicit discussion of the priorities of development, and on issues such as military spending, inequality in wealth and living standards, and gender. It thus goes some way to meet O'Riordan's (1988) criticism that the original WCS omitted the debate about basic needs, and it takes at least some account of political economy at sub-national and international scale (Adams 1990).

There is also considerable attention to implementation, including a notional budget to implement priority requirements. There is not, however, a clear statement on economic growth. Attention to Lélé's first core issue is still obviously beyond the range of what is possible in terms of international consensus-creation.

Whatever its theoretical eclecticism and inconsistencies, there is no doubt that sustainable development has succeeded in drawing attention to a series of significant problems and real issues. Furthermore, much of the strength of the insights it brings depends not on debate about the macro-level of theory but on the micro-level of practice (B. Arts, personal communication). The insights of neo-populism and the moral discourse about poverty, powerlessness and welfare are both driven by field experience of people at the global periphery. It is the way in which sustainable development has the potential to bracket the plight of the poor, the state of their environment and the structured political economy within which they are situated that is important.

In terms of 'sustainable development theory', what is needed is a discourse that embraces micro and macro scale, from peasant to transnational corporation, from field to biosphere. Above all, what is needed is a theoretical discourse that is lodged in practice, within the daily realities of people's lives and the planning environments within which their conditions are restructured. After all, even if sustainable development offers no more than a renewed focus on power and wealth, poverty and environmental degradation, it does promise to increase the trickle of resources directed at these issues.

Sustainable development has won an important place in the lectionary of development. If agendas such as that of Lélé are followed, the phrase may come to represent a theoretically clearer concept, and may retain its place within development discourse. This makes it all the more important to remember, as Redclift comments, that 'our very definition of sustainable carries cultural and political bias' (Redclift 1990: 5). For the moment, 'sustainable development' is, like development itself, a word which can have many meanings. It should be used with great care.

Relevant Literature

Adams, W.M. 1990. *Green Development: Environment and Sustainability in the Third World*. London, Routledge.

Amin, S. 1985. 'Apropos the "Green" Movements'. In H. Addo *et al.*, *Development as Social Transformation: Reflections on the Global Problematique*, Sevenoaks, Hodder & Stoughton, for the United Nations University.

Aseniero, G. 1985. 'A Reflection on Developmentalism: from Development to Transformation'. In H. Addo *et al.*, *Development as Social Transformation: Reflections on the Global Problematique*, pp. 48–85, Sevenoaks, Hodder & Stoughton, for the United Nations University.

Beckerman, W. 1974. *In Defence of Economic Growth*. London, Jonathan Cape.

Blaikie, P. 1985. *The Political Economy of Soil Erosion*. London, Longman.

— & H. Brookfield. 1987. *Land Degradation and Society*. London, Methuen.

Bookchin, M. 1979. 'Ecology and Revolutionary Thought'. *Antipode* 10(3)/11(1), pp 21–32.

Brandt, W. 1980. *North-South: a Programme for Survival*. London, Pan Books.

— 1983. *Common Crisis North-South: Cooperation for World Recovery*. London, Pan Books.

Breitbart, M. 1981. 'Peter Kropotkin: the Anarchist Geographer'. In D.R. Stoddart (ed.), *Geography, Ideology and Social Concern*. Oxford, Blackwell.

Brown, M.B. 1976. 'The Crisis of Capitalism and Commodity Production'. In M.B. Brown, T, Emerson and C. Stoneman (eds.), *Resources and Environment: a Socialist Perspective*, pp. 5–9, Nottingham, Spokesman Books.

Brundtland, H. 1987. *Our Common Future*. Oxford, Oxford University Press (for the World Commission on Environment and Development).

Chambers, R. 1983. *Rural Development: Putting the Last First*. London, Longman.

Conroy, C. 1988. 'Introduction'. In C. Conroy and M. Litvinoff (eds.), *The Greening of Aid: Sustainable Livelihoods in Practice*, pp. xi–xiv, London, Earthscan.

Corbridge, S.E. 1982. 'Interdependent Development? Problems of Aggregation and Implementation in the Brandt Report'. *Applied Geography* 2: 253–65.

— 1986. *Capitalist World Development: a Critique of Radical Development Geography*. London, Macmillan.

Cotgrove, S. 1982. *Catastrophe or Cornucopia: the Environment, Politics and the Future*. Chichester, Wiley.

Dasmann, R.F., J.P. Milton & P.H. Freeman. 1973. *Ecological Principles for Economic Development*. Chichester, Wiley.

Daly, H.E. (ed.). 1973. *Towards a Steady-state Economy*. New York, W.H. Freeman.

— 1977. *Steady-state Economics: the Economics of Biophysical Equilibrium and Moral Growth*. New York, W.H. Freeman.

Devall, B. & G. Sessions. 1985. *Deep Ecology: Living as if Nature Mattered*. Salt Lake City, Peregrine Smith.

Ehrlich, P.R. 1972. *The Population Bomb*. London, Ballantine.

— & A.H. Ehrlich. 1970. *Population, Resources and Environment: Issues in Human Ecology*. New York, W.H. Freeman.

Enzensberger, H.M. 1974. 'A Critique of Political Ecology'. *New Left Review* 8, pp. 3–32 .

Forrester, J.W. 1971. *World Dynamics*. Cambridge, Massachusetts, Wright-Allen Press.

Fosberg, F.R. 1963. *Man's Place in the Island Ecosystem*. Hawaii, Bishop Museum Press.

Friberg, M. & B. Hettne. 1985. 'The Greening of the World: Towards a Non-deterministic Model of Global Processes'. In H. Addo *et al.*, *Development as Social Transformation: Reflections on the Global Problematique*, pp. 204–70, Sevenoaks, Hodder & Stoughton, for the United Nations University.

Galois, B. 1976. 'Ideology and the Idea of Nature: the Case of Peter Kropotkin'. *Antipode* 8, pp. 1–16.

Goldsmith, E., R. Allen, M. Allaby, J. Davoll & S. Lawrence. 1972. 'Blueprint for Survival'. *The Ecologist* 2, pp. 1–50 (also 1972, Harmondsworth, Penguin Books).

Goodland, R.J. & G. Ledec. 1984. *Neoclassical Economics and Principles of Sustainable Development*. Washington DC, World Bank Office of Environmental Affairs.

IUCN. 1980. *The World Conservation Strategy*. Geneva, International Union for Conservation of Nature and Natural Resources, United Nations Environment Programme, World Wildlife Fund.

— 1991. *Caring for the Earth: a Strategy for Sustainable Living*. Geneva, IUCN, UNEP, WWF, 1991

Kropotkin, P. 1972. *The Conquest of Bread*. London, Allen Lane (ed. P. Avrich; first published in English as a book in 1906, London).

— 1974. *Fields, Factories and Workshops Tomorrow*. London, Allen & Unwin (ed. C. Ward; 1st ed. London, Hutchinson, 1899).

Lélé, S. M. 1991. 'Sustainable Development: a Critique'. *World Development* 19, pp. 607–21

McCormick, J. 1986. 'The Origins of the World Conservation Strategy'. *Environmental Review* 10(2), pp. 177–87

Meadows, D., J. Randers & W.W. Behrens. 1972. *The Limits to Growth*. New York, Universe Books.

Mies, M. 1986. *Patriarchy and Accumulation on a World Scale: Women in the International Division of Labour*. London, Zed Books.

O'Riordan, T. 1981. *Environmentalism*. London, Pion (2nd. ed.).

— 1988. 'The Politics of Sustainability'. In R.K. Turner (ed.), *Sustainable Environmental Management: Principles and Practice*, pp. 29–5, Boulder, Colorado, Westview Press.

— & R.K. Turner. 1983. *An Annotated Reader in Environmental Planning and Management*. Oxford, Pergamon Press.

Pepper, D. 1984. *The Roots of Modern Environmentalism*. London, Croom Helm.

Redclift, M. 1984. *Development and the Environmental Crisis: Red or Green Alternatives?* London, Methuen.

— 1987. *Sustainable Development: Exploring the Contradictions.* London, Methuen.

— 1990. 'Beyond the Buzzword: Defining Sustainable Development'. *New Ground* 24 (Spring), pp. 4–5.

Rich, B. 1991. 'World Bank – Green Frankenstein'. *ECOS: A Review of Conservation* 12(1), pp. 82–3.

Shiva, V. 1988. *Staying Alive: Women, Ecology and Development.* London, Zed Books.

Stewart, I.A. 1988. 'The Brundtland Commission: Pathways to Sustainable Development'. In A. Davidson & M. Dence (eds.), *The Brundtland Challenge and the Cost of Inaction*, pp. 117–21, Halifax, Nova Scotia, Royal Society of Canada and the Institute for Research on Public Policy.

Strange, S. 1986. *Casino Capitalism.* Oxford, Blackwell.

Talbot, L.M. 1984. 'The World Conservation Strategy'. In F.R. Thibodeau & H.H. Field (eds.), *Sustaining Tomorrow: a Strategy for World Conservation and Development*, pp. 10–15, University Press of New England.

Turner, R.K. (ed.). 1988. *Sustainable Environmental Management: Principles and Practice.* Boulder, Colorado, Westview Press.

About the Contributors

Bill Adams is a Fellow of Downing College, Cambridge, and a university lecturer in geography. He works on environment and development issues and has a particular interest in water resource development and the impact of hi-tech dam and irrigation schemes on indigenous systems of water management. He is the author of *Green Development: Environment and Sustainability in the Third World* (London, Routledge, 1990). He is currently engaged in research projects on agriculture and conservation in East Anglia and on the sustainability of farmer-managed irrigation in Kenya and Tanzania.

David Booth lectures in sociology and is Director of the Centre of Developing Area Studies at the University of Hull. He has done research in both Latin America and Africa, much of it concerned with the political sociology of developmental reform. He is the editor of *New Directions in Social Development Research* (Cambridge, Cambridge University Press, forthcoming) and is currently completing a book on the social dimensions of structural adjustment programmes in rural Tanzania.

Stuart Corbridge is a fellow of Sidney Sussex College and teaches in the Department of Geography, University of Cambridge. He is the author of *Capitalist World Development: A Critique of Radical Development Geography* (London, Macmillan, 1986) and *Debt and Development* (Oxford, Blackwell, 1992). His main research interests are tribal politics in India, and development theory and international finance.

Michael Edwards has a Ph.D. in Geography. For the last 10 years he has worked for a variety of development agencies in Africa, Asia and Latin America. From 1984 to 1988 he was Oxfam's Regional Representative in Lusaka, Zambia, and is now Head of Research and Information at Save the Children Fund in London. He has published on urban housing in the Third World and on the relations between development theory and practice.

Norman Long is Professor of Sociology of Development at Wageningen Agricultural University in the Netherlands. Prior to that, he was Professor of Anthropology at the University of Durham in the United Kingdom. He has published extensively on the sociology of agricultural knowledge and practice, economic anthropology and planned intervention. His books include *An Introduction to the Sociology of Rural Development* (London, Tavistock Publications, 1977), *Miners, Peasants and Entrepreneurs* (with B. Roberts) (Cambridge, Cambridge University Press, 1984) and *Battlefields of Knowledge: The Interlocking of Theory and Practice in Social Research and Development* (edited with A. Long) (London and New York, Routledge, 1992).

Ronaldo Munck was born and educated in Argentina before coming to the United Kingdom where he subsequently did his doctorate at the University of Essex. He is Reader in Sociology at the University of Ulster. His research interests have ranged widely and include Latin American politics and development, Irish social history, and labour studies. His books include: *The New International Labour Studies: An Introduction* (London, Zed Books, 1988), *Politics and Dependency in the Third World: The Case of Latin America* (1984), *Latin America: The Transition to Democracy* (London, Zed Books, 1989), *Belfast in the Thirties: An Oral History* (Blackstaff Press, 1986) and *Ireland: Nation, State and Class* (Boulder, Colorado, Westview Press, 1985). He is currently working on a new Foucaultian 'archaeology' of the socialist experience in the Third World.

Frans Schuurman is a Senior Lecturer at the Third World Centre and at the Department of Non-Western Geography at the Catholic University of Nijmegen in the Netherlands. He has published on a variety of Latin American issues, including agricultural colonisation in the Amazon Basin, urban transport problems and patterns of intra-urban migration. He has coedited (with T. van Naerssen) the volume *Urban Social Movements in the Third World* (London, Routledge, 1989) and co-authored (with Ellen Heer) *Social Movements and NGOs in Latin America* (Saarbrucken, Breitenbach, 1992). He is currently engaged in a research project on democratisation and decentralisation in the Southern Cone.

David Slater is Associate Professor at the Inter-University Centre for Latin American Research and Documentation (CEDLA) in Amsterdam. He has written extensively on issues of territory and state power in Latin America. In addition to numerous articles in learned journals including *The International Journal of Political Economy, Society and Space* and *Development and Change*, he has edited a book called *New Social Movements and the State in Latin America* (Dordrecht, CEDLA, 1985). He is currently doing research on theories of development and politics in the post-modernist era.

Janet Townsend has been a Lecturer in Geography at Durham University in the UK since 1970. She was educated at the University of Oxford where she did her D. Phil. Most of her fieldwork has been in Colombia, although she has visited most of Latin America, including Mexico, on study tours. Her particular research interest is on the colonisation of rainforest areas. In addition to various scholarly papers and journal articles, she is the author of *Women in Developing Countries: A Select Annotated Bibliography for Development Organisations* (Brighton, Institute of Development Studies, 1988). She has also done consultancy in Nigeria and India.

Magdalena Villarreal is a Research Fellow in Sociology at Wageningen Agricultural University, the Netherlands. Prior to that she carried out field research in western Mexico which she is writing up as a doctoral thesis focusing on issues of countervailing power and the negotiation of identity in the face of state intervention, with special reference to gender.

Index

ZED BOOKS LTD

is a publisher whose international and Third World lists include:

- women's studies
- development
- environment
- current affairs
- international relations
- labour studies
- children's studies
- cultural studies
- human rights
- indigenous peoples
- health

We also specialize in Area Studies where we have extensive lists in African studies, Asian studies, Caribbean and Latin American studies, Middle East studies and Pacific studies.

For further information about books available from Zed Books, please write to : Catalogue Enquiries, Zed Books Ltd, 57 Caledonian Road, London N1 9BU. Our books are available from distributors in many countries (for full details see our catalogues), including:

IN THE USA
Humanities Press International Inc., 165 First Avenue, Atlantic Highlands, NJ 07716
Tel: (908) 872 1441 Fax: (908) 872 0717

IN CANADA
Fernwood Books Ltd, PO Box 9409, Station 'A', Halifax, NS, B3K 5S3

IN AUSTRALIA
Peribo Pty Ltd, 26 Tepko Road, Terrey Hills, NSW 2084

IN INDIA
Urvashi Butalia, B26 Gulmohar Park, New Delhi 110 049

NEW FROM ZED BOOKS

Wolfgang Sachs (Editor)
THE DEVELOPMENT DICTIONARY
A Guide to Knowledge as Power

'Sach's ideas are dynamite. They call into question the whole phase of human activity which we are used to describing as 'development''
— *New Internationalist*
Hb 1 85649 043 2 £36.95 $59.95   Pb 1 85649 044 0 £14.95 $25.00

Wolfgang Sachs (Editor)
GLOBAL ECOLOGY
Conflicts and Contradictions

'In his seminal *Development Dictionary*, Wolfgang Sachs and his colleagues convincingly showed that economic development was the problem rather than the solution. Now, in his equally seminal *Global Ecology*, Sachs and his colleagues show us, equally convincingly, that it is only at the local, grassroots level, rather than at the global and hence institutional level, that the sustainable society we are all talking about can be brought into being.'
— Edward Goldsmith, co-editor, *Ecologist*
Hb 1 85649 163 3 £36.95 $59.95   Pb 1 85649 164 1 £14.95 $25.00

Serge Latouche
IN THE WAKE OF THE AFFLUENT SOCIETY
An Exploration of Post-Development

'A sober, sociological account of the unviability of our present system without ideological *a prioris*. It has the power to convince those who are not of his opinion. It is sociology at its best.'
— Professor R Panikkar, Professor Emeritus, UCLA
Hb 1 85649 171 4 £32.95 $55.00   Pb 1 85649 172 2 £12.95 $19.95

WOMEN AND WORLD DEVELOPMENT SERIES
– Published with UN/NGO Group on Women and Development

The series makes available the most recent information and debate about world development issues and their impact on women. Each fully illustrated book provides an overview of its particular subject, an introduction to resources, and guidance for workshops and seminars. The series aims to bring women's concerns more directly and effectively into the development process, and to help improve women's status in our rapidly changing world.

The series includes:

- Women and the World Economic Crisis *by Jeanne Vickers*
- Women and Disability *by Esther Boylan*
- Women and the Environment *by Annabel Rodda*
- Women and Health *by Patricia Smyke*
- Refugee Women *by Susan Forbes Martin*
- Women and Literacy *by Marcela Ballara*
- Women and Human Rights *by Katarina Tomaševski*
- Women and Work *by Susan Leather*
- Women and the Family *by Helen O'Connell*
- Women and Participation *by Marilee Karl*

'As a source of up-to-date information about issues affecting women, this is an authoritative and valuable series.' *– Literary Review*

The UN-NGO Group on Women and Development brings together 80 United Nations agencies and international NGOs in the production of the Women and World Development Series with Zed Books. All titles in the series are available free of charge through NGLS to developing country organizations. Please contact Kirsi Floor, NGLS, Palais des Nations, 1211 Geneva 10, Switzerland.

For further details about books in the series, please request the series leaflet from Zed Books Ltd, 57 Caledonian Road, London N1 9BU, UK.